col/LOC ref.

D0409607

BUILDERS OF REPUTE
The Story of Reader Bros.

Josephine Boyle

The Suitable Press

© Josephine Boyle 2002
Builders of Repute: The Story of Reader Bros.

ISBN 0 954 1688 0 1

Published by:
The Suitable Press
55 Monkhams Avenue
Woodford Green
Essex IG8 0EX

The right of Josephine Boyle to be identified as author of this work
has been asserted by her in accordance with the Copyright,
Designs and Patents Act 1988.

All rights reserved. No part of this publication may be produced in
any form or by any means – graphic, electronic or mechanical
including photocopying, recording, taping or information storage
and retrieval systems – without the prior permission, in writing, of
the publisher.

Design & production co-ordinated by:
The Better Book Company Ltd
Havant
Hampshire
PO9 2XH

Printed in England.

Cover design by MusicPrint

CONTENTS

To all our Readers

ACKNOWLEDGEMENTS

The research for this book has stretched over ten years and been assisted by many people. It has also been incalculably aided by the invaluable Alan Godfrey Maps, and readers will find the topography of building developments much easier to grasp if they keep the relevant one to hand.

First, my thanks to all family members who have kept attics, drawers, cupboards, cardboard boxes, plastic bags and in one case a garage bulging with paperwork, photographs, mementoes and ephemera, and who have been so forthcoming with information, namely Jacqueline, Richard, Howard, Nicholas, Frank and Bernard Reader, Madeline Langham, Stephanie Bilton, Martin Koster, Non Thornicroft and Mary Schavieren.

Helpful co-operation was received from the Building Control and Planning departments of the London Boroughs of Barnet, Bromley, Harrow, Redbridge, Tower Hamlets and Waltham Forest, and those of Brentwood and Epping Forest District Councils; also from The Local Studies Libraries and Archives of the London Boroughs of Barnet, Bromley, Camden, Croydon, Enfield, Finsbury, Greenwich, Hackney, Haringey, Harrow, Islington, Newham, Sutton, Tower Hamlets, Redbridge, Waltham Forest and West Ham, also the City of Westminster and the Royal Borough of Windsor & Maidenhead.

Personal thanks to David & Eileen Anderson, Paul Barrick, Geoffrey Clarke of White & Mileson, Alan Cox of the Royal Commission on Historic Monuments Survey of London, John Dann, Len Davis, Ian Dowling, Chris Embling, Grahame Farrell, Harold Fitchett, Bill Flanagan, Rodney Fraser, Michael Kirkland, David Mander, Cyril Newman, Brian Nicholas, Guy Osborne, Peter Reid of Thames Water Reading, Karl Reveley, David Ruddom, David Salter, A.E. Sheppard, Martin Taylor, Derek Walden, Mr. J.Williams of the Loriners' Company, Isobel Watson and the Rev. A.S.Atkins of St Dionis Parsons Green, who allowed me to see the fittings from St Dionis Backchurch.

Thanks also to the staff of Beaulieu Motor Museum Reference Library, the Bishopsgate Library, Bushey Museum, Chingford Cemetery, the Corporation of London Record Office, Epping Forest Museum, Essex Record Office Southend and Chelmsford, the Family Record Centre, Flamingoland Kirby Misperton Yorkshire, Gateshead Local

Studies Collection, Guildhall Library, Hackney Archives, the Imperial War Museum, the Centre for Kentish Studies Maidstone, London Metropolitan Archives, the London Transport Museum, Loughton Library, the Ministry of Defence Archives Dept., Newington Reference Library, North Yorkshire County Library, the Public Record Office, the Royal Institute of Chartered Surveyors, the Harry Simpson Memorial Library, the Skinners' Company, Surrey History Centre Woking, Tyne & Wear Archives and Vestry House Walthamstow.

If anyone has been left out I apologise, also for any mistakes which have eluded my repeated but not necessarily infallible checking.

FOREWORD

Our urban areas are a patchwork, and there are reasons why the patches are that particular shape and the buildings on them of that particular period. This is an attempt to reveal some of them by recording the work of one small London building firm, and to explain how this work multiplied by thousand upon thousand resulted in the townscapes we live with today. The main source has been the eighty-year collection of plans, archives, ephemera, photographs and objects kept in the firm's offices until its closing, and afterwards in the homes of the partners.

The period covered, from the 1890s to the 1970s, saw the countrywide development boom continuing, and the town travelling by leaps and bounds into the countryside at London's gates and into the heart of every home county. When the firm started, Reader Brothers built in Leyton, Wanstead, Finchley, Woodford & Clapton. Their last housing estate, built in the 1960s, was in Chelmsford. Like the rest of humanity, builders do not function in isolation, and one of the most interesting aspects of researching them is discovering tenuous connections, physical and personal, cropping up all over the place and proving that so-called local history cannot be confined by uncrossable boundaries. For example, the reasons that Reader's built their first houses in Wanstead were 1. an aristocrat ruined himself in 1822, 2. a railway was built in 1856, 3. Alice Caroline Pailthorpe married a widowed cutler from Fleet St named Charles Kearney in 1863 and produced a son called Fred, and 4. a life assurance company collapsed in 1869.

Before and after pictures usually tend to provoke melancholy. There are few places whose scenic beauty is enhanced by comprehensive development, and when examining photographs of the countryside before and after the firm passed over it it is difficult not to feel nostalgia for vanished fields and buildings; the isolated village of Chingford on its hill above the Lea marshes; the gardens of Monkhams House with its famous fountains; Wades Hill when it was a lane of old cottages and Thomas Hood was living round the corner; the wonderful views which could be enjoyed before they built the houses in between. But if Reader's had refrained from covering these pretty places with suburb, someone else would only have done it instead. There was no Green Belt then, and little foresight of the problems unregulated suburbanisation was to lead to. Even now, the Belt has too often led to development hopping over it and proliferating farther afield, where historic country town centres have been knocked down to build shopping malls and absolutely anywhere can be destroyed for yet another road.

The study of the growth of the Great Wen in the nineteenth and twentieth centuries is an absorbing one for those interested in buildings, fashion, people and lifestyle, and over that period firms like Reader Brothers were feverishly active. The demand was there and the land available, and just as today, cowboys rode in and out of the business. The original brothers Reader were not cowboys – they built solidly and well, but were probably not the best of businessmen and on occasions seem to have survived by the skin of their teeth. The figures for builders going bankrupt have always been high, right down to the present day, and at least they escaped their locksmith father's experience of that disaster.

Due to the wide spread of their developments, many council records and archives have had to be consulted, but in tracing the beginnings of the firm I have started from family legends & anecdotes. We may know what our ancestors did, and where they lived, and what happened to them, and yet have no idea at all what they were like as people or how they affected those about them, and family legends provide something which any number of researched facts and dates do not - insights into character. However, it is generally unwise to accept a story handed down like a Chinese whisper with blind faith, particularly in a family of raconteurs like the Readers. If a story has been travelling for a long time it is wise to check its credentials, but there is always a genuine fragment in there somewhere. Some of these stories have turned out to be pretty accurate, others have retained only a vestige of fact and a few still remain a puzzle.

When I decided to write up the firm's archive, someone asked me "Do you realise what you're taking on?" I didn't. In possession of a complete set of plans, I had assumed that making a list of Reader buildings and their dates would be reasonably straightforward, but when I started looking at local councils' Planning Application Indexes it all became much more complicated. To start with, not all early records have survived, as they take up a great deal of valuable shelf space and authorities are no longer required to preserve any previous to 1947. Then it is difficult to marry up maps with applications and with actual houses, because the building may not have been built, or the plots may have been doubled, halved or changed in shape. Plans can be changed several times, designs can be passed and then abandoned, applications can now be missing altogether. Money can run out, as can bankrupt builders, and most irritating of all, street names and numbering may have been changed, and more than once. All I can promise is that I have searched widely and done my best to pin down the truth.

THE READER FAMILY TREE

Joseph Reader *m.* Elizabeth Hughes

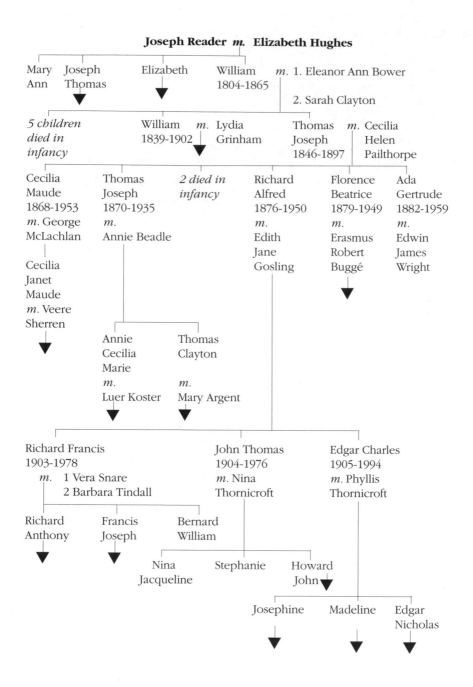

Mary Ann   Joseph Thomas   Elizabeth   William 1804-1865   *m.* 1. Eleanor Ann Bower

2. Sarah Clayton

5 children died in infancy

William 1839-1902   *m.*   Lydia Grinham

Thomas Joseph 1846-1897   *m.*   Cecilia Helen Pailthorpe

Cecilia Maude 1868-1953 *m.* George McLachlan

Cecilia Janet Maude *m.* Veere Sherren

Thomas Joseph 1870-1935 *m.* Annie Beadle

2 died in infancy

Richard Alfred 1876-1950 *m.* Edith Jane Gosling

Florence Beatrice 1879-1949 *m.* Erasmus Robert Buggé

Ada Gertrude 1882-1959 *m.* Edwin James Wright

Annie Cecilia Marie *m.* Luer Koster

Thomas Clayton *m.* Mary Argent

Richard Francis 1903-1978   *m.*   1 Vera Snare   2 Barbara Tindall

John Thomas 1904-1976 *m.* Nina Thornicroft

Edgar Charles 1905-1994 *m.* Phyllis Thornicroft

Richard Anthony

Francis Joseph

Bernard William

Nina Jacqueline

Stephanie

Howard John

Josephine

Madeline

Edgar Nicholas

CHAPTER 1 1804-1888

The Reader family

William Reader was christened on 26 August 1804 in St.Mary's parish church beside Lambeth Palace. He was the child of Joseph and Elizabeth and his father was a whitesmith or worker in metals. The fact that older siblings were born in Holborn and Westminster shows that like most people in a time of practically universal rented housing, they moved around.

In 1820 his elder brother Joseph Thomas, also a whitesmith, was living in Margaret Street Clerkenwell.[1] In the 1813 edition of Richard Horwood's London map, there are still fields between Islington and Clerkenwell, interrupted only by the New River Head, a tile works and the rural resort of Bagnigge Wells, but most of this land belonged to the New River Company and was soon sold off for development. At last only the Cattle Field belonging to the Skinners' Livery Company remained opposite their market. It was bounded by Myddelton Street, St John's Street, Corporation Row & Plumber's Place, and in 1818 was leased from the Company by James Whiskin and covered with closely packed terraced housing on a plan so irrational it verged on the perverse.[2]

Slanting from north west to south east across the site was Coburg Street, where in November 1822 Joseph Reader the younger sub-leased number 6 from the builder.[3] The development was criticised as sub-standard from the start and many houses were to be rebuilt in 1888, by which time not only the leases were falling in. Joseph Thomas's sister Elizabeth and her husband Richard Beach, an organ builder, also moved into the estate, while back in Lambeth William Reader and Eleanor Ann Bower married on Christmas Day 1828, along with another fifteen couples for whom it was one of the few days off work. He joined his brother in Coburg Street and his first child Eleanor Elizabeth was born at number 24 on 2 October 1829, Matilda following in 1831. On 11 November 1832 Eleanor Ann was interred in the new burial ground of St James Clerkenwell,[4] aged 22, and William was in the tragic situation of so many men of his century; a young widower with small children.

In those circumstances it was quite common to look around quickly for a new wife; the children needed a mother, the house needed a housewife, the husband had a living to earn. William's parents were witnesses to his second marriage at St Mary Islington on 6 July 1834, and William Joseph Reader was baptised at St James's Clerkenwell a mere three months later, which suggests the match had at least some affection about it. His new wife was Sarah Clayton, born 1804 in Godstone, Surrey, and it was from this union that William's builder descendants were to come.

The story handed down is that Sarah was connected to the Clayton baronetcy associated with that area of Surrey, and even that she was Lady Sarah. As at the time of their marriage William was a "smith" living in a teemingly populous and largely unfashionable district, the natural corollary of this legend was that marrying beneath her resulted in severance from her distinguished family – the world lost for love. No proof of this story has yet come to light. Sarah and her four younger sisters were certainly born in Godstone, as were her father and grandfather, but there is no obvious connection with the great Sir Robert Clayton who became Lord Mayor of London under Charles II, extremely and conspicuously rich and a great benefactor. The illustrious descent is from his nephew, the first baronet, and although the Mormons' International Genealogical Index reveals that Marden Park, Godstone, Oxted, Limpsfield and Addington were full of Claytons in the eighteenth and nineteenth centuries, plenty of them were already there in the sixteenth and seventeenth, long before Sir Robert came down from Northamptonshire to seek his fortune. Sarah's grandfather Thomas was born in 1740 and he and his two wives have quite respectable gravestones in front of the east end of Godstone church, but her father was described on his wife's death certificate as a labourer. Any upper class blood in the Claytons may have been illegitimate.

* * *

In Pigot's Directory for 1840, William Reader appears for the first of many times as a locksmith and bellhanger in business at 14 Cullum Street in the City of London, and through the 1841 Census, that ten-yearly exercise so blessed by anyone searching for their roots, it is possible to catch a first glimpse of the Readers at home in Coburg Street.

Georgian and Victorian terraces evoke romantic pictures of their first tenants; top-hatted fathers off to the City, well-dressed mothers and children waving goodbye from the steps, servants in white caps bustling in the basement. It is unlikely that this picture prevailed in any but the more pricey areas. In general, it appears that the minute a man signed his lease or paid the first instalment of his rent he immediately began to sublet, fitting provincial clerks, lady annuitants, retired couples and whole families into the spare rooms of his home. The Skinners' Estate was no different, as the enumerator recorded.

Next door to the Skinners' Arms at number 24, the children Eleanor, Matilda and William Joseph were already dead and gone, but the thirty-five-year-old William and Sarah now had a five-year-old Thomas Clayton and another William aged two. The name Clayton was to turn up fairly regularly in the family from now on, a respectful nod in the direction of Sarah's proud ancestry. The house also contained a 45-year-old widowed lodger with two daughters.

Number 6 housed brother Joseph and his wife Susannah, their five children and two servants, a Scottish jeweller with a wife and daughter, a watchman with a wife and two grown children, and a sempstress. Perhaps it was a larger house than number 24, but it must have been pretty cramped and about the norm for Clerkenwell.

It was not only crowding which made Clerkenwell a dubious place to live. It was smoky, of course, like all towns, and the soot must have settled very quickly onto the new brick, but on the Skinners' Estate there was the high wall of a Remand Prison on the other side of Corporation Row and a health hazard of a literally deadly nature just beyond Rosoman Street in the shape of the Spa Fields Chapel burial ground. This leased-out two-acre site had been receiving burials since 1777, and was now so packed with bodies that bonfires were lit there each night, cremating last week's burials in order to provide room for tomorrow's. In such circumstances, a high local mortality rate was only to be expected.[5]

By September 1842, when a daughter was born and quickly buried, William Reader had moved his family to 17 Cullum Street; like nearly every tradesman in London, he now lived over the shop. Thomas Clayton died the next year, and the sole surviving William junior must have become the object of much attention and anxiety. He was probably only too aware of his own mortality, and a sense of insecurity could have led to a habit which would cause the family a lot of trouble. William senior's seventh and last child, Thomas Joseph, was born on 8 April 1846 and christened in the parish church of St.Dionis Backchurch round the corner.

In contrast with the conglomeration of vast commercial buildings which makes up the modern City, Dickensian London was crammed with small shops and homes. Every street, alley and court contained houses full of citizens, and although commerce was in evidence everywhere it was often of the old-fashioned kind which involved providing actual services, and making useful articles, and exchanging them across the counter for visible money.

Cullum Street was a short cut between Fenchurch Street and Lime Street, built following the Great Fire by Sir John Cullum, a sheriff of the City. Although it has been entirely redeveloped since William's day, its narrow, crooked shape makes it easy to imagine as it was. The numbering is still consecutive, the remnants of an inn yard remain at its east end and the approximate site of the locksmith's shop is occupied by a sandwich bar. At the 1851 Census the premises housed William, his wife, two sons, a twenty-one-year-old apprentice and a tailor and his wife. He was doing well, if the will drawn up a few years later by John Taylor of Grays Inn is anything to go by. When William signed it on 22 May 1854 he owned number 17 leasehold and number 20 freehold, four leasehold houses in Frederick Place,[6] Tottenham Road, Kingsland and the lease of 24 Coburg Street which he had been renting out to three families (seventeen people in all) since the move to the City. He also had investments.

In the manuscript section of the Guildhall Library, a bill is preserved dated 12 April 1858, addressed to St Dionis Back Church and receipted 31 January 1859 by William Reader junior, aged eighteen. The letterhead describes William senior as "Ironmonger, Locksmith, Bell Hanger" (i.e.house bells) "and Smith in General. Stoves, Ranges, Railing and Balconies Made. Gas work in all its branches. Work done in all parts of the town or country."[7]

One cannot know how many of the skills and facilities here offered were regularly called upon by the people of the City. The two Williams and their apprentice(s) may well have travelled for miles around and produced custom-made ironwork for some of the many houses then being built, but the bill is for repair and maintenance on locks, doors and chandelier in the very dilapidated parish church, and this sort of work must surely have been a large part of the firm's trade.[8]

Just after his twelfth birthday Thomas Joseph acquired three new schoolbooks, with "Master Reader 25th May 1858" written on the flyleaves; G.F.Graham on English Composition and Lindley Murray's English Grammar, both of which look fit to paralyse the brain of the student, and a more interesting volume with maps and fine steel engravings; "A Grammar of General Geography for the use of Schools and Young Persons with Maps and Engravings by the Revd. J.Goldsmith, Revised corrected and greatly enlarged by Edward Hughes F.R.G.S. & Head master of the royal Naval Lower School, Greenwich Hospital." This contains a wealth of pleasing quotes. "The inhabitants of Iceland are poor, but virtuous and intelligent." "The Russian Government is despotic." "The free and admirable constitution enjoyed by Great Britain, the intelligence, industry and perseverance of her people, have raised her to the highest pitch of greatness." "London, the metropolis of Great Britain, is in 5½ degrees north latitude, and contained, in 1851, above 2,363,141 inhabitants. It is the largest city, and the greatest seat of commerce, in the world." William Reader, and all other inhabitants of that City who were doing nicely, would have agreed.

In addition to his usual Post Office Directory entry, in 1860 William inserted a dramatic half page advertisement, extolling what seems to have become his chief line.

"FIRE, THE DEVOURING ELEMENT, SUBDUED. W.Reader, of 20 Cullum Street, City, E.C., Begs to offer to the public, at very Reasonable Prices, his IMPREGNABLE FIRE-RESISTING SAFES, Which stand unrivalled for Quality and Workmanship, having Additional Security, with Private Escutcheon, and HOBB'S CELEBRATED DETECTOR AND POWDER PROOF LOCKS. A liberal allowance made for all safes taken in exchange. Also a general assortment of second-hand safes and chests always in stock. N.B. Price lists sent free on application."

By Census 1861 William & Sarah were fifty-five, the "unmarried" William junior was twenty-one, and the "scholar" Thomas Joseph was one day short of his fifteenth birthday and probably on the point of becoming apprenticed to his father. Prosperity meant that there were no longer any lodgers, and the only other person sleeping at number 17 Cullum Street that night was a "visitor" from Godstone. Lydia Grinham, twenty-one, was the daughter of a deceased bricklayer and a straw bonnet maker, and would have known Sarah's mother and sisters; and on 6 February, two months previously, William junior & Lydia had been married at St Mary's Lambeth like his father, witnessed by Lydia's brother Thomas and a member of the Abel family with whom Sarah's mother had lodged for the last years of her life.

Presuming it was he who filled in the Census form, why didn't William senior know this? It could be that no-one dared tell him because he was a stereotype heavy Victorian father who didn't want a dependent son getting married, but there is another possibility. The accuracy of information recorded upon death certificates in the present day has recently been estimated at only 40%, so the reliability of Victorian doctors' diagnoses must be regarded with strong suspicion. Medical dignity, not to say pride must seldom have allowed cause of death to be honestly stated as "don't know," but the symptoms recorded on William's certificate a few years later seem pretty unambiguous.

"Congestion of liver and portal system. Many years. Vomiting and purging of blood 4 days. Haematemesis and Haematuria."

Metalworking was not a healthy occupation, particularly when it involved lead, but William was identified in the family legend as "a bottle a day man", and there seems little doubt that his extremely nasty end owed something to alcoholism, or at least unwisely heavy drinking. The loss of a very young wife and five children must have required the drowning of sorrow at times, and on the up side, he was a member of the Loriners' Livery Company with all the enjoyable eating, drinking and getting merry that went with it. His ignorance of the true status of the visitor in his home on the night of 7 April 1861 could be explained by his being ill, forgetful, drunk, or all three.

Or again, in such circumstances it may have been Sarah who filled in the form, and she who was kept in the dark about a marriage of which she would have disapproved – back in Godstone, the Claytons might have looked down upon the Grinhams. Whatever the explanation, while William was still enduring his many years with a shot liver, his wife died at 17 Cullum Street on 24 August 1862 of phlebitis, hectic (i.e. habitual or continual) fever and coma, aged 57.

William's Will of 1854 mentions a family grave at Beaumont Cemetery, Mile End, now a recreation ground with a few disconsolate tombstones leaning against the wall onto Shandy Street, and it is very possible that his five dead children were laid there. But the 1852 Burial in Towns Act [9] had led to the closing and clearing of hundreds of overcrowded burial grounds like the notorious Spa Fields, poisonously wedged between the houses of Londoners. Beaumont was included, the remains being removed to the City of London Cemetery Ilford between 1857 and 1871, and the records last being reported in a rusted-up safe in the Beaumont Institution office, Beaumont Square in 1913.

In 1862, then, William bought a new plot at Abney Park Cemetery and Mr Biggs of Houndsditch turned his plumed horses down Bishopsgate, along Shoreditch High Street and up the Kingsland Road for two and a half miles. All Victorian families were cursed with frequent hearses, and with five to ten burials taking place in the Stoke Newington ground every day, the local passers-by may not always have taken off their hats. Sarah Reader was buried on 30 August near the spired brick chapel, one row back from the path, and the mourning party of William, his two sons, probably his brother Joseph and family, presumably his daughter-in-law Lydia, and possibly some of Sarah's Surrey relatives, returned to Cullum Street.

If Sarah had been the problem, perhaps William junior and Lydia announced their marital status over the funeral refreshments, or perhaps they just repeated the news once more and hoped their chronically inebriated father would finally take it in. Certainly the couple were living with him and Thomas at number 17 by 20 November 1863, when their daughter Lydia Sarah Ann was born. William's health would have been poor and getting worse, and if his sons and daughter-in-law nursed him it must have been a ghastly business.

He died on 18 April 1865, aged 60, and on the 21st Mr Biggs carried him off to be buried in the same grave as Sarah. Probate was granted to the surviving executor on 1 June, William not having named another after his wife's death. Edward Crucknell Sandy, a City merchant engaged with William in property business, was also appointed Guardian of any minor children, which meant William was free of his jurisdiction and Thomas still subject to it. The estate was sworn at just under £4,000, and the family legend states with absolute certainty that the seeds of a split between William and Thomas were now sown, because William was a compulsive gambler and a large part of the brothers' inheritance went to pay his debts. But gambling among the unfashionable classes in the 1860s left few records, and whether William played the horses, cards or the stock market there is little hope of finding out now. The Post Office Directory for 1867 records him as living at 3 Bishops Rd Victoria Park, which may confirm bad feeling between the brothers, but perhaps he just wanted to better himself; out of the dirty City, into the new suburb.

* * *

The Readers now become people with faces and figures. In the earliest surviving family photograph album, Thomas Joseph Reader appears to be of no more than average height, stocky, with a round, stolid face and side whiskers. As he matures, he becomes plumper.

Little has been passed down about his character, but a few clues remain. All his children were to be musical, so it seems likely that he was; nineteenth century parlour music was as universal as twentieth century radio and television, the standard of the former varying as widely as that of the latter. He painted in watercolours, as most Reader descendants were to do, again, a popular occupation in the nineteenth century. His mahogany paintbox survives, with T.J.R. carved on the front. Beneath the box is a drawer intended for a sketch book, but which contains evidence of a boyhood romance: a handpainted valentine addressed to Master T.Reader, 17 Cullum St, Fenchurch St and postmarked City February 1859, and a heart-shaped birthday card addressed in the same hand-writing, postmarked 7 April 1861 and sent from Hastings. The fact that this was a census day should mean that the writer could be identified, but certain pages are missing. As Thomas kept the cards for the rest of his life they were probably from the girl he married.

The most revealing source for getting to know him is a personal ledger 9 inches by 6 inches, which he started in September 1867. His father's estate had been wound up and the first pages are a summary of his assets and investments, nearly all of them owned jointly with his brother. From now on it is possible to monitor the state of the business and to catch glimpses of family relationships, all written in Thomas's own hand. The impression one gains from it is of a conscientious, responsible young man trying to do his best, perhaps against odds quoted by his gambling brother, and in that autumn of 1867 things probably looked quite hopeful as he could now afford to marry.

All great cities make themselves over at regular intervals. In the 1860s London was once again changing fast and public works were being undertaken everywhere, especially great new thoroughfares such as Queen Victoria Street and the Thames Embankment. When, therefore, on 13 October 1867 the couple arrived at St.Andrew's Holborn, the surroundings were not exactly picturesque. This six hundred-year-old church occupied a prominent position at the top of Holborn Hill, and since 1863 had been surrounded by a dusty demolition shambles and then a building site as the enormous engineering feat of the Holborn Viaduct was undertaken. A slice of the churchyard had been commandeered and its occupants also carted off to Ilford, so that the church's high, arched windows would now look out at a raised road, very like the predicament of modern buildings which have their space, light and air invaded by stilted motorways. Somehow, the wedding party negotiated the mess and climbed up the steps into the grubby, neglected interior.

Like William and Lydia, the couple were very young. He was 21, she 20, and although Thomas was fortunate to be a partner in his own business they appear perilously vulnerable. No wedding photograph exists, but a probable engagement one shows the bride-to-be as pretty, fair-haired, ringleted and rather apprehensive, and as she is seated, surrounded by crinoline, it is possible she was taller than her husband.

Cecilia Helen Pailthorpe lived in Grays Inn Passage, Holborn, the eastern end of an alley which ran from the south-east corner of Red Lion Square to Bedford Street (now Sandland Street), where the beginning of this vanished thoroughfare can be seen in the curve of the Three Cups public house. She was born at number 7 about 1847, the youngest of eight children two of whom died in infancy, and when she married only her older brothers Frederick William and Edward were left at home. Photographs taken in Kent about that time reveal the two to be tall, thin, alternative-looking young men in baggy clothes; Edward was a "photographic artist" and Fred an artist and engraver who worked for George Cruikshank. Cecilia remembered sitting on this great man's knee when she was a child, and it would be nice to believe he gave her a wedding present.

Their father, Richard Pailthorpe was a tailor turned book and print seller, and the family lived over the shop. A magnificent, life-sized photograph of him with mutton-chop whiskers, tousled white hair, a black silk stock and a grim expression, was taken by Gush and Ferguson of Regent Street in the 1870s, and it later hung in his grandson's home and alarmed his great-great-grandchildren. A more human glimpse of him can be caught in the Robson & Kerslake edition of the Pickwick Papers which Fred illustrated in 1882, where he is depicted looking out of the door of his shop.

Cecilia's mother, born Cecilia Avis in Bath, was dark-haired and large-jawed, and as she was to promote Cecilias throughout the family for at least a hundred years she must have been either much loved, much feared, or from a better class than her husband. Her sister Frances Sarah was married to a butler in Park Crescent Regent's Park, and another relative is said to have been clerk of the works on Lansdown Crescent Bath.

As Fred and Edward seem to have been of a raffish disposition and lifestyle, and Cecilia Helen was a lively, entertaining soul to the end of her long life, it is possible that the Pailthorpe blood introduced a streak of humour and a touch of anarchy into the rather glum Reader family, not to speak of a tendency to grow tall.

After a three-week honeymoon (Ledger; "Mrs.Bower, Hastings ech. Oct 14th Nov.4th £13 17s 4d"), Thomas and Cecilia settled in at 17 Cullum Street, doubtless with the pleasures and problems of all very young newly-weds, and their first child, Cecilia Maude, was born on 7 August 1869 and christened in November at St.Dionis Backchurch. Thomas Joseph junior followed in 1870.

In 1871 the Census was taken again. At number 17, Thomas "smith and safe maker" and family were attended by a 16-year-old servant, Phoebe Fitch, born in Bishopsgate. At number 20 William ("smith and gas fitter") was back with his wife Lydia, three young children and another teenage maid he may have brought back with him, as she was born in Bethnal Green. At number 21, Cecilia's oldest brother John was running coffee rooms, though living at 110 Minories. The proximity of the three families and the partnership of the brothers in the thirty-year-established business suggest Dickensian cosiness, with frequent get-togethers around a candle-sconced piano and a shared goose on Christmas Day.

In fact, things were desperate.

* * *

The family legend always blamed William's gambling for the downfall of the family business. William senior, it said, was a very wealthy man, "carriage trade", an Alderman, next in line to be Lord Mayor, married to a near-aristocrat with a private income. His immense inheritance was frittered away by his irresponsible son William while his responsible son Thomas tried desperately to save it. In short, it was all William junior's fault.

Investigation has revealed that most of this is overblown if not totally inaccurate, but it can be understood if we see matters through the eyes of Cecilia, who seems to have been the main channel by which the story passed down to children and grandchildren. William was wealthy from the Pailthorpe angle, though it seems unlikely that he kept a horse and carriage among the confined buildings of Cullum Street; a horse and van for business purposes, yes. But although he had the glamour of Livery Company membership, he paid the Steward's fine rather than take his turn at an official position, and he doesn't appear on the list of City of London Aldermen. Even if he had, capital of only £4000 would have been totally inadequate to cover the expense of living for a year as Lord Mayor of London. Yet one can understand how the trouble caused after his death by William junior's bad habits would naturally have made Cecilia blame her brother-in-law for all her husband's problems.

The clue to what really happened lies in a play written in the middle of the twentieth century by one of Cecilia's grand-daughters,[10] with whose parents she often stayed and whom she regaled with the family history. The thinly disguised characters have gone up-class and act out the strife between the brothers against the background of a prosperous City counting house. The play starts on a racecourse where William and Lydia are enjoying the high life and teasing "Edwin" and "Kitty", whom they have persuaded to accompany them, for their dull, careful ways, and yet the financial disaster doesn't come via gambling – in fact, she seems to continue with a completely fictitious plot-line, bearing no resemblance to anything which survives in oral history.

But it turned out to be accurate; enlarged, even glorified, with vast sums of money mentioned as being in the family's possession, but the actual situation was the true one. The crash of the Reader locksmith's business and the loss of all their property occurred because shareholders then had unlimited liability for a company's debts, an archaic and unreasonable practice which still survives for Lloyd's Names and which has caused a City scandal of global dimensions.

Among the investments recorded by Thomas at the beginning of his ledger were two hundred shares in the Albert Life Assurance Company, Waterloo Place, Pall Mall, these being held jointly with William. It had started out in July 1839 as the Freemasons' and General Life Assurance Company and had since, in the way of businesses, swallowed a large number of other assurance and insurance companies, taking on their liabilities in the process. The Dividend for the half year ending 25 December 1868 was paid, but on 17 September 1869 the Company was wound up by the Court of Chancery, having found it impossible to fulfil the obligations of no less than nineteen absorbed companies, including the dodgy-sounding Indian Laudable Mutual Life Assurance Society, a name which surely protests too much.[11]

On the day before the census, 1 April 1871, Thomas made the last formal entry in his ledger, receiving rent for two first floor rooms at 20 Cullum Street let out as offices. A loose sheet of paper lists the financial situation up to June 30, and includes a section headed "Debts to pay" and an estimated valuation of the stock in trade plus tools and fixtures as £500. The brothers made efforts to protect number 20 by putting it in the hands of friends and relatives and then claiming it was part of Lydia's and Cecilia's dower; this subsequently involved them in stressful appearances before the Lord Mayor and his court. [12]

The effects of this City scandal were so widespread and complicated that on 25 May 1871 the Albert Life Assurance Company Arbitration Act 1871 was passed to deal with them, to be followed on 30 June 1874 by another. Presumably calls for money continued, but as the ledger was no longer kept up there is no way of knowing the exact events which led to the notice in column 2888 of the London Gazette a year later on 21 June 1872.

"The Bankruptcy Act 1869

"In the London Bankruptcy Court

"In the Matter of a Bankruptcy Petition against William Reader of 20 Cullum St in the City of London, Fire Proof Safe Manufacturer.

"Upon the hearing of this Petition this day, and upon proof satisfactory to the Court of the debt of the Petitioner, and of the trading and of the act or acts of Bankruptcy alleged to have been committed by the said William Reader having been given, it is ordered that the said William Reader be, and he is hereby, adjudged bankrupt – Given under the Seal of the Court this 20th day of June, 1872

"By the Court, P.H. Pepys Registrar

"The First General Meeting of the creditors of the said William Reader is hereby summoned to be held at the London Bankruptcy Court, Basinghall Street, in the city of London, on the 9th day of July, 1872, at eleven o'clock in the forenoon, and that the Court has ordered the bankrupt to attend thereat for examination, and to produce thereat a statement of his affairs, as required by the statute.

"Until the appointment of a Trustee, all persons having in their possession any of the effects of the bankrupt must deliver them, and all debts due to the bankrupt must be paid to Philip Henry Pepys, Esq, one of the Registrars, at the office of Mr. Peter Paget, Official Assignee in the London Bankruptcy Court, Basinghall Street. Creditors must forward their Proofs of Debts to the Registrar, at the same address."

It was at least fortunate that imprisonment for debt had been abolished in 1869, but despite all efforts, a Sergeant at Mace to the Sheriffs of London executed a writ of possession on number 20 Cullum Street in January 1873,[13] and William moved in with his coachman brother-in-law in Streatham.

By March Thomas and his family had moved to 27 Addle Hill, Carter Lane, being coffee and dining rooms listed in the City Directory as belonging to Cecilia's brother, Frederick William Pailthorpe; (art has rarely ensured the artist a living wage, and when he married in 1871 he had taken over a similar business in Duke Street, London Bridge). The reason we know of this move is because Thomas and Cecilia's troubles were compounded by the sort of tragedy which gets preserved in official records.

Addle Hill was a narrow thoroughfare once leading from Carter Lane to Upper Thames Street but now blocked by the offices of the British and Foreign Bible Society, which must have made it dark. The buildings were small and old and housed a variety of fairly humble occupations, including a laundress and makers of boots, straw hats and packing cases.

In addition to Maude and Thomas junior, the Readers had a six-month-old daughter named Alice Gertrude. On 8 March she was found dead in bed, and on top of their grief the young parents had to undergo ordeal by inquest before a jury largely made up of local residents.[14]

The inquest was held on the 12th at the Bell Tavern[15] the other side of the street from the coffee rooms. The jury included Mr Thomas Spikes, boarding house keeper of 2 Addle Hill, the deputy coroner was Samuel Frederick Langham junior of 22 Caversham Rd Kentish Town, and the doctor was Mr Key Hardy. The proceedings are best conveyed in the witnesses' own words, although the coroner's abbreviations and hurried scrawl make decipherment difficult.

"Cecilia Ellen [sic] Reader 27 Addle Hill Wife of Thos Josh Reader Coffee Ho Keeper being sworn saith that Decd Alice Gertrude Reader was her child she was 6 months old – has been quite healthy … On Friday night I went to bed at half past 11. She was well then – the child took the breast freely – at 2 o'clock and at 5 it took the breast and it appeared well then – I turned child back to me on the pillow – my husband was in bed at the time – At 8 o'clock I got up and my husband had got up at 6 o'clock – I looked at the child's face which appeared very white and I went and kissed it and found it dead – the whole of the face was exposed – I called my Husband who came up immy [immediately] and got a warm bath and the child was placed in a bath directly a Dr was sent for and he came immy and pronounced him [sic] dead –"

"Thos Josh Reader 27 Addle Hill Coffee Ho Keeper – On Saturday morning I got up at 6 o'clock – I saw Deceased with the face up turned – I noticed nothing particular and believed both to be asleep I did not come up until 10 to 8 when I awoke my wife – I went down stairs about ¼ to 20 past 8 I heard my wife scream. She [cried] Oh Tom the Decd dead I fetched a warm bath –"

"Key Hardy 4 Wardrobe Place Doctors Commons Surgeon being sworn saith I was called in on Saturday morning at half past 8 to see Decd – Decd was in the Bath – Child was quite dead and right side slightly discoloured. No external marks of violence hands clenched. all the appearances consistent with Death from Convulsions. Decd well nourished –"

Mercifully, the verdict was that Victorian catch-all, "Natural death from Convulsions". Today, we would almost certainly use the catch-all of cot death. Poor little Alice Gertrude was taken up the Kingsland Road by Mr Hearley of Clerkenwell but her grandparents' grave was not opened – that would have been too expensive for Thomas's reduced means. She was buried in a public grave away in the north west corner, along with fifteen others.

Another child, Egbert Clayton, was born at Addle Hill the next year, but by the birth of Richard Alfred on 21 September 1876 the family had moved out of the City to 34 Annis Road, South Hackney, a ten-year-old street of terraced houses with bay windows and iron-railinged front gardens, situated off Victoria Park Road.

William's bankruptcy was declared closed on 23 January 1877, and as for the brothers' inheritance from their father, "so much of the property as could be realized had been realized for the benefit of creditors of the bankrupt," and "the balance of £32 15s 10d as appeared by the statement thereunto annexed, was not more than sufficient to pay the costs and charges." In 1878 both Cecilia's father and little Egbert died, and by Census 1881 the family had moved to 10 Eastwood Terrace,[16] Hornsey Rd, its numbers swelled by the one-year-old Florence Beatrice and Cecilia's widowed mother. Also mentioned is "unmarried" brother Edward Pailthorpe.

There are interesting things to be discovered about the Pailthorpe brothers. The undeniably talented Fred comes across as the most extrovertly bohemian, with a liking for tobacco and alcohol and a disconcerting sense of humour which didn't improve as he grew older, but Edward had his secrets. After a few years clerking he became a painter of miniatures based on photographs, and by the early 1870s had a daughter living in north London, born to a woman who claimed on both birth and death certificates (the child died aged 4) to be his wife. Despite the 1881 census statement that he spent the night in Hornsey Rd, he was also recorded at Hammersmith in the company of this lady, and she turns out to be the wife of George Bruce Shepherd, the Tunbridge Wells photographer who took the brothers' pictures some time between 1865 and 1867. Edward and Elizabeth finally married in 1883, no doubt on hearing that her husband had died, and left immediately for Australia.

By the 1880s William and Lydia were living in a succession of small terrace homes in Stratford, including a grocer's shop in Channelsea Square, while their three teenage daughters had started their working lives as maids of all work in local homes.

Thomas and Cecilia had fared rather better. He was now the manager of a lock factory, and by the christening of their last child Ada Gertrude in 1888 at St.Augustine's, Victoria Park, the family were at 4 Dagmar Road, parallel to Annis Rd and pretty well identical to it. The Readers were to stay in South Hackney for the next fifty years.

Frederick Willliam and Edward Pailthorpe.

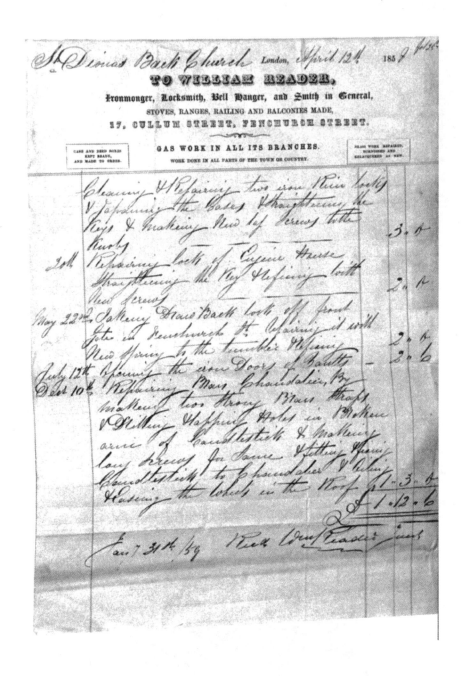

Bill for work on St Dionis Back Church, Lime St.,
presented by William Reader 12th April 1858.
Guildhall Library

Thomas Joseph Reader & Cecilia Helen Pailthorpe c.1867

CHAPTER 2 1891-1905

Wanstead, Leytonstone, Finchley.

In many families the same names crop up again and again down the generations and cause great confusion. Among the Readers, Thomas was shortened to Tom or Tommy, Cecilias became Cis or Cissie and Richards were usually called Dick or Dickie, but in order to differentiate one version of a name will be used for each person. Thomas Joseph's eldest son will therefore be referred to as Tom and his surviving brother as Richard.

By the 1891 Census Thomas was 44 and an engineer draughtsman. Cecilia was 42. Maude was 22 and "an artist in watercolours", which meant tinting photographs at a high-class West End photographer's. Tom was 20 and an engine fitter; Richard 14, Florence 11 and Ada 9 were scholars.

It is now that building starts to appear. There was a lot of it about in 189l. In the countrywide workforce there were 37,815 builders and 11,830 auctioneers, appraisers, valuers & house agents. The combined numbers of bricklayers, brick/tile makers, carpenters/joiners, chalk/clay/sand/gravel labourers, surveyors, road contractors and inspectors, plasterers, whitewashers, paperhangers, plumbers, stone and slate dressers, slaters, tilers, and timber dealers, to name but a few, was at least 621,000. [1]

In London the total for building-associated tradesmen was over 116,000, and there can have been very few people without relatives involved in the business of building. Even the upper classes had long been leasing their land for development, particularly in the capital.

Thomas's two sons had grown up with plumbing, gasfitting, metalworking, engine-fitting and technical designing. There were carpenter in-laws on both sides; Cecilia's brother John had progressed from carpenter to builder[2] whilst keeping a financial foot on the ground in the coffee rooms, and Aunt Alice Caroline Kearney née Pailthorpe had a twenty-one-year-old son in the trade. Nearby, sons of the developers of South Hackney still occupied houses their fathers had built, whilst reaching beyond Hackney, quite literally, to fresh fields and pastures new made available by agricultural depression. There were, in fact, widespread opportunities open in building.

Here, the family legend introduces the Queen's Hall, Langham Place. In 1886 Francis Wall Mackenzie Ravenscroft was flirting with the idea of erecting high-class residential flats on the site of an incongruous mess of poor-quality buildings, including the Portland Bazaar, left over from the time before Nash's great redevelopment. By May 1887 the Crown lease had been acquired by a company intending to erect concert rooms between St George's Hall and Riding House Street, their prospectus being issued on 18 June.[3] This enterprise would be conveniently central for its patrons, and would blend well with the elegant Portland Place and the last word in modern luxury provided by the twenty-two-year-old Langham Hotel opposite. A design was commissioned from joint architects Thomas E.Knightley and Charles R.Phipps, an experienced designer of theatres.

Various dissensions followed between owners and architects and between the architects themselves, in fact the argument about who had actually originated the plan simmered on in the correspondence column of The Builder for some time. It is possible to detect deep acrimony and rage beneath the formal phraseology of these letters from Knightley and Phipps, and the dispute was eventually referred to the President of the R.I.B.A. in December 1893. The final adjudication balanced itself carefully on the fence.[4]

Work was started in spring 1891 and the resultant building, at first known with yawning predictability as the Victoria Hall, was to be held in great affection by Londoners during its fifty years of existence. It was a splendid piece of fin-de-siècle architecture, hung with stone garlands, dignified by busts of great musicians and ringed by naked ladies; few fin-de-siècle buildings seemed able to do without them. Due to the adjacent All Souls' Church and Schools standing up for their right to light and air, and who could blame them, the hall entrance was at balcony level and the rest of the building sunk into the ground. This idea was conceived by Phipps, but Knightley took immense pains over the acoustics and the sound of Queen's Hall concerts was to become legendary. On 21 November 1893 the finished hall was licenced by the London County Council, Knightley transferred the licence to the new manager Mr Robert Newman, and the building opened with a children's party on the 23rd.

This means that when work started Richard was fourteen and at school. When it finished he was seventeen, so if he worked there as a plumber and gasfitter, as the story goes, it must have been as an apprentice either to his father or to another. It is not known whether

Tom worked there, too, or continued with his job elsewhere as an engine fitter (there were 87,510 of those in England & Wales at the Census). Plans and elevations were published in The Builder, and various originals and papers to do with the project are in the Public Record Office; those for Edwardian alterations are at London Metropolitan Archives.[5] The main contractor was Charles Wall of Ashburnham Works, Lots Rd, Chelsea, but with the exception of a few firms of specialised experts, subcontractors have disappeared from public ken.

* * *

While large public and private projects such as this were going up throughout central London in the 1890s, developers continued to nibble away at the green fields around its edge. Landowners had roads and services put in at their own expense; builders large and small descended on the newly available sites and leased plots at so much per foot frontage. They then put in planning applications for anything from one to several hundred houses, built and sometimes moved in, sold, leased or rented out, then bought another plot elsewhere and moved on as soon as there was a new house available. Their progress is often marked by initials on terrace ends or by the names of streets; their own surnames, their wives' and children's christian names, the place where they were born, the British heroes they most admired. In addition to these personal choices, royal and military events generally produced a rash of loyal tributes, so there is no problem dating Sebastopol Terrace, Jubilee Crescent or Mafeking Road.

In 1840 the Northern & Eastern Railway built a line up the Lea Valley from Stratford,[6] and in 1856 its lessees the Eastern Counties Railway took a right turn off this line and passed through the delightful village of Leyton on its way out to Loughton. From then on the rural retreats of Essex gentlemen gradually began to fall before lower middle and working class dormitory developments, laid out with the standard late Victorian terraces which ring London like a tidemark.

The Leyton Tithe Map of 1839 shows a large part of the southern part of the parish in the hands of the Hon. William Pole Tylney Long Wellesley, formerly of Wanstead House and now living on a pension from his brother, the Duke of Wellington. This deservedly execrated man had acquired a huge estate and fortune (plus two more names) in 1812 when he married Catherine Tylney Long, and within ten years had squandered the lot. The house was gone and the remaining estate mortgaged, and when he died on 1 July 1857, receiving the distinction of one of the very few truthful obituaries ever published,[7] the land passed to a son who died unmarried six years later. A cousin, Henry Richard Wellesley, first Earl Cowley and Viscount Dangan, now took on the burden and began to shift it by means of sale for building.

In 1878 the City of London Corporation was empowered to acquire undeveloped land around London for the public benefit by the City of London (open spaces) Act, and in 1880 negotiations were opened with Lord Cowley about Wanstead Park; plans for it had already been mooted in 1871, with a military exercising ground included.[8] The entirely peaceful pleasure ground eventually created was declared open to the public on 1 August 1882 by the Chairman of the Epping Forest Committee, the price having been £8,000 and a make-weight of 50 acres of land. This land was made up of oddments of "waste" scattered about among existing development and not suitable for inclusion in the main sweep of forest. They did, however, have potential as building sites, and as the suburbanisation of Essex villages connected to London by rail was now moving fast, the Earl, along with other local landowners, was on to a good thing.

The field numbers in Tithe and Ordnance Survey maps are different and those of the Epping Forest map different again, so care has to be taken to keep the three separate or total confusion ensues. Those quoted hereafter in this chapter are from the Leyton and Wanstead Tithe Maps.

The Wellesleys' field 449 to the south of Ruckholt Rd had already been crossed by the two railways, and the piece between the High Road and the curve in the line which now carries the Central Line underground was developed during the 1880s by Adolphus Charles and Edwin Isaac Rayner. There were several Rayner families in the 19th century London building trade, but A.C. and E.I. belonged to one of the most successful, not least because their father William Rayner had at least twelve children to help put up further estates.[9] Just over the border in Wanstead Parish Slip, they built Rayner Terrace along the western edge of field 10 and were also busy in the new Downsell Rd. A passage in Edwin Isaac's Will, which received probate 17 August 1923, demonstrates the complexity of business arrangements behind development, and the number of people or organizations who might hold an interest in it; an indenture made 8 May 1885 involved 1. the Rt Hon William Henry Earl Cowley, 2. the Hon Francis Leveson Bertie of the Foreign Office and Andrew Alfred

Collyer Bristow, solicitor of 4 Bedford Row, 3. A.C.Rayner of St James Rd Overcliff Gravesend builder, and 4. E.I.Rayner of Wanstead builder.

The first Earl Cowley died in 1884 and his son continued to develop his land. The Ordnance Survey Map of 1894 reveals the suburbanisation of Leyton High Road as almost complete, and the Post Office Directory for the same year is evidence that the area had been settled by the men who built it. At 6 Hughenden Terrace (111 High Rd Leyton) were Rayner & Bridgland house agents, and at 30 (159 HRL) lived Charles Spurgeon Rayner. E. I. Rayner had an office at 40 Rayner Terrace (78 HRL) and also owned a builders's merchants' on the corner of Maud Road. At 36 Hughenden Terrace (171 HRL) lived Charles Kearney, husband of Cecilia Reader's sister Alice and father of Frederick Kearney, who was working for the Rayners. It was almost certainly Fred who introduced his Reader cousins to Edwin Isaac Rayner and gave them their start in the trade.

* * *

The original definitive map of Epping Forest is vast, rolled, boxed and in store somewhere in the City of London Corporation Record Office, while the reduced copy is still large enough to take up most of the table space in the reading room.[10] Study of this reveals that among the pieces of forest waste land given to the first Earl were some woodland near Snaresbrook Station, which still survives on the corner of New Wanstead, and an area to the south west of Spratt Hall Green which consisted largely of arable and pasture. E.I.Rayner and other builders had been working there since 1886, the estate having been laid out as Spratt Hall, Gordon, Chaucer, Dangan, and Addison Roads,[11] in fact Rayner's home at that time was 3 Claremont Villas, later 13 Spratt Hall Rd. Fred Kearney put in applications under his own name for houses in Addison Rd on 5 October 1894, 9 December 1895, 20 July 1896 and 4 October 1897. In 1898 application was made on Rayner's behalf by architect Douglas Matthew for 16-66 Dangan Rd, and although no confirmation exists in any surviving paperwork, it is known that they were built by the Readers. By the end of the century, therefore, T.J. & R.A.Reader were an established building and contracting firm working in north east London.

* * *

In April 1896, about the time of his 50th birthday, Thomas Joseph Reader senior was diagnosed as having cancer of the oesophagus. There is a photograph of him taken shortly before that time, a small man with a slight smile, smartly dressed in grey hat and suit and sitting leaning on his stick in the garden of 14 Christie Rd South Hackney. His plumpness had gone, and his troubles must have reduced his resistance to illness. No doubt he smoked – most men did.

His death on 6 July 1897 only days after Queen Victoria's Diamond Jubilee celebrations, was registered by the twenty-year-old Richard, who was to live in dread of dying as his father had done for the rest of his life. The two brothers were very different in character; simplistically, it might be said that Richard was a Reader, quiet, thoughtful, sensitive and a worrier, and Tom a Pailthorpe, extrovert and cheerful, boisterous and sometimes coarse. The contrast between the two caused their men to nickname them husband and wife, but of course each had his reverse side. Tom had a fiery temper and on at least one occasion was observed to literally dance with rage, while Richard had a mischievous sense of humour and a tendency to come out with sallies reminiscent of his Uncle Fred.

Thomas was buried in his parents' grave at Abney Park, and no doubt his widow and five surviving children experienced the mixed anguish and relief that follows such a death. It must have given a welcome lift to their spirits when Tom got married at Christ Church, Gore Rd, on 30 October.

Annie Beadle was a dressmaker of 22, daughter of a piano tuner and cabinet maker and with two older brothers and four younger sisters. Her family had moved to Hackney from Globe Road, Mile End some time between 1887 and 1891, and by 1892 they were living in Victoria Park Road.[12] She was a handsome young woman, with the sort of looks fashionable at the end of the nineteenth century; an oval face with large, dark eyes, a rather heavy jaw, up-swept dark hair and a well-built figure which looked its best in a corset, in fact she had more than a passing resemblance to Lillie Langtry. She was of course aware of her beauty and therefore carried herself with great dignity. She is said to have admonished a bus conductor with the words "You can stop looking at mc likc that, young man, I am another's" and it takes a lot of poise and self-assurance to deliver a line like that. The newly-married couple moved into lodgings over a tailor's shop at 20 Mare St.

Richard would have known his own future wife by now, as she lived in the next street at 14 Christie Road. Her father Francis William Gosling, known as Frank, was a commercial travellor in drapery for Ryland's of Wood Street, City. He was born in Eltham Kent, the son of a plumber who must have been an oppressive character, as Frank was a difficult prude and his brother and sister were quiet and subdued, though much more lovable. Frank's wife Sarah was the daughter of a detective sergeant in the City of London Police and seems to have suffered from ill health from early years. This cannot have helped Frank's disposition or eased his relationship with his three daughters.

The Gosling girls were not beauties but Edith Jane was tall, dark and quite handsome, Florence Esther (Florrie) was cheerful and likeable and the equally likeable Jessie Elizabeth had a certain prettiness. In some respects their father treated them like boys, taking them rowing, climbing, swimming and tennis-playing, and he also took many photographs of them including one of the 15-year-old Edith in Roman dress and chains entitled The Captive, which provokes thought about how he and she may have seen their relationship. Perhaps in an attempt to escape his domination, she was engaged to be married by the time she was seventeen to Frederick Jones of 40 Annis Road, nine years older, a merchant's clerk and an only child. When he died of perforated peritonitis in the London Hospital in 1894, his parents gave Edith a watch engraved "In memory of Fred," and both this and the engagement ring with a gipsy-set ruby and two diamonds remain in the family.

Edith worked variously as an assistant in the S.P.C.K. bookshop and as a piano and class singing teacher expert in tonic solfa; in her old age she spoke with pride of how she could sign one vocal line with her left hand and another with her right. She also played the organ for some services at St Augustine's in the park on the other side of Victoria Park Road, but as the years went on her time must have been more and more taken up with nursing her mother and running the house.

Frank Gosling had the use of the 1890s equivalent of the company car. A brougham with a smartly dressed driver called for him at his own front door and spent the day ferrying him from customer to customer. Refreshment was sometimes offered, so there were certain days when Edith was hovering at the front window when her father was due home. As soon as the brougham drew up she was out on the pavement to propel him inside, before the neighbours noticed his condition. All in all, the Gosling household had its fair share of stress.

* * *

About 1900, the brothers Reader had their photographs taken in the dining room of 60 King Edward Road; the wallpaper matches the upholstery so wasn't left over from a previous tenant, and it seems possible they did it themselves as some of it is upside down. Cecilia and her four unmarried children had moved there since the death of her husband, as a larger property would make it possible to take in boarders. It is interesting to see the two young men as they were, aged 29 and 23, at a significant moment in their working lives.

Spratt Hall Rd Wanstead was nearly filled up, and Fred Kearney had built a terrace numbered from 32 to 37 with no architect's name stated on either application or plan. Speculative builders of all periods have worked from standard plans and elevations in the current fashion but varied them according to individual fancy, and so it may have been his own design. He now started the adjacent terrace, 26 – 31, using a slightly more florid frontage. The lower bay is canted instead of square, the window and porch surrounds are more ornate, the glazing is more interesting with squared upper sashes.[13]

The presented plans also had differences. The first was much as late-Victorian terraces had been built for years, with front and back parlour divided by folding doors, the back part of the hall squeezing between the stairs and the robbed back parlour, the kitchen and scullery beyond in the back addition and the outdoor W.C. stuck on the end. Upstairs, the back addition was reached from a half landing and contained a cramped bathroom and the third bedroom.

The design for the second terrace was based on a plan which turned up all over London at that period. There was a much larger bay in the front reception room and access to the kitchen, scullery, back door and outside W.C. was under the staircase, which started with a three-step curve and then rose in a single flight. Connected with the front door by a long straight hall, the second reception room was as large as the first and had french windows onto the garden. The first floor was all on one level with an additional tiny bedroom for a servant squeezed in beside the bathroom. If the plan is truly to scale, the length of the house was fifty-seven feet.

On 15 March 1900 T.J. & R.A.Reader applied for numbers 22 to 25, to be built to the same design. Tom's confident and florid handwriting announced that he was the owner and builder now residing at 14 Navarino Road, Dalston, and the plans and elevation are so obviously drawn by him that it seems very likely the design was his also. It was their first ever application under their own names and received approval from Wanstead Urban District Council on 7 April.

Where the brothers borrowed the money from to finance this enterprise is not obvious. Their father left no will, which indicates little to leave, and none of their relatives immediately spring to mind as affluent. Probably Rayner gave them a deal or perhaps they went to a bank, a solicitor or a building society, but however they managed it they had made the transition from tradesmen and contractors to master builders, and it must have been a heady moment for them. They marked the occasion with date stones in the gables; they don't seem to have done this ever again, but Fred had already marked his houses 1899, and 1900 was a date worth remembering for Tom and Richard.

By September the job must have been well ahead, and in true East London style they hired a brake and went for a celebratory picnic at Ambresbury Banks, just off the Epping New Road in Epping Forest. Cecilia Reader and Sarah Gosling travelled separately in a brougham as Sarah was now very frail, in fact a holiday photograph taken at Littlehampton that year shows her in a bath chair. Both Readers and Goslings were excellent photographers and Frank Gosling was a keen member of the Hackney Photographic Society. A very large number of his beautiful pictures survive, mostly in the form of lantern slides, and most of the extended family are immortalised in the ones he took of this occasion. Among the trees and earthworks the family sit in straw hats, shirtsleeves and moustaches, or in small-waisted summer dresses. The young women's hats are covered in bows and feathers, the older women wear dark, frilly capes and high dressy bonnets. There are a lot of beer bottles lying about, and the journey home must have been rowdy. Among a few unidentifed faces, those present at the outing appear to be

Frank, Sarah, Edith, Florrie & Jessie Gosling. Frank's sister Esther Gosling.
Cecilia, Maude, Richard, Florence & Ada Reader.
Tom & Annie Reader.
Fred Beadle and his other daughters Nellie, Edith, Hettie and Ada.
Elizabeth, Sam & Kate Witherick (descended from Cecilia's oldest sister Frances) and Kate's fiancé William Sharpe.
Alice, Fred and Charles Kearney
Fred and Clara Pailthorpe.

* * *

Sarah Gosling died of tuberculosis on 19 January 1901 aged 47, and was buried at Manor Park Cemetery, Forest Gate.[14] Edith was now free to marry but the proprieties of mourning had to be respected for at least a year. Frank photographed Jessie and Florrie in full black in the parlour of 14 Christie Road, studying an album which doubtless contained photographs of their mother. In the summer the Goslings went on holiday to the Arundel area and to North Devon, standing on the shore in black blouses, skirts and boaters while Frank took dramatic pictures of rough seas. They visited Aunt Esther and Uncle Will Gosling in the weatherboarded Jubilee Cottages, Eltham High Street where they had been brought up, and Edith was photographed in black in the churchyard where her Gosling grandparents were buried. They even played tennis in black.

Frank was probably quite happy about this compulsory hiatus in Edith's romantic life. Apart from his resentment at the prospective loss of a daughter, he and his future son-in-law didn't get on well personally. They seem to have differed on politics, religion and most other things, and the run-up to the wedding is unlikely to have been smooth. Another awkward occasion occurred when Richard first took his fiancée to Amity Rd West Ham, where they found his uncle Fred Pailthorpe happily merry amid artist's disorder and piles of engraved copper plates. Edith came away considerably flustered.

Meanwhile the next generation of Readers got started with the birth on 26 March 1901 at 21 Groombridge Road of Tom and Annie's daughter, Annie Cecilia Marie (Cissie).

* * *

It is not possible to make a tidily chronological list of the building estates worked on by the Readers, or indeed any other builder. There was almost always an overlap between the last houses of one development and the first of the next, sometimes two sites were in full swing at the same time and in any gaps they subcontracted on other men's sites. Like all self-employed men, they took whatever was going wherever and whenever it was offered and this custom still prevails, accounting for the sudden mysterious disappearance of builders for days at a time, and their equally sudden reappearance if the customer is lucky or insistent enough. However...

On 15 March 1902 Herbert C. Clare of The Briars, 469 Grove Green Road, Leyton put in an application to Leyton U.D.C. for a terrace of eighteen houses on one of the few pieces of undeveloped land left in that street, the site of Dyer's Hall Farm. The builder William James

Johnson had lived there between 1899 and 1901, and presumably Clare had bought it from him. The architect was Alexander Martin of 4 Connaught Road, on the other side of the Gospel Oak to Barking Line railway bridge, and the work must have gone ahead quickly, as at least one was to be ready for occupation by September. But the amended drainage plan for numbers 325 – 359 was prepared and signed by Thomas J.Reader builder, so Clare must have contracted the actual building out to Reader's.[15] Numbers 248 – 270 on the other side of the road are the same design, but the only extant application is for a different design in 1893.

While this development was going on, the wedding of Richard Reader and Edith Gosling finally took place on 7 June 1902 at St John of Jerusalem, Church Crescent, South Hackney, The bridesmaids were Florrie and Jessie Gosling, and Florence and Ada Reader, and the wedding groups in the back garden of 14 Christie Road were for once not taken by a member of either family, but by the Honorary Secretary of the Hackney Photographic Society Walter Selfe. But either Frank or Richard photographed the wedding presents, set out in the front bay of 14 Christie Road against a backdrop of loyal decorations for the coronation of King Edward VII. Many can be recognised as still in the family.

Being in the drapery trade, Frank was able to supply items for the couple's new home and the bill survives, stamped F.W.Gosling and receipted over a penny stamp on the second of June, five days before the wedding.

"Dick

1 Tap Square, 2.7.0. l 14ft Rug 9.6., l 12ft Rug 4.10.,

1 Grey Goat 5.11 [a hearthrug, not a pet], 4/12 Marts 21/6 8/2/. 2 prs Lac Curtains 6/9 13.6., 2 prs. Lace Curtains 10/- 1.0.0., 1 Quilt 9.11, Floor cloth 1.14.8. 1 pr Blankets 115.0."

A bill was also presented -

"To 3 Carriages at 21/- ea £3. 3. 0.

Wedding Card[s] 10. 0."

The bride's father normally pays for such things, but on top of everything else Frank was notoriously tight and Richard stumped up the entire £12. 0s. 6d. total.

Edith and Richard honeymooned in Ventnor, Isle of Wight, which had long holiday associations for both of them. On their return they set up home near Tom and Annie at 47 Groombridge Road, between Victoria Park Road and Well Street Common and within easy walk of South Hackney Parish Church.

At that time Richard was of the Low Church persuasion, possibly Baptist with a certain interest in Swedenborg, while St Augustine's, which Edith attended, was High. It had incense, candles, Stations of the Cross and a vicar who wore cassock and biretta, and had been thus from its building in 1869. The couple met each other halfway by adopting St John of Jerusalem, a huge building with a commanding spire, put up in the 1840s to relieve the old parish church at the top of Mare Street and to serve the newly developing area north of Victoria Park.

On 11 September Tom and Richard's sister Florence married Erasmus Robert Buggé[16] at the same church. "Ras" came from a Norwegian seafaring family which had lived in East London for some years, and had studied chemistry at The People's Palace polytechnic in Mile End Road. The wedding photographs were taken by Walter Selfe in the back garden of 60 King Edward Road and Edith wore her wedding dress with a dark hat and accessories. Ras and Florence moved into one of the first completed houses in the Grove Green Road development – number 327, next but one to the southern exit of Dyers Hall Road, thus for the first time introducing into the Reader family the time-honoured custom of builders housing their relatives.

Richard and Edith may still have been in the Isle of Wight when Tom put in a building application to Finchley Urban District Council on 13 June, for 33 private residences in Prince's Avenue, Ballards Lane on behalf of the owners and builders, Messrs T.J. and R.A.Reader of 2l Groombridge Road, South Hackney.

Ballards Lane (a name at least five hundred years old), was one of several old routes from London to the north. Like all such main roads it had become lined with large-gardened villas, and in 1894 the east side remained practically untouched between Finchley Station[17] and Long Lane. The buildings were The Vines, where the station master lived, Finchley House, Edenbrae, the Presbyterian Church, Redbourne Cottage, Dalkeith Villa, Field Cottage, Claverley and The Hollies. By 1902 Redbourne Avenue had gone in beside the church and Prince's Avenue had replaced Field Cottage, sold after the death of its owner Robert Turnham of "Woodlands".[18]

The Reader houses were to occupy the whole of the south-west side of the road and to be numbered 1-65. The architect for numbers 1-23 was Alexander Martin, and the design similar though not identical to 27-32 Spratt Hall Road. Again, if the plan is accurately to scale, they were rather larger than average, being 24 feet wide and 64 feet deep. There were four bedrooms, a dressing room, bathroom, internal and external W.C.s, 2 reception, kitchen, scullery and coal cellar. The General District Rate for April 1903 records Tom as also owning the site of 12 – 18, but the style of the erected houses is that of James Ellwood who designed all that side of the road except 2 – 10, which were put up by Pappin along with part of Prince's Parade. It seems possible that Ellwood bought the site from Tom to complete his development.[19]

An application for the remaining 21 Reader houses went in in August 1903 and they were nice, fat, self-satisfied Edwardian terraced homes with five bedrooms and lots of fashionable, florid detail. A preliminary unsigned drawing exists in the Reader collection, but there is no indication whether it is Tom's or Richard's.

It is rarely possible to trace the original begetter of houses. As mentioned before, there were fashionable standard plans and fashionable standard frontages, and plans presented to councils for approval often bore names and addresses which one suspects were largely a matter of convenience. A house design is a difficult thing to copyright and builders sometimes claimed openly that a particular dwelling had been "inspired by" or rather lifted from a famous architect's design. Any builder with a few years' experience behind him could knock up a passable set of plans, and at some time or other most of them did. The Boards of Health which studied applications at that time were mainly concerned about drains and the ventilation of W.C.s, the root causes of so many deadly epidemics in the past.

By 1905 number 1 Prince's Avenue had become both the official Reader estate office and Tom and Annie's new home. It must have felt palatial after their successive lodgings in Mare Street, Navarino Road and Groombridge Road, and no doubt Annie had a wonderful time furnishing it. At number 49 lived Ada Reader and her new husband Edwin James Wright, a manufacturer's agent (commercial traveller) known as Teddy. Gertrude Ethel "Cherry" Meadows, a friend of Ada's, moved in with them as a temporary measure and stayed till they died and beyond.

It was a nice place to live, once building was finished in the immediate vicinity. A good shopping centre was developing, there were trams at the bottom of the road in Ballards Lane and the railway was within ten minutes walk. There was plenty going on socially, too. Tom, with an excellent baritone voice which could be pushed into a tenor, joined the new Finchley Amateur Operatic and Orchestral Society and appeared in their initial production of Balfe's The Bohemian Girl at the Woodside Hall in June 1906. The Finchley Press, Muswell Hill Mercury and Highgate Post (all one paper) gave him a good notice; "Mr T.J.Reader, as the mincing, affected courtier-nephew, was in excellent form, and he got the best out of the character." His son Thomas Clayton was born on 29 May 1906 and Tom adopted this more distinguished name for future operatic performances. He even appeared thus in the 1914 street directory – the legend of Sarah Clayton's ancestry was still potent.

In 1912 Florence and Ras Buggé were living at number 13 Prince's Avenue, and by 1918 Tom and Annie were at 53 and his cousin Kate Sharpe and her husband had moved into number 1. The Reader-built side of the street backed onto the grounds of Dalkeith, 68 Ballards Lane, which was to have a varied future life. In 1912 a cinema and winter garden named the Alcazar was built before and behind this house, and the following year it was sold and reopened as a showy Moorish structure called The Bohemia Theatre. This closed by 1920 and the site later became a boot polish factory.[20]

Today, a fair amount of period detail and stained glass remain in Prince's Avenue, and number 11 is so well preserved and cared for that it might have been built yesterday. But modernisation and window-changing are advancing, along with conversion into flats. Double occupancy actually started soon after the building of the large five-bedroom houses, but didn't necessarily involve permanent physical division until some time later. 13 and 15 have been removed to provide access to Dorset Mews,[21] an attractive development of 46 terraced houses built on the Dalkeith/Bohemia/boot polish factory site. The shops of Prince's Parade shield it from the noise of Ballards Lane and the old factory gate is for residents only. Numbers 1-11 and 17 Prince's Avenue, whose garden boundaries had once been part of the demolished factory, have been provided with a new 2.1 metre brick wall to preserve their security. Number 17 was used as the estate office and has since been thoroughly spruced up and given a new front door.

* * *

Maude had married in June 1904, and with all her children now gone Cecilia gave up her home and spent the rest of her life moving around between those of others. This arrangement probably had a lot to do with money, but it was a usual way of life for a widow and seems sad from the viewpoint of our present times. However, her household furniture was divided amongst her five children, so she must have felt quite at home wherever her perpetual odyssey took her.

      16-66 Dangan Rd Wanstead

      22-25 Spratt Hall Rd Wanstead

      325-359 Grove Green Road Leyton

      1-65 Prince's Avenue Ballards Lane Finchley

Tom's drawing on plan for 22-25 Spratt Hall Rd

Front: Elevation

*The Gosling Family at 14 Christie Rd. South Hackney, early 1890s.
L to R: Florrie, Jessie, Sarah, Frank, Edith.*

*14 Christie Rd, 1899. Back: Florrie Gosling, Annie Beadle, Edith
Gosling, Hettie Beadle, Jessie Gosling; Front: Tom Reader, Richard
Reader.*

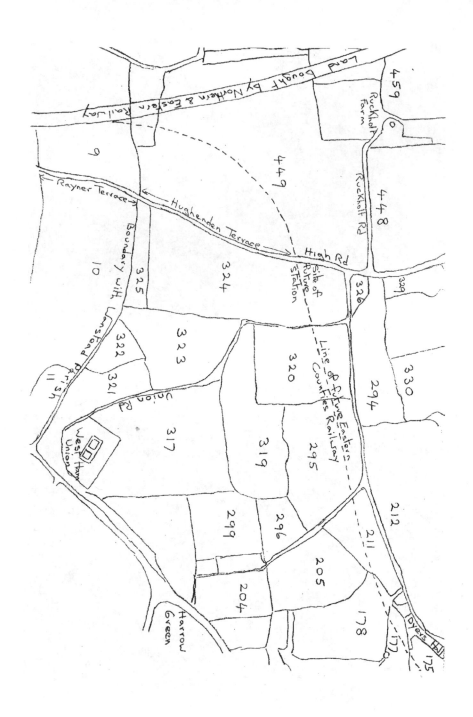

Field pattern of Leyton with 1839 Tithe Map numbering.

30 Dangan Road, E11, 1988

Picnic at Ambresbury Banks, Epping Forest, September 1900. Standing: Maude Reader, Esther Gosling?, Fred Pailthorpe, Ada Reader, Sam Witherick Jnr., Fred Kearney, Ras Buggé, Florence Reader, Fred Beadle, Ada Beadle, Tom Reader, William Sharpe, Kate Witherick. Seated: Alice Kearney, Elizabeth Witherick, Cecilia Reader, Jane Pailthorpe (widow of John Woodyer), ?, ? Sitting on ground: Florrie Gosling, Nellie & Annie Beadle, Edith Gosling, Charles Kearney, Hettie Beadle, Jessie Gosling.

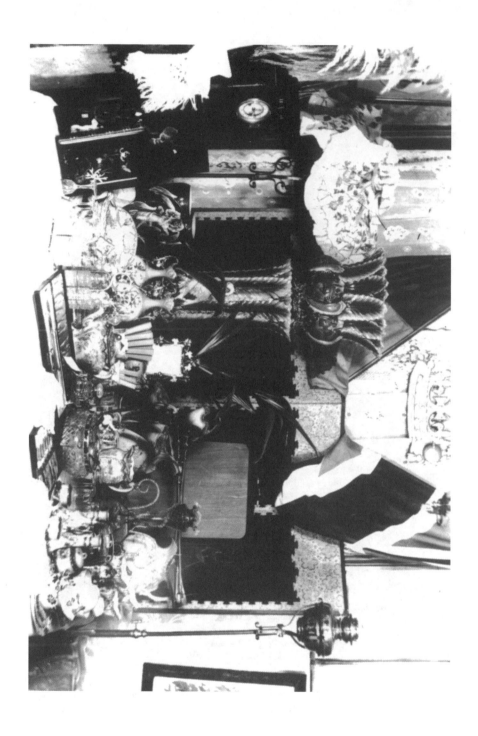

Richard and Edith Reader's wedding presents, 1902.

Wedding of Richard and Edith Reader, 7th June 1902. Back row standing: Esther Gosling, Tom Reader, Alice Kearney, Jane Reader (widow of Thos Joseph senior's cousin), Maude Reader, Fred Pailthorpe, Hilda Witherick, Sam Witherick Jnr., Elizabeth Witherick. Next row standing ?, ?, Florence Reader, Richard Reader, Edith Reader, Ada Reader, Ras Buggé, Will Gosling, Frank Gosling, Florence & Cecilia daughters of John Woodyer and Jane Pailthorpe. Seated: Clara Pailthorpe?, Annie Reader, ?, Cissie Reader, Florrie Gosling, Jessie Gosling, Cecilia Reader, Jane Pailthorpe.

PRINCE'S AVENUE, FINCHLEY

LEFT: Number 1 c.1909 with Cissie & Clayton Reader

CENTRE: Number 49, the home of Edwin James and Ada Gertrude Wright from 1905 until 1959

LEFT: Number 53, Tom and Annie Reader's home c1918-25.

CHAPTER 3 1903 – 1914

Monkhams Estate Woodford, Craven Estate Clapton Common

Richard Francis Reader was born on 31 March at 47 Groombridge Road, where Frank Gosling photographed his grandson in the arms of the monthly nurse and captioned the resultant lantern slide "1903!!" Dick was a ferocious-looking child from the moment he was born, although he was to become a handsome and attractive man, even with the large Gosling nose he had inherited. Cecilia Reader examined him and remarked "Oh, poor little dear," which is not the sort of comment a mother cares for, especially from her mother-in-law.

John Thomas Reader was to follow on 5 July the next year, and Edgar Charles on 15 August 1905. In the photographs taken soon after all three births, Edith looks ill and worn, and the effort of coping with three very small children was as wearing as it is for anybody. She recalled, after a difficult day, doing a last minute bed-make and tidy-up before Richard came in for his evening meal, and hearing the crash downstairs as Dick pulled the tablecloth off the laid table. He was also a bolter, a problem she solved by marking him with a brilliantly coloured sash which would be easy to pick out as he disappeared into the distance. Edith's health appears to have become persistently debilitated for some years, and there were no more children.

The two younger boys were born at 28 Christie Road, the house which was to contain their childhood memories and to which Edith became deeply attached, not least because her father and sisters were only seven houses away. It was, of course, rented, had two parlours linked by folding doors, kitchen, scullery, outside W.C., three bedrooms and no bathroom. There was a small garden which became for a while the setting for seriously authentic games based on the four males' passion for railway engines, and Frank took pictures of the "Chief Engineer and Staff" with their engines, signals and signalbox.

The house also contained music, and the boys went to sleep to the sound of violin and piano duets in the parlour below; for all three, Raff's Cavatina, Meditation from Thaïs and the slow movement of the Mendelssohn concerto would always recall childhood. Amateur music-making flourished at that time in South Hackney, when few middle class homes were without at least one musical instrument.

Concerts and musical evenings were widely attended, choral and operatic societies provided entertainment for their friends, occasionally of the wrong sort, and the boys joined the choir at St John of Jerusalem, acquiring a valuable musical education from the choirmaster, R.Bernard Elliot in the process.

* * *

On 24 June 1903 the mansion and estate of Monkhams at Woodford Green, Essex were auctioned by Messrs Trollope.[1] Part of this property had belonged to the Abbey of Stratford Langthorne until the dissolution of the monasteries, and from then on it had had a restless history; divided, added to, changed and renamed until the early nineteenth century, when its house was rebuilt on a new site. By 1864 it had passed into the hands of Henry Ford Barclay of the banking family and seventy acres of fields had become park.

It lay between Woodford Green and Woodford Wells, a few minutes from Epping Forest and near the top of the hill which stretches from South Woodford to the beginning of Loughton. Knighton Wood was to the north, the mansion looked east down a slope to the Roding Valley, and its main entrance came out into Monkhams Lane where it began to run across Woodford Green to the High Road. The southern part of Woodford around St.Mary's parish church had already been developed with streets of Victorian villas, and Snakes Lane was edged with roomy houses, but the Monkhams Estate was open land from the green to the Great Eastern railway and beyond.

On Barclay's death in 1892 the estate was bought for £36,350 by Arnold F.Hills, ironmaster and shipbuilder of the Thames Ironworks, Bow Creek and thereby, due to a philanthropic enterprise on behalf of his workers, the founder of West Ham United Football Club. He proceeded to lavish yet more love and money on Monkhams, including illuminated ornamental fountains. In addition to the gate lodges there were other buildings scattered around the mansion's demesnes; a farmhouse of about 1649, a timber-framed house known as Little Monkhams, a brick farmhouse of the second quarter of the nineteenth century and a scattering of small cottages. In 1895 Hills now added a row of seven brick and timber styled cottages with a single one known as Orchard Cottage in Monkhams Lane, and in 1899 a similar group of four with a laundry and drying ground at the end was erected nearer to the mansion, backing onto the boundary wall with the next estate, Harts House.[2] The intention was to use all sewage from these to feed the adjacent orchard, but it is not clear whether this was carried out; it really doesn't sound the kind of arrangement a Board of Health would warm to. Finally, in 1901 a pair of cottages was built by the farm gates where Monkhams Lane turned sharply north west between Knighton Wood and Lord's Bushes.[3]

Despite the apparent affluence suggested by these improvements, the Thames Ironworks was starting to decline,[4] not least because the Admiralty had begun commissioning ships from other yards, and in May 1900 Hills mortgaged his estate with the National Provident Institution for £30,000. But if he was in financial difficulties this tactic didn't disperse them. The sale catalogue described the many beauties and advantages of what must have been a truly wonderful place to live, and its photographs reveal late Victorian opulence installed within late Georgian simplicity and set among conservatories and gardens. It wasn't derelict, run-down or in any way "ripe for development", but a fully operative mansion and estate on which a great deal of money had only recently been spent. Perhaps the surrounding area was no longer rural and exclusive enough for the really wealthy, but a prosperous businessman could have been very happy there. If any such were bidding, the price produced by the pressure of the building boom was apparently too much for them. Instead of welcoming a new resident ready to cherish its great beauties, Monkhams fell to James Robert Twentyman for £60,300.

This man is something of an enigma. He had just returned from the Far East at the age of 59, and to the end of his life still banked with the Chartered Bank of India Australia and China and the Hong Kong and Shanghai Bank, but his background turns out to be humble. He was born in Gateshead in 1843, the son of a postman, and appears to have gone out to China c.1883 as a widowed foreman for an engineering firm building bridges. By the time he returned in 1903 he had acquired a second wife, five children and an immense fortune.

Twentyman may or may not have moved into his lavish new home, but his intentions for the estate were unambiguous from the start. In March 1904, nine months from the date of his purchase, he submitted plans to the Woodford Urban District Council for the first roads,[5] produced by the architects Cockett and Henderson of 72 Bishopsgate Street and the surveyors Mabbett and Edge of 127 Mount Street, Grosvenor Square. Cockett had received approval for an estate agent's shop, office and flat[6] by the railway level crossing in February, and the plan shows the southern part of the park near Woodford Station very much as eventually built, although King's Avenue is called Barclay Drive. Whether this refers to Henry Ford Barclay or to the builders of that name who worked with Twentyman is not clear. The road and services contractors were to be local firm W.C.French of Buckhurst Hill. An amended road and drainage plan was put in almost immediately and approved on 31 May, and the details of drains for King's Avenue and Queen's Avenue were passed by 20 September.[7]

It is immensely rewarding to research an estate for which full source material survives. In addition to the plans in the Reader archive, all other builders' planning applications have been retained by the present London Borough of Redbridge, though the oldest are very fragile, and there is even a Building Inspector's book for 1909 – 1914 extant.

On 13 December 1904 the very first building application for the Monkhams Estate was approved by the council. It was for twelve villas to be numbered 2 – 24 Monkhams Drive and the owners and builders were T.J. and R.A.Reader of 1 Prince's Avenue, Church End, Finchley.[8]

Others followed. In February 1905 H.C.Clare applied for nos 19 and 21 Monkhams Drive,[9] and the local firm of Sheppard Brothers put in applications for three large detached houses overlooking Woodford Green soon after.[10] During the first ten years houses were built by Reader, Barclay, Lee, Edmondson, Clare, Sheppard, Osborn, Flaxman & Wright, Starke, Young and Peachey.[11] Twentyman himself put in several building applications for Monkhams Lane,[12] and in 1913 for twelve semi-detached houses in Monkhams Drive to be built by Alistair Barclay (73-95).[13]

The presence of all these different builders on one estate naturally produced intense competition, and not always of a gentlemanly character. There is a Reader story illustrating this situation, though not necessarily at Monkhams, in which a big builder swaggers onto their site and tells Richard "You'd better sell this lot quick and get out, I'm coming in." It is interesting to try and work out who this unappealing man was, but impossible to come to a conclusion; there must have been so many likely candidates.

The first Reader Bros houses in Monkhams Drive were a big step-up for them. They were and are large, handsome, double-fronted, semi-detached middle class villas, each with three reception rooms, lounge hall, six bedrooms with fitted wardrobes, a "fine" bathroom and a box room. They sold for £1,100, and again one wonders about finance. Sales documents reveal Twentyman as the first part, the builders as the second part and the buyer as the third. Whether Reader's obtained their stake from the bank, a building society or from Twentyman, the outlay on these houses must have been considerable, and they were quickly followed during the next three years by many others. But study of the Post Office Directory shows that they were being bought fairly quickly, and at the same time the brothers were contracting for other firms on the site. In King's Avenue, for instance, James Edmondson of Muswell Hill started building on the east side of the south end by 1906,[14] and although the plans and elevations presented to the council name Edmondson's as both architects and builders, preparatory pencil drawings of these houses marked Edmondsons Plan F survive in the Reader plan collection, and the porch design includes bulbous pillars reminiscent of ladies' legs which were said to be a favourite feature of Tom's. It seems more than likely, then, that the Readers contracted out both their building and their designing skills. Purchasers visiting the estate to choose plots would sometimes ask the master builders working on site to design a house for them and there are several of these in the folder which contains the earliest Reader designs, one labelled "for Mr.Edmondson" and not all of them eventually built. Postcards were also produced for prospects to take away.

Two large houses built for Edmondson were 26 and 28 Monkhams Drive.[15] The first has Edmondson named as architect on the application, but it is remarkably similar to other houses on the same side of the road designed by Reader's, and Richard was photographed outside it with his men. The second was a complex construction called The Gables.

This huge house, with four reception rooms, conservatory, extensive domestic quarters, seven bedrooms, two bathrooms and a roof which must have been a headache both to construct and to maintain, was built for David Skene Barclay,[16] a timber merchant and developer whose nephew Alistair was building in Queen's Avenue, Monkhams Drive and King's Avenue. Grubby linen copies of elevations and plans exist in the Reader archive, signed Edmondson 9 The Broadway Winchmore Hill with "architect" in very afterthought writing, and Reader's were certainly the contracted builders even if not the designers of this impressive residence. In 1920 a garage with flat above was built in the grounds by Dove Bros. of Islington no less, and the house survived until the sixties, when it was demolished and the cul-de-sac Broad Oak built upon its site.

Although the plots were sold off numbered, houses were at first known only by their names,[17] which added to the high-class atmosphere and gave residents the feel of owning a country house as opposed to living in a suburb. But this could result in confusing duplications; for instance, a Hillside in both Monkhams Avenue and Monkhams Drive, which must have caused the sort of postal misdelivery which still afflicts an estate with three roads called Monkhams. There was also a significant proportion of Scots, Irish and Welsh names, the rationale presumably being that Celtic meant cosy, for as Georgian and Victorian development sought class with royal or noble titles, so the Edwardians yearned for the healthy seaviews and misty hills of British country life.

Of course, during the early years of the estate the residents were indeed living in the country. The station to London might be at the bottom of the road and amazing parades of shops being erected by Edmondson with every fashionable Edwardian twiddly bit stuck on somewhere, including looming false gables;[18] and the Woodford Urban District Council might have bought a piece of ground on the fork between Monkhams Avenue and King's Avenue for Council Offices, but behind the new houses fields stretched away to Buckhurst Hill and Woodford Bridge, and the adjacent mansion of Harts House was still the seat of a gentleman who hosted garden parties in aid of the Liberal cause. In rural style, some of the local firms building on the estate continued to double as undertakers.

Reader's took further plots in Monkhams Drive,[19] and in 1909 applications were also put in for smaller property in Monkhams Avenue,[20] which the advertising leaflet produced for this new enterprise claimed had been regularly inquired for over the previous five years. Buyers were offered either freehold or leasehold, the difference in price being approximately £200. The Reader estate office was a wooden building between 35 Monkhams Avenue, built by Osborn's of South Woodford, and 39, the first of the Reader houses. The footpath kerbs were turned in towards this piece of land, ready for a road to be put in should Mr. W.H.Brown of Harts decide to sell up for development. At the time the possibility must have looked very likely, but it was actually to take ninety years to happen. Edith brought the three boys over to watch the building and explore the half-built houses, and they picnicked in Knighton Wood or walked to the baker's at the bottom of Queen's Road Buckhurst Hill for tea and cakes on a green-tiled table. The children remembered these outings as idyllic, with corn head-high in the fields of Monkhams Farm and butterflies to be chased and collected.

Unfortunately, whether the Readers were really doing well or merely keeping their heads above water, they were soon to be affected by something completely beyond their control. At auction, the land had been described as "free of title and land tax, with timber included in the sale", but in 1909 Lloyd George introduced his proposal for the taxation of all land in order to raise sixteen million pounds of extra revenue, and the bottom dropped out of the house sale market, even though the measure was to be fought tooth and nail through both Houses of Parliament. In May the Conservative member for Finsbury Holborn Division, James Farquarson Remnant declared "Of all the fallacies that ever entered into the minds of men there are none perhaps more ridiculous than this idea, that in the case of land and land alone, you can assist progress by clapping on heavy taxes, by driving away the prudent investor, and by subjecting such person as may still be willing to develop into exceptional risks and disabilities."[21] At the second reading, Austen Chamberlain also lambasted the Chancellor. "You can force [land] onto the market, and you may make it impossible for them to hold it, but you cannot force builders to build. Men will not risk their money in property until there is a reasonable chance of finding occupants for the houses. The process of development is nearly in all cases slow and costly... What man today would offer the same price for property subject to these taxes as he was willing to give the day before the Budget statement was announced?"[22] Tom and Richard, stopped in their financial tracks by the Chancellor, must have felt like heaving bricks over Mr Brown's Liberal fence.

Buyers dropped off quickly and anxiety became a daily companion. It must have added extra emotion to Tom's performance when at the beginning of July "the singing of 'Vain! in vain do I call' by Mr.T.Clayton Reader as Faust was highly commendable and his acting quite above the usual average."[23] Tom's daughter remembered driving over from Finchley with her parents on Saturdays, and sitting in the car or in the estate office on the site of the flower bed in the present Hutton Close while absolutely nothing happened. Richard doesn't seem to have run a car at that time, although he had a motorcycle, and on one occasion was standing on Woodford Station in the depths of despair when a man digging up onions on the other side of the railings boasted to him that it was the best crop he'd ever had in his life. The story handed down is that Richard found this joy in small things cheering, but it is hardly obvious why; he might well have envied the onion-grower. The Land Tax was not brought into operation until 1911 but its shadow fell over development from the moment it was announced, deputations of master builders hurrying to lobby M.P.s and Lloyd George himself. And it was not only builders who would be affected; landowners such as Twentyman would suffer as well, hence the outraged opposition of the land-wealthy House of Lords.

In 1910 Reader's built a house named Shepreth, later numbered 76 Monkhams Avenue,[24] for Thomas Collins, a nurseryman in business on the Monkhams House kitchen garden site next to the stables, and the building of their part of the Monkhams Estate dragged on into 1914. In March of that year a further piece of land was taken in Monkhams Avenue for ten more houses but only two were to be built, numbers 63 and 65.[25] It seems probable that Twentyman eventually bought unused land and unsold houses back at a lower valuation, as the brothers are said to have barely broken even on their investment, a disastrous start for houses which are now so admired and so sought after.

The Reader memories of James Robert Twentyman were bitter, in fact Tom's daughter referred to him at the end of her life as a crook. But he was probably just an astute and unsentimental businessman, which can look very like the same thing to those at the sharp end of the astuteness. Certainly his Will is full of family affection and religious sentiment, and the inscription on his grave what the Victorians used to call "affecting."

In the same year that he bought Monkhams he also acquired the Lordship of the Manor and the Hall at Kirby Misperton near Pickering in North Yorkshire; Prince's Avenue and Madeira Grove, Woodford Green were originally to be called Misperton Road and Misperton Crescent. A great deal of money was spent upon the Yorkshire estate, including ornamental gardens built by Chinese labourers, one of whom is said to haunt the place, and according to Twentyman's Yorkshire obituaries he dispensed philanthropy in every direction and was active in all branches of the local Establishment e.g. Alderman, Freemason, J.P. etc.[26] He retained ownership of much of the Monkhams Estate until his death in 1928, his agent Stephen Harper being officially in residence at The Swiss Cottage (the brick farmhouse halfway down Monkhams Lane now 9 Prince's Avenue) as well as having a house in Kirby Misperton. All Twentyman's real estate including that in the Far East was then supposed to be sold off, but Kirby Misperton Hall was still in the hands of his trustees in 1937. His testamentary prayer that God would give his children the grace to sort things out amicably perhaps suggests that he thought they might need it.

* * *

At the same time as the break-up of the Monkhams Estate, the sloping landscape between Clapton Common and the River Lea was also suffering death by development. The Ordnance Survey map for 1868 delineates a paradise of large-gardened villas surrounded by open fields, with the back windows of Buccleuch Terrace on the Common commanding views of the Lea Valley and Essex beyond. At the north west end is the early nineteenth century Craven Lodge Estate, skirted to the south east by a path to Baileys Lane called Craven Walk. This estate was sold to a developer, Reuben Button, and by 1894 had been laid out in roads, with some houses already built in Baileys Lane (Craven Park Rd), Olinda Rd, Ravensdale Rd and Castlewood Rd.[27]

Neighbouring land was also under pressure. In 1908 applications were made to Hackney Urban District Council by a neighbour of Tom Reader's, James Ellwood of 50 Prince's Avenue Finchley, for the laying out of Leadale, Ashtead and Lingwood Rds for the Barclay brothers[28] on Tyssen land behind Buccleuch Terrace. David Skene and Samuel Headrick Barclay had been putting in applications at the Craven estate since 1906, and by 1911 had houses built or building in Moundfield Rd, Castlewood Rd, Spring Hill, Lingwood Rd and the widened Craven Walk. This last had been diverted towards the Lea, where "Rivulet Rd" was eventually intended to run along the towpath. But from 1912 onwards, S.H.Barclay's name no longer appears on applications. Instead they are put in by D.S. Barclay or by Richard Reader, working as Barclay's manager. This must have been welcome work, given the problems at Woodford, but he was providing designing skills as well and Barclay was an exacting man to work for. There are many houseplans designed by Richard for the Craven Lodge Estate in the Reader archive, but by no means all were used. One is not signed, and he possibly supervised construction of work already in progress. He kept a foot in both developments; on the back of his designs for 51 – 69 Lingwood Rd he roughed out a plan for the new garage at Dunnottar 26 Monkhams Drive.

The three-bedroom houses were less expensive than those at Woodford and mostly built in terraces, but they have the same hallmarks of self-confident Edwardian architecture; bay windows, ornate woodwork and plenty of stained glass, including some displaying the number of the house. A motorshed was added to 1 Leadale Road by the end of 1913, but this was still an unusual request. Ironically the estate benefited from a campaign to stop further development before the complete destruction of what had once been a beauty spot, and was thus able to enjoy the amenities of the Upper Clapton Cricket and Lawn Tennis Club and the new Springfield Park.

For many years the area has been widely adopted by the Hassidic Jewish community, and there are few doorposts which do not bear a mezzuzza. The condition of the houses ranges from well-preserved through "improved" to utter dereliction, as if in Chancery.

* * *

Few clear answers lie in planning applications. The first approved plan for an estate will not always, in fact is fairly unlikely to be built exactly like that. There will be second thoughts, alterations, problems, sometimes complete abandonment and the selling on of the land to another builder. The Barclay-Reader aspect of the Craven Lodge Estate is complex and confusing, and the final decision on whose houses are which is best made by going and looking at them. With this criterion, the Reader-built houses appear to be as follows:

> Ashtead Rd 12-44
>
> Craven Walk 44-58
>
> Leadale Road 1-69 2-46
>
> Lingwood Rd 51-69 and possibly 1-49 10-36

On the Monkhams Estate Woodford, definite Reader houses are:

> Monkhams Avenue 39-65 2-4 8-30 76
>
> Monkhams Drive 3-15 23-25 2-28 (28 dem.)

Those recorded in the planning index as Edmondson but probably designed and built for them by Reader are:

> King's Avenue 3-13 2-10

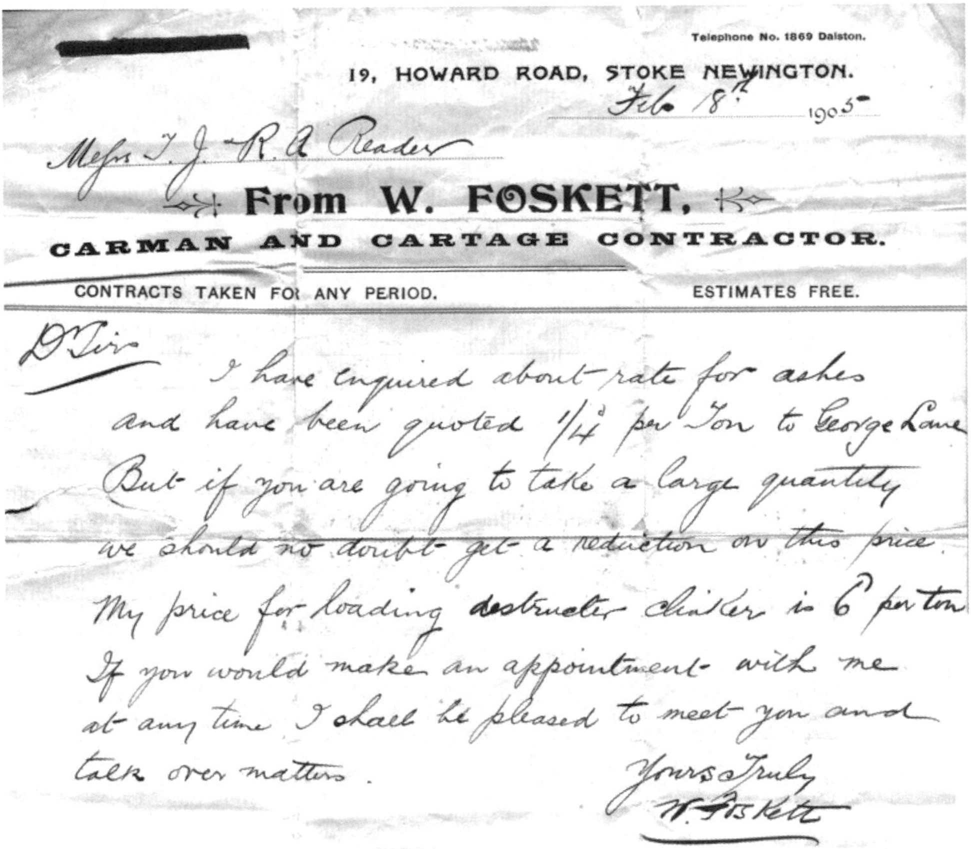

Telephone No. 1869 Dalston.

19, HOWARD ROAD, STOKE NEWINGTON.

Feb 18th 1905

Messrs T. J. & R. A. Reader

From W. FOSKETT,

CARMAN AND CARTAGE CONTRACTOR.

CONTRACTS TAKEN FOR ANY PERIOD.   ESTIMATES FREE.

D'Sir

I have enquired about rate for ashes and have been quoted 1/4d per Ton to George Lane But if you are going to take a large quantity we should no doubt get a reduction on this price. My price for loading destructor clinker is 6d per ton If you would make an appointment with me at any time I shall be pleased to meet you and talk over matters.

Yours Truly
W. Foskett

W. Foskett's estimate re the Monkhams Estate. The destructor clinker was probably used to build garden walls.

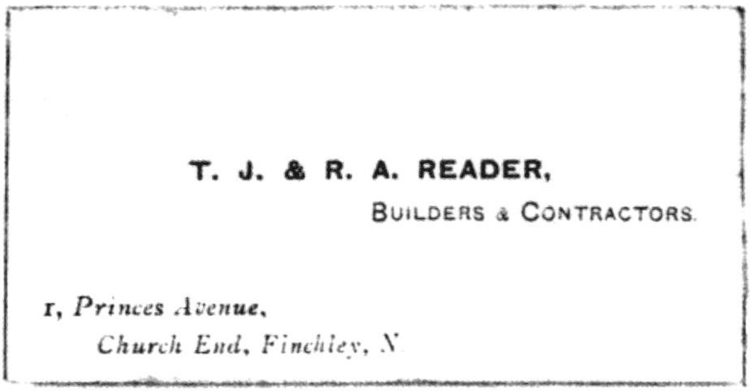

T. J. & R. A. READER,
BUILDERS & CONTRACTORS.

1, Princes Avenue,
Church End, Finchley, N

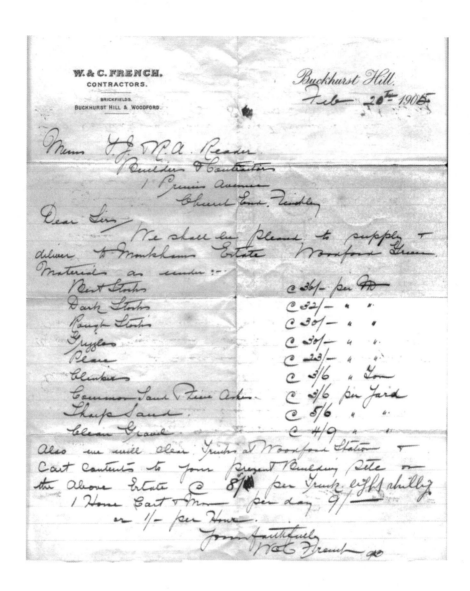

Estimate from W.C. French for building materials
on Monkhams Estate Feb 20 1905.

Opposite page above : Postcard given to prospective buyers:
Rosemount, 14 Monkhams Drive and Fritton Lodge, number 20.
Below: Plan of Fritton Lodge and Fernbank,
but with dormer windows.

Monkham's Drive.

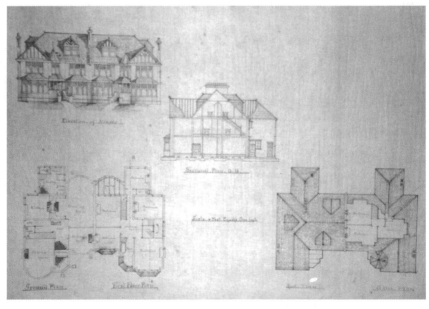

Richard Reader (back row with bowler hat) outside Dunnotar, 26 Monkhams Drive. Many of these men died in the 1914-1918 war.

The bottom of Monkhams Avenue. Left, The Nursery at No 1, Edmondson's 3-17. Right, space left for council offices then 2 & 4. Ahead, nos 3 & 5 Monkhams Drive. Pre 1914.

The Chief Engineer and Staff, 28 Christie Road, 1909. Photograph by F.W. Gosling. Richard built the three engines.

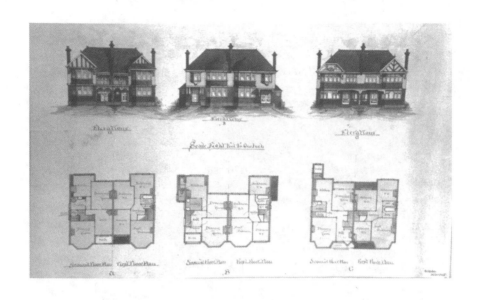

Monkhams Avenue

Above: Plans A, B & C

Below: Plans D, E & F.

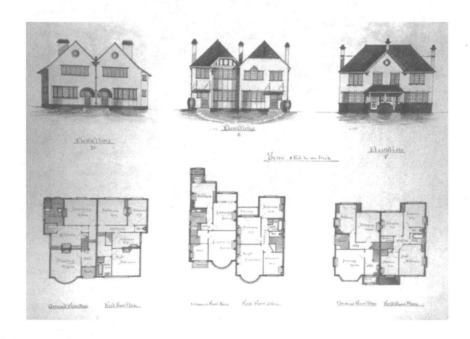

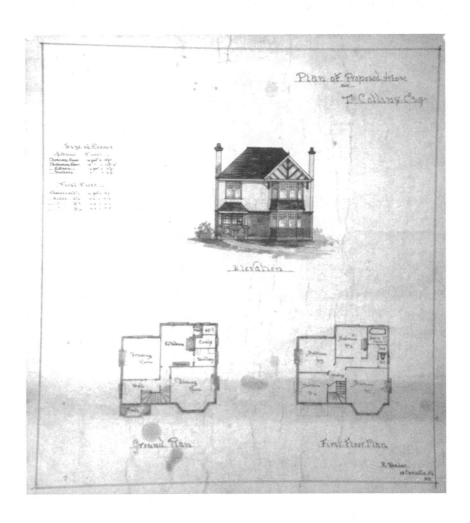

Shepreth, 76 Monkhams Avenue.

Monkham's Drive.

Frontage 110 ft.; entire depth of Land 148 ft.
Entire finish to choice.

SPECIFICATION:

It is quite impossible to describe these houses in a few words. They are a copy of one of our most eminent Architect's designs. They have magnificent Rooms, and the Hall and Staircase is fit for a Mansion. One of them has accommodation for a Motor Garage at the side, fitted and finished in keeping throughout.

SIZE OF ROOMS :

	GROUND FLOOR.
Dining Room ...	15 ft. 6 in. by 23 ft.
Hall Parlour ...	16 ft. „ 20 ft.
Drawing Room ...	15 ft. „ 24 ft.
Kitchen ...	16 ft. „ 15 ft.

Tiled Scullery, large Stove, Cupboards, etc., etc.

SIZE OF ROOMS : —

	FIRST FLOOR.
Best Bedroom ...	24 ft. by 15 ft. 6 in.
Small Dressing Room	
Front Bedroom ...	12 ft. 6 in. „ 12 ft.
Billiard Room or	
Side Bedroom ...	22 ft. 6 in. „ 15 ft.
Servant's Bedroom ...	15 ft. „ 13 ft.
Back Bedroom ...	14 ft. „ 13 ft.

Wardrobes, Linen Cupboards, etc., etc.

PRICE :—

Freehold.—£1,200. Motor Garage Extra.

THE BEST VALUE TO BE HAD ROUND LONDON.

2 Monkhams Avenue, then called 2 Monkhams Drive,
from the Sales brochure. The plan was nearly used again
at Child's Hill in 1923.

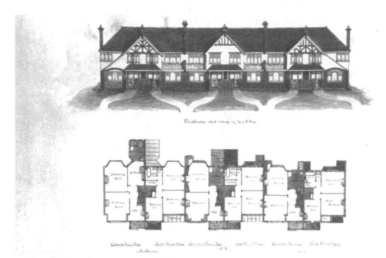

Elevation of a Group of Six Villas.

Ground Floor Plan   First Floor Plan   Second Floor Plan   Attic Floor Plan   Basement Floor Plan   Sub Floor Plan

Previous page:

TOP: Plan by Richard Reader for Ashtead Rd. Clapton

MIDDLE: Numbers 30-38 Ashtead Road, Clapton c.1914.

BOTTOM: Numbers 30-38 Ashtead Road, Clapton 1994.

19 - 1 Leadale Road, Clapton, c.1914.

CHAPTER 4 1914 – 1920

War. Hackney Council's first housing estate.

Richard and Edith's sons started their education at Miss Elizabeth Winter's school, 1 Meynell Rd, behind Well St Common. Its numbers were small, but there were as always a few rough characters among the boys; Jack is said to have turned on a bully amidst the general acclamation of his schoolfellows, and a deep rage against cruelty and injustice remained with him all his life. In the spirit of imperial times, the boys were provided with wooden rifles and marched around the small school yard to the accompaniment of Miss Winter's piano, but by 1914 she had closed down and they were moved to the Board School at Lauriston Rd.

At the end of July Tom was supervising in Monkhams Avenue and Richard managing for Barclay's at Clapton. Richard took his family down to one of their favourite holiday resorts and settled them into lodgings with Mrs. Matthews at Katella, New Road, Littlehampton, and Dick, Jack and Edgar got down to the business of swimming, paddling, sailing model boats and building sandcastles on Climping Sands.

On the evening of Bank Holiday Monday 4 August, the three boys leant out of their bedroom window and watched people gathered around a street lamp, reading the evening newspapers which announced Britain's declaration of war on Germany. The next day ships could be seen out in the Channel moving towards France, and Richard returned to London to see what was happening to trade (it was "in a state of chaos") and report back to his family.

"My dear Pets, Just a line to let you know all is well – The train was very late getting to London Bridge nearly an hour, we were held up for a long time near Spa Road and then an enormous troop train flew past, 2 Engines a train full of soldiers shouting, with 8 cannons on trucks at the back with horses in Waggons complete off to the Front somewhere. Those Ships we saw on the Sea yesterday at regular intervals, crossing the Channel I heard on the Train and again in London on good authority were taking troops to Belgium & France, in any kind of old tramp Steamer they could lay their hand on. 180,000 men crossed the Channel in 14 hours with Sir John French in Command, when it becomes known it will be a record in Mobilizing troops but nothing of this is in the papers. Mr Barclay came to day and decided to put the men on three quarter time for a while, some of the men had been called up for the Reserve in the week all their tools left behind 2 of them expecting Babies this month, there is Luck for their poor little wives 10/- a week and 2/6 for each child till their husbands return. . . God bless you all till I see you Saturday."

Frank Gosling sent cards from Bude with his own pencil cartoons – the three Goslings watching the coast for invasion, "England for Ever. Many people coming home, all very quiet...." On Friday 14 August Edith sent a postcard to 28 Christie Road, catching the 5 p.m. post. "We are just sending these hoping you will wait for the post, have you given the garden some water, if not leave the garden door for Polly just try and see her dear Try and catch train between 1 & 2." It crossed with another letter from Richard.

"My Dear Sweetheart, Once more I send you a few lines of Greeting . . . this has seemed a long week to me sweetheart – I have just spent 2 hours on Victoria Park Station . . . My Word what excitement – on the side where the Stratford trains should be was a line of G.E.R. expresses and troop trains were being pulled up one after the other with Great Western & L.& N.Western Engines, they pulled up just outside the Station and Changed engines the G.E.R. taking them on somewhere, trains full of Soldiers with trucks full of Horses, I felt I could not come away and leave it all. . . . Mr Barclay is in a very worried state I had strict orders today to pay nobody at all, and put off several tomorrow, which he altered afterwards to knocking 1½d per hour off which will be better for them but I am expecting a very warm time tomorrow..."

On Tuesday 18th "Once more I sit down in the kitchen all alone to write you a few lines but I am quite all right having been in with the Dad and Girls for the past 2 hours they are very brown and blistered . . . I can't forget my blessed Dat & Dagy [Jack and Edgar] racing up the platform after the train . . . Well Darling I have plenty of work and business on unfortunately rather unpleasant, I have seen Tom to-night and he seems worried and upset, it has got on my nerves a bit I am afraid otherwise I am quite well and fit, have a good time My Dears ..."

This could be a reference to the buying back of the unsold Monkhams land and houses by Twentyman, or to laying off men at Clapton due to the retrenchment of David Barclay.

On the 21st Edith sent a card of the Promenade. Her health was poor again – "My dear, just a card, shall see you soon, I felt rather worried about you but we must hope for the best...Have you seen the eclipse? I am feeling a bit better today but shall not bathe this holiday, we are just off crabbing, looking forward to to-morrow..."

From Richard next week – "To My Dear Ones – I was so pleased to get your packet this morning 3 fine pictures and a dear message from you.. . . Dear Dat's picture of you all having dinner without your Old Daddy is beautiful. . . I have got a very busy week this week, having got the 12 sets of plans back from the plan printers.[1] I have got to colour them all and put the red drains in and send them in to the Town Hall and Spring Gardens [L.C.C.County Hall] and very glad I shall be to see the back of them once more. Mr Barclay was on the job twice on Monday as he came up on Sunday night he has got the fidgets and is very funny but I am not going to worry myself, I expect he has got the War on the Brain.....all the schools round Hackney have got Soldiers quartered in them now...Kenton Rd School has about 200 there . . . Love and kisses to you all Darlings from Daddy."

* * *

The young men flooded out to France, where events soon shattered the nation's illusions about a quick, clean victory, and the country settled into the rhythms of War. Belgian refugee children stayed in the road and played with the Reader boys. A neighbour's son came to say goodbye to his parents in officer's uniform and hitched his horse to a lamp-post. Victoria Park was partly turned over to allotments and an anti-aircraft post, and in May 1915 bombing started and the Goslings had their windows blown out. There was another Littlehampton holiday in August, when Edith was told off by a mounted officer for ignoring the warning flag on Climping Sands and Richard again came down at weekends – "great joy at thought of your arrival –"

On the night of Saturday 2 September 1916 the whole of Christie Rd turned out to watch the Zeppelin going down over Cuffley. Two months later, their conscripted next-door neighbour Mervyn William Irvine wrote from Rouen asking how much now for Zepp front seats? The boys drew complex, detailed battle scenes and Edgar started writing a stirring boy's story called Jack Neville (Chapter 1 – I make a friend). The neighbours were seen at St John of Jerusalem in tears because their officer son had been killed.

Tom had finished off at Woodford and then found a job as traveller with a petrol company, booking orders from depots. Building probably continued at Clapton until October 1916 when the forty-year-old Richard was medically examined, found fit for service in garrison or provisional units and drafted into the Woolwich Arsenal as a First Class Examiner of big guns.[2] Unfortunately, the records of all civilian workers at the Arsenal during the First World War were automatically destroyed when the workers reached or would have reached their 85th birthday, so information on his life there is sparse. Of course the job meant long hours in dangerous conditions. There was much sickness, particularly among women filling shells, and the perils of bombing were added to the situation. The severest danger of all, however, had little to do with the Boche, despite its taking place on the Kaiser's birthday.

Like numerous others, the works of Brunner, Mond & Co. by the Thames in North Woolwich had been taken over by the Ministry of Munitions, and was now engaged in the purification of T.N.T. At about 6.52 p.m. on 19 January 1917 an explosion was heard all over London and as far away as Cambridge. As the sky to the south-east of Hackney was seen to become a red glow Edith jumped to the same conclusion as most of the population, that the Arsenal had gone up. She grabbed the children and made for Victoria Park Station in search of news.

Richard had just finished his shift, and he emerged from the northern exit of the Woolwich foot tunnel to find that the world had turned to flame. All buildings within 400 yards of the works were totally demolished. Up to 500 yards everything was beyond repair, beyond 650 yards most buildings had broken windows, collapsed ceilings or other damage. Flying metal added to the devastation – a gas holder on the south bank was destroyed by a white-hot boiler plate. The whole area was cut off from communications and it was at least half an hour before help began to arrive, so by the time Richard was able to reach home his family were frantic.

Until Sunday afternoon fire raged over a square mile, and as it finally subsided the water from fire engines froze on everything. Richard's escape was nothing short of miraculous, for at least a thousand people had been injured, 73 of them fatally.[3]

* * *

For the 1917 summer holidays Edith and the boys stayed in a terraced cottage at 8 Doods Rd Reigate, amidst the wonderful scenery and wildlife of the North Downs. Postcards went back and forth between there and London, and Cecilia wrote from Eastbourne in July. On 14 August Richard sent a card of the Woolwich Ferry from a temporary hostel in Archery Rd Eltham. On the 18th Frank Gosling sent hand-drawn postcards from Leigh-on-Sea. The boys reported exciting news of seeing German prisoners being marched around Reigate.

 They returned to a new school, Coopers Company, the other side of Victoria Park in Tredegar Square, Bow.[4] The boys were growing fast and were not to stop for some time. Now 5'9", 5' 5" and 5' 1", they were eventually to measure 6' 3", 6' 5" and 6' 4", heights which were so unusual at the time that people would turn and stare at them in the street.

Towards the end of the year they were taken to see round the Arsenal, despite the events of the previous January and the fact that normal safety precautions had been abandoned. Scattered over the vast complex there were 172 buildings which each contained at least a ton of explosive, and only 15 of which were in accord with distance regulations. It was estimated that in all no less than three and a half thousand tons were within 100 yards of the river bank, and that an explosion would have demolished it and caused catastrophic flooding.

The huge naval gun used by the boy hero Jack Cornwell[5] was in for repair, and the Reader boys peered into great sheds full of munitions waiting to be loaded onto ships at the Arsenal's own quay. Of course they drew it all afterwards (surely illegal in wartime?) and Richard received pictures of himself and his colleague Bob Grant at work in their brown overalls. In Bristol, Fred Pailthorpe's widow Clara got a full description and wrote to Edith on notepaper which probably came from Pailthorpe's bookshop.

 "I have been a long time in writing, and I hope you are feeling better and have not been scared by the Bombs but last nights raid seemed serious enough. Tell your Boys I quite enjoyed the description they gave about the guns . . . You will see what very old fashioned paper I am writing on I think it must be sixty years ago since they were sold. Does Dick still have to go to Business on Sundays Fredy's days begin quite early and does not get home until past eight at night. He is at a large aeroplane works at Filton . . ." Another letter the following April revealed that Frederick William Pailthorpe's two sons had not spoken to each other for two years.

Bombing raids continued, now mostly by Gotha bombers, and it may have been at this time that the park building used to house model boats was hit, destroying the expert work of many enthusiasts, Richard among them. It was a small tragedy among so much carnage, but personal enough to make him shed tears.

In contrast to most of the population, the Readers and their immediate relatives suffered no fatalities and only minor casualties. John Woodyer Pailthorpe's son Edwin, for instance, contracted trench foot at Passchendaele and had part of it removed. Very many others in Hackney were not so fortunate, and George Marston from number 26 Christie Rd was killed in 1916. When news of the Armistice came through Edith called across the fence "The War's over, Mrs. Marston!" "It's too late for me," was the bitter reply.

Frank Gosling, who had been suffering from lung trouble for some time, died in November 1918. Despite the difficult side of his nature his departure must have left a gap in the family, particularly for the grandsons he doted on. However, the passionate enthusiasm he had had for the War prompted a cynical obituary from one member. The Armistice, he said, had left Frank nothing to live for.

* * *

The end of a war releases overwhelming relief and hope, but in a country where actual fighting has not been taking place it brings only small changes in everyday life for some time. The Arsenal gradually changed over to the making of railway engines and other engineering, and Richard stayed there for at least a year, with little chance yet of taking up his own trade again. Both he and Edith had been ill, and this is very obvious from their photographs.

But the return of huge numbers of demobilised servicemen brought Lloyd George's National Government face to face with the serious shortage of decent homes for working class heroes. To meet this dire emergency the "Addison" Housing and Town Planning Act 1919, named after the Minister of Health, made local authorities responsible for providing housing and accepted for the first time that central government should subsidise it. There was anxiety in all organizations connected with building that the standard of the imminent rush of council development should be of good quality, not the run-up-quick, short-life jerry-building which had so often distinguished privately-built lower class housing. On 14 April and 29 November 1919 the Society of Architects sent circulars to all Local Authorities, urging that competent architects should design the work, and repeated their request on 6 March 1920, while the London House Builders' Association later held a conference at Caxton Hall Westminster on 8 December 1921, in the same bid to raise standards and presumably business.

The building of estates was pursued as quickly as dealing with government departments allowed. The cost was largely to be met out of loans raised by local councils, but in the capital any loss on schemes approved by the Ministry of Health would be paid for by a penny rate levied all over London, and the shortfall made up out of Imperial Funds. For this reason costs were scrutinised rigorously by Whitehall, and as changes often had to be made in designs and specifications to satisfy them the councils were by no means masters of their own proposed houses.

In order to keep everyone concerned in this great enterprise fully informed and galvanized, the Ministry of Health Housing Dept. issued a journal entitled Housing,[6] its first number coming out at the time of the Peace Celebrations in July 1919 when, it pointed out, "there could scarcely be a better way of celebrating the termination of a desolating war than to unite in a determined effort to sweep away the evil slums and wretched cottages which disfigure our towns and our countryside, and to raise up healthy and pleasant houses for our people."

No-one could argue with such a programme, but alongside it another went in step. Architecture can be a pretty snobbish business, more concerned with what people ought to have than with what they want. Planners, architects and housing officials of every period invariably deplore and run down previous building, particularly if it has been largely speculative and popular (though greater and more worthy items like Euston Station have still received their share of contempt). They themselves have found the right answer and the correct style at last, and the old is always going to be "swept away" (like Euston Station). These fascinating periodicals contain their share of sniping; at coloured glass, "fantastic" metal door plates, carved woodwork and other enjoyable and surely harmless fripperies, and we are left in no doubt that a moral crusade is on the move. Yesterday's architecture is not only out of fashion, it is <u>wrong</u>, and this attitude crops up again and again at all dates. For instance, Design for Today, published by the Design and Industries Association in 1934, was to go into a puritanical huff about how "ornamentation is unnecessary on any modern shop-front. It is offensive on the exterior of a butcher's shop, where present day standards of hygiene demand plain surfaces & dark or neutral colours." Unnecessary maybe, but offensive? These outraged cries of "Rubbish!" were to grow even louder after 1945 and reach their intolerant and destructive peak in the sixties.

* * *

Like all Inner London areas, the Metropolitan Borough of Hackney had housing problems before 1914, and there had been a fair amount of bomb damage and neglect to make things worse. A housing committee was set up in July ready for the new Act, and the conversion of existing property was set in hand. They then began to look for vacant sites on which to erect new estates, lighting on an area immediately south of Clapton Station. Just before the coming of the railway in 1866 the site had been occupied by some of the large villas and gardens lining Lower and Upper Clapton Roads, plus brick fields 134, 135 and 136 behind them and a small field marked 137 in the 1868 Ordnance Survey map. By 1894 field 137 was fully built up, and roads were being laid out on the remainder.

In Gunton Road, Woodruff put in applications for 1-51 and 2-52 in the 1890s, and Osment for 53-63 and 54-64 in 1907 and 1908. In Cleveleys Road, Chillingworth put in applications for 1-91 and 2-88 between 1912 and 1914, but by 1920 only 1-67 and 2-68 had been built. In Casimir Road, he had applied for 1 – 69 between 1913 and 1915, but only 39-69 had been built.[7] In 1919, therefore, the east side of the estate, overlooking the North Millfields Recreation Ground, remained empty. Hackney[8] Council submitted plans to the London Housing Board of the Ministry of Health for finishing the development with houses similar to the existing ones, only to be told that they were too large and too expensive.

In November 1919 the council election brought a majority Labour Council to power in Hackney for the first time, though with a very small over-all majority. By now the site's landowners were about to sell the land for factories, and the new Housing Committee became so frustrated by the Housing Board's "difficulties and delays" that they were talking of organising a deputation. The Borough Engineer's Department had produced a plan for 80 terrace cottages by February 1920, but it was not until 18 March that the Ministry approved both site and purchase for £12,610, exclusive of costs.

Even then, the Council's problems were not over. On 5 May the lowest tender, £87,931 9s 6d, was put in by W.E.Davey of Southend on

Sea, but the London Housing Board refused to allow acceptance unless the cost was reduced by no less than £90 per house. Also, the present residents of the estate complained that the erection of much cheaper houses would affect their own values, in response to which the Committee could only agree, express sympathy and explain that they had Government on their backs. To compound the difficulties, the London Building Trade Federation now increased the prices of materials and wages, and Davey first increased his price by £5,300 then withdrew his tender altogether.

* * *

Richard Reader had left Woolwich Arsenal by this time and former employees had started to call on him in the hope of work. Many of his men had been killed, and it must have taken time to recruit a large enough workforce with which to start up again. Both Dick and Edgar were working in the City, Dick as a stockbroker's runner and Edgar as an office boy, but Jack was enthusiastically interested in building and joined his father in the reviving firm, where he was put under the tutelage of Walter Moore the carpenter. And yet when tenders for Hackney's first post-war housing scheme went in, there was none under the name of Reader Bros, 1 Prince's Avenue Finchley, only of R.A.Reader, 28 Christie Rd E9.

Tom was finishing off at Clapton, where the estate office was still in operation until at least 1921 and the last Barclay/Reader houses didn't appear in the post office directory until 1923, but there seems to have been no question of the two Reader brothers getting together as they were before. Tom's son Clayton was soon to be working with him, and although the family tie was close and enduring, the business relationship between two different personalities had always had its stormy side and an attempt to make it work with four people was unlikely to improve things, though Clayton got on very well with his cousins as friends. From now on, the two branches of the firm travelled on parallel tracks which occasionally converged and then separated again. How down-to-earth matters such as taxation were dealt with in this situation is not recorded. Both brothers seem to have been of the "ignore it and it will go away" turn of mind on such matters. It didn't, of course.

Richard had put in the second lowest tender for the Casimir, Clevelys and Gunton Roads estate, and after Davey's withdrawal he was interviewed and asked to modify his price. By July 1920 he had got it down to £84,818 19s 2d, but even then the contract was only his if the London Building Trades Federation didn't put in a lower one for direct labour. By 10 September the land purchase was completed and the work started, but still the Ministry continued to complain, wanting the contract broken, insisting on economies, changing specifications, stipulating the future rents. At the same time there were shortages of materials, particularly tiles, yet despite these problems, all 80 dwellings were occupied by 30 June 1922, at a rent of 14s 6d per week exclusive of rates, taxes and water, although the council had wanted to charge at least a shilling less.

The cottages were compactly planned and had gas boilers and gas lighting, still the norm for lower class building, but the secluded green location made them very pleasant to live in, and as early as 1926 a few requests to buy through a mortgage from the council were made and granted; one went for £680.[9] It is still a quiet, attractive estate, now with new doors and windows and presumably modernised within as well. At the time of writing only 90 Gunton Road retains its original, unmistakeable, 1920s public housing frontage, and is none the worse for that.

A development of maisonettes on empty sites was planned by Hackney Council in Daubeney Rd and Adley St off Marsh Hill Homerton, but again the Ministry of Health was stipulating costs. After the third lot of tenders on 25 October 1921 Richard had managed to reach second lowest, but the accepted figure was put in by F.& G.Foster of Norwood Junction.

Cooper's College, Tredegar Square, Bow

BUILDERS OF REPUTE: THE STORY OF READER BROS.

Miss Winter's School, 1 Meynell Rd. S. Hackney, c.1912.
Back row left: Jack Reader; next row seated 3rd from left: Edgar;
in front of him, Dick.

Staff photograph from Woolwich Arsenal c.1917/18.
Richard Reader in cap and overall behind pillar on left.
The man to his left may be his friend Bob Grant.

The 11-year-old Edgar's picture of the Zeppelin going down over Cuffley on the night of 2nd September 1916.

L to R: Richard and Edith Reader at the gate of 28 Christie Rd., the Irvines from number 30 (Mervyn waving his stick), the three Reader boys with Dick pointing, Phil Stevens from number 24 with Eton collar, Roland and Margaret Koster from number 19 and, with his braces trailing, Mr Greenaway from number 40 who collected the rents. Many neighbours had moved out to escape the bombing, and the people in the background are French and Belgian refugees who had moved in.

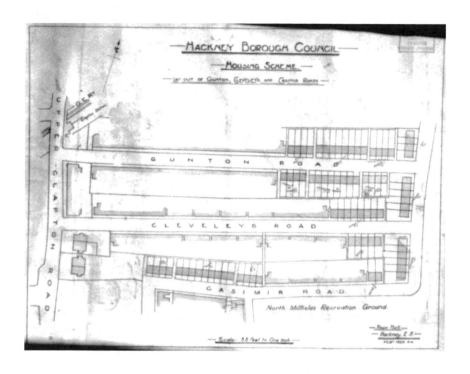

Plan of Hackney Council's first housing estate, 1920.

CHAPTER 5 1920 – 1926

Poplar, Child's Hill, Blackheath. The General Strike.

In the Metropolitan Borough of Poplar, Bromley and Bow, public housing was getting under way via the missionary zeal of another Labour Council. These areas of east London, stretching from Victoria Park down to the tip of the Isle of Dogs, were in a worse state than Hackney, blighted by slums, poverty and ill health, and devastated by the bombing of docks which were their heart and their livelihood. In addition, the dockers suffered the degradation of having literally to fight for work, due to the casual labour system in operation.

The Poplar Special Committee on the Housing of the Working Classes[1] met for the first time on 22 July 1919, one week before the Addison Act came into force, and deliberated on a schedule of houses suitable and available for quick conversion into flats or tenements. For future purpose-built estates, the sewers, roads and drainage were to be constructed by the council's Works Dept and the building then put out to tender.

In co-operation with the Office of Works, Griggs & Son of Manchester Road started work on the first of these sites in December 1919, at Chapel House Street near the south end of the Isle of Dogs, though the ceremonial sod-cutting wasn't performed until 30 January by the equally celebrated and deplored Mayor of Poplar, George Lansbury. It is somehow fitting that this great new experiment in public welfare should have begun where the only building on the entire marshy peninsular, bar the ferry house and the mills on the west wall, had been erected by monks in the middle ages for the shelter of pilgrims on their way to Waltham Abbey in Essex. Its last traces could still be seen in a farmhouse wall at the beginning of the 19th century and only finally disappeared with the building of Millwall Dock.

By 5 January 1920 tenders had been received for another fifteen houses, designed by the Borough Engineer and Surveyor Harvey Heckford and to be built on empty plots in Baldock and Ridgdale Streets, off Fairfield Road Bow. The highest was £17,100 from Marrable, the second lowest was £14,968 put in by Heckford for building by direct labour and the lowest and accepted bid was for £12,705 5s 6d, from R.A.Reader. The first sod was cut on 3 February, the navvies started clearing the sites and digging the foundations, and by the Housing Committee meeting of 8 March "fair progress had been made having regard to the scarcity of skilled labour".

Despite this problem, Richard also put in an accepted tender of £8,057 5s 0d for nine flats in St.Leonard's Road Bromley, again underbidding the Borough Surveyor. It has to be remembered that the Casimir Rd site at Hackney was finally started about this time, proving that Richard and Jack could now field two large gangs of men and contemplate providing more for other contracts.

On 16 September 1920 tenders for six flats on the site of Oriental Terrace,[2] Grundy Street, Poplar were considered and once more Richard beat Heckford's bid, this time by a mere £17. The Council pleaded with the Ministry of Health for permission to accept the second lowest figure, on the grounds that direct labour would provide much-needed local employment, but it was refused. Since such a method would have dealt with two problems at once, this would seem to be another example of the perennial tendency of governments to be penny wise and pound foolish.

By the meeting of 15 November the 15 houses were on the point of completion in Ridgewell and Baldock Streets and the tenants had been selected. The Grundy Street Flats, numbered 45A – F and to be renamed Heckford House some years later, were completed by the middle of 1921, although problems with the hot water system on these and the St Leonard's Road flats continued into 1922. Few of the housing schemes built by councils under the eye of the London Housing Board were to be free of this sort of problem; it was the inevitable result of penny-pinching and speed. On the other hand, problems may also have arisen because some tenants were unable to handle novelties like running hot water, or any sort of piped-in water. As late as 1928 Richard drafted a letter in his notebook explaining how such a system worked on another site and complaining that "Our Man has been in to the House at least 20 times to try and remedy supposed & Real Faults and the whole system is in perfect working order, As a domestic supply of Hot & Cold Water, but not for a public Baths Washouse [sic]." But the standard of housing produced was generally good, and in Poplar developments were finished with shrubs and hedges, planted in soil from the fertile dock dredgings of the Port of London Authority's Mud Chute.

The Casimir Rd estate for Hackney Council was completed and occupied by the end of June 1922 and no further work was immediately available in either Borough.

Baldock St 1-11 odd
Ridgedale St 41-55 odd
St Leonard's Road   Flats 1-9 between Chadbourn St and
Clutton St
Grundy St   Heckford House 45A-F

* * *

Quite apart from the succession of public housing estates undertaken by R.A. Reader during the 1920s, he was also engaged in private development under the name of Reader Bros. The first of these fitted neatly into the pause in the Poplar building and was at a place variously referred to as Cricklewood, Hendon, Golders Green and West Hampstead; one of those indefinite topographical areas lying between more easily identifiable places, on the border between Hendon and Hampstead and called Child's Hill after a mediaeval local family.

It had once been an isolated hamlet on the lane between Watling Street and Hampstead, but the building of Finchley Road changed that. The old main road from St Giles to Finchley lay via Camden Town and the steep, tortuous highways of Hampstead. By the 1820s, Colonel Henry Samuel Eyre was developing his St John's Wood Estate to the north-west of Regent's Park, and he conceived the idea of a new turnpike road which would bypass Hampstead altogether. Despite the usual protests by people who would have to put up with the through traffic, an enabling Act of Parliament was passed in 1826, and during the following nine years the road sliced down through rural Middlesex, gathered up Child's Hill on the way and deprived it for ever of its quiet isolation.[3]

Inevitably, villa development started along its length. Soon after the completion of the road in 1835, Henry Weech Burgess started to develop his Great and Little Temple Woods, just inside the parish of Hampstead, and his son Major Ardwick Burgess continued the process, laying out Burgess Hill, Ardwick Road and the Eastern part of Ranulf Road.

But over the border in Hendon, the fields and farms of Child's Hill remained. In 1840 the ground landlords of the hamlet were Augustus William Freake Hoffman[4] and the churchwardens of St.John's Hampstead, but all surrounding land was owned by the Dean and Chapter of Westminster.[5] In 1854 a new parish was taken out of Hendon and a church and vicarage built on part of Lower and Upper Oxgate fields, marked 1590 and 1624 in the tithe map. By 1870, Gurrey Lodge faced the Finchley Road, with vicarage glebe land absorbed into its garden, and by 1881 Prospect Road and Prospect Villas covered the nursery ground to the north-east of the vicarage, and Lyndale had been laid out on more of Upper Oxgate and on Harman's Hills (field 1623), in fact Ardwick Burgess was living there.

The remaining land to the south of Child's Hill Lane was still part of Cowhouse Farm, tenant Henry Dickers. At the beginning of the 20th century it consisted of an eighty-year-old farmhouse surrounded by much older barns and outbuildings, and with 120 acres of land on both sides of the lane. Although its gate was flanked by Victorian terraces, the house was still approached by a superb avenue of ancient elms, mentioned in 14th century records and known locally as Buckhams Grove after previous tenants.[6]

In 1907 the Charing Cross, Euston and Hampstead Railway Company finally reached Golders Green after four years' tunnelling and construction, and a house building boom followed it. When Farmer Dickers died the Ecclesiastical Commissioners sold off the remainder of fields 1590 and 1624 and part of 1623 (Harman's Hills) leasehold. Leasehold sale was much more common than freehold until well into the twentieth century, and it was only in the sixties that the Commissioners were legally obliged to offer freeholds to property owners on Church land. By the outbreak of the Great War, development of the two new roads, Lyndale and Lyndale Avenue, had not exactly been rapid; Lyndale Avenue had a row of fourteen semi-detached on the south side put up by Alfred Bretzfelder of Cricklewood Broadway, and Lyndale contained only four detached houses.

With the post-war resumption of private building, Robert Hart & Sons Ltd. of Heath Drive Hampstead restarted the development of Ranulf Road and Lyndale early in 1922, and on 29 September the same year Reader Bros. received planning approval for semi-detached houses which would fill up the last gap in the south side of Cricklewood Lane, numbers 270 to 308. The plans were designed by Richard and the applications sent in from 28 Christie Road.

The houses were of three slightly differing designs, with either three or four bedrooms. Motor garages were provided, by now expected in a house of any pretensions, but for the still motorless, electric trams ran past the front gates giving easy access to Cricklewood Midland Railway Station and the Hampstead Tube.

The road is now tramless but busier and noisier. When first visited in rush hour and pouring rain the houses appeared unattractive, but the next visit in bright sunshine changed this first impression considerably. The building line is slightly staggered, which adds interest, and they have the pleasant detailing Richard was so fond of, attractive gables, stained glass, unusual porches. Number 308 on the corner of Lyndale Avenue was built with a surgery at the back for Dr.John Precope and named Lyndale House to add professional dignity. Of course, very few are as Richard left them; most people know better than the builders of their homes and chop them about accordingly, but number 292 is nearest to its original state.

On 29 January 1923 approval was given for "seventeen private dwelling houses" at the west end of Lyndale Avenue. The originally drafted layout takes account of the old right-of-way which ran from Child's Hill probably to Watling Street (Edgware Road), and which was known as Hocroft Walk after House Croft Field which it crossed. Since the building of the church institute in Cricklewood Lane, now the library, its northern outlet had been in Lyndale Avenue which it approached at its old slant. Richard's plan assumed that this portion of "The Farmway" as he labelled it would be made up in its present position and he therefore introduced three large detached houses, pretty well identical to 2 and 4 Monkhams Avenue, Woodford Green. But the course of the track was later realigned with the church entrance, and the layout changed to consist entirely of semis.

There were two designs, one an enlarged version of Plan C in Cricklewood Lane, the other an attractive "Old English" style with a four-centred arched front door. The hall-parlour had a brick fireplace flanked by built-in settles and a three flight staircase beyond an arch as on the Monkhams Estate. Again, motor garages were provided, in this case tucked behind the houses to economise on frontage.

In 1924 Arthur van Zwanenberg of Gurrey Lodge started to erect houses in his garden along Lyndale Avenue, and by 1925 other roads were spreading across the fields now given the "nicer" name of Avenue Farm. Richard was back in Poplar, but Reader Bros. 53 Prince's Avenue, Finchley sent in an application in February for sixteen houses in Hocroft Road, which had swallowed another stretch of the right-of-way. Tom's designs were recognisably different from Richard's and often L-shaped.

The estate continued to spread. In 1925 A.J.Reynolds of Golders Green began the building up of the farm avenue, later going on to build Hocroft Avenue and Harman Drive off it. The magnificent elms were lopped but left standing, though they have all since disappeared.

Tom started on 14 and 16 Lyndale Avenue in the second half of 1926, and this time the application was sent from 2 Hocroft Road, on the corner with Farm Avenue and opposite the bedraggled farmhouse in which lived Farmer Dickers' daughters. Tom and Annie's new house was a brick and timbered, pebble-dashed, leaded-windowed, 5 bed 3 recep. detached with a double motorhouse. It is still in good repair but the shaped window frames and leaded lights which sparkled in the background of family photographs have been removed.

Building continued on the Avenue Farm estate until at least the early 1930s, particularly the erection by Robert Hart of numerous opulent-looking double-fronted Georgian villas, a great deal nearer to genuine Georgian than houses claiming that description in the 1990s. In 1929 Hendon Way Arterial Road, which had been gradually travelling south, crossed Cricklewood Lane and pressed on to its final destination, the Finchley Road. Numbers 278 and 280 Cricklewood Lane were demolished and Gurrey Lodge and the three houses on the west side of Lyndale also disappeared, but no others had stood in its way. Presumably for the last few years the event had been, as they say of deaths, expected. 282 Cricklewood Lane went later when Hendon Way was widened.

The farmhouse and barns of Cowhouse/Avenue Farm were finally demolished and their sites built on in 1932, but the farm's remaining fields were saved for recreation and Hocroft Walk still runs through them, made up into streets at each end.

> Cricklewood Lane 270-308 even
> Lyndale Avenue 1-15 odd 2-16 even
> Hocroft Rd 1-9 odd 2-22 even

Some Reader houses at Child's Hill underwent changes after the second war, partly due to bombing and partly to the housing problem which once more followed it. In Lyndale Avenue numbers 16 – 24 had to be rebuilt, and numbers 4 and 11 were converted into flats.

* * *

By 1923 Poplar Council was planning its next estate,[7] involving Kingfield St, Billson St, Parsonage St and Stebondale St, between Manchester Rd and Millwall Park on the Isle of Dogs. The land, bought from the Charteris Estate, consisted once more of vacant plots between existing terraces, and the prospective houses were an Office of Works design previously used for the Chapel House Street estate. The Survey of London suggests that Heckford was probably trying to avoid time-wasting red tape.

Tenders for the first 28 houses were considered by the Special Housing Committee on 25 July 1923 and once more Richard's lowest estimate was accepted. It was also decided in advance that he would be given first option on the remainder, as he had "satisfactorily carried out other housing contracts for the Council." The entire scheme was to consist of fifty-five houses and six flats.

However, Richard quickly realised that this time he had quoted too low; it would not be possible to build for that price and make a profit. He informed the Committee of the situation and suggested various modifications to the plans, one of which was taking six inches off the height; with these, he could deliver the work at his quoted price. The Committee put the new specifications out for a repeat tender but Richard's figure was still the lowest, despite the fact that his bid must now have become known. It was and probably still is customary to put in your tender at the very last moment, so that the figure could not be leaked to another firm by an interested party, enabling them to undercut you.

Labour was still a problem for all builders, much of the valuable wealth of British skill having been squandered in Flanders.[8] It is remarkable just how many sites Reader's managed to juggle during the 1920s, considering this lack. For this job, a list of building workers was obtained from the Poplar Workhouse Guardians for Reader to employ "if suitable", but it was the trained, experienced, reliable tradesmen who were hard to find. As a result, the minutes for both Poplar and Hackney record minor disasters on all schemes by all builders; cracked plaster, ill-fitting joinery, badly-done paintwork etc.

The first houses were ready in May 1924 and the rest completed early the next year, the six flats having been replaced by six houses; strangely, they were cheaper.

> Kingfield St 1-27 odd 2-28 even
> Billson St 18-26 even
> Parsonage St 13-39 odd 18-32 even
> Stebondale St 40-50 even

* * *

Richard had been beaten to the lowest tender for twenty-four flats in Lower North Street, between Poplar High Street and the East India Dock Rd, by the local builder William Simms,[9] but although this meant there was no immediate prospect of another job for Poplar, he had already bought another small plot for private development.

It was in Kidbrooke, Kent, to the south of where the Old Dover Road met Shooter's Hill Road. On the tithe map the expanse of fields is interrupted only by four farmhouses; Kidbrook, Kidbrook Upper, Kidbrook Lower and Kidbrook Hill, but by the end of the century villas were advancing from the west and more of them lined Shooter's Hill. The newly-built Hervey Road ran round behind them with a few houses at the east end. By 1925 the road was filling up and Richard bought land on the south side. His plan is dated 5 January 1925, and the drainage system was approved by the Metropolitan Borough of Greenwich on 18 March. Consent for "bay windows, oriel windows, porches, sham half-timberwork & wooden brackets under gables" was given on 13 May.

The farmland behind was still in use, and in the fields women were hand-planting cabbages from apron pockets. In time-honoured fashion, Reader's men whistled and shouted builders' greetings, only to receive replies of such vulgarity that the 19-year-old Edgar was considerably startled; he probably regarded his mother and his Gosling aunts as the norm for women's behaviour. Frank Gosling's upbringing had marked his daughters for life, so that the occasion when Jack tried to be a helpful boy by making his aunts' bed led to a horrified scene at such impropriety. Edith, Florrie and Jessie were lovely people with a strong sense of humour, but they were paralysed by a prudery that made it unwise and unkind to say certain things in their presence. Tom Reader was sometimes scolded as "naughty" by his sister-in-law, and Uncle Fred Pailthorpe had been a real trial.

The Hervey Rd houses were two groups of three pairs with garages and four bedrooms, numbered 68 – 78 and 82 – 92. Jack's notebook covering this development survives, and contains the memorandum "Pay bills, order Aunt Maud's wallpaper, demonstration house, Miss Fountain [buyer of number 84], take stock of tiles." Richard's sister Maude, her husband George McLachlan and their daughter Janet moved from 104 Marlborough Rd Bowes Park into number 92. Maude looked like Queen Mary, very dignified, with late Victorian forehead curls and a black velvet band around her neck, and George's many brothers are said to have proved an occasional problem for her, especially when they came down from Glasgow for a football match.

The development was closely similar to those erected in Cricklewood Lane, but these houses now look better than those because their situation has been kinder to them. Despite the proximity of Rochester Way, Hervey Road is quiet and leafy and the residents keep their homes looking their best.

* * *

At much the same time as he started the Kidbrooke job, Richard won the contract for a scheme to the south of Millwall Park, Poplar, involving Manchester Rd, Manchester Grove and East Ferry Rd and to be built on allotment land bought again from the Charteris Estate.

The Borough Surveyor gave a very good report on Reader's work to the Committee, and his ability to deliver a low price is particularly remarkable in this case. His figure for building seventy-two houses was £35,856 7s 2d, (the 2d appears a nicely scrupulous touch), but the highest tender among the other nine builders was an enormous £53,537 from Perry & Co. of Bow.[10] The explanation may lie in lower overheads. All three sons were now working with him and learning the skills of the trade. Jack was studying at Hackney Institute for membership of the Institute of Builders and was to obtain his Licentiate in December 1926. Dick had re-organised all the paperwork including accounts and tax, which had never been his father's strong point; Richard's system consisted of stuffing all pieces of paper into a drawer. His offices were his own home and the site sheds, which travelled around with them, while other builders had purpose-built yards which cost money just by being there. Labour costs don't appear too great a problem from this distance, but it is difficult to grasp the value of money at a time when a shilling made all the difference between a working man being able to afford his rent or not. As a matter of record, however, a letter sent by the Borough Surveyor's Dept. on 15 June 1921 mentions hourly pay as being bricklayers and plumbers 2s 2½d; carpenters, plasterers and masons 2s 2d; painters 2s 1d and labourers 1s 1d.

In January 1926 Reader's tender was accepted for twenty-four houses and forty flats at Glengall Grove, now Tiller Road, on the west side of Millwall Dock. Unfortunately, the strip of land along the north side of the road had been John & Edwin Wright's Universe Rope Works, built when the Dock was first planned in 1859 and working until 1914, after which it was used by a sailmaker. Preparation of the site therefore involved excavating several feet of tar, hemp and wire, and digging out the iron wheels upon which the rope was spun. Buildings, also, had to be removed, including a boiler house chimney at least fifty feet high with a Portland stone top made in four pieces. Expert steeplejacks were called in to demolish it in the way now made familiar to television viewers by Fred Dibnah of Bolton. In this case, scaling ladders were put up the side of the chimney and held by bands, the brickwork being cut into to hold them. At the top, the man left the ladder and scrambled across the overhang, leaving himself no way of getting down until he had broken up the crown of stone beneath his feet with a pickaxe and pushed the pieces down the flue. The chimney itself was then felled by the traditional method of mining the base, shoring up with timbers and lighting a fire.

The next month Reader's won the contract for flats in St.Leonard's St, Bow[11] and demolition of existing terrace houses (137-159) started in April 1926. The site had a railway goods yard to the north, a saw mill to the east, and to the south was a private road which led across the River Lea and Bow Creek to the Gas Works on the Essex bank. The Readers spent the whole of one morning setting out the rather intricate plan with wooden pegs, only to discover on returning from lunch that children had taken them all for firewood. This large, long block later became known as Twelvetrees House[12] and was to last into the 1960s, when the Blackwall Tunnel Approach Road virtually wiped out the ancient St Leonard's St. A slip road from the southbound carriageway circled the block to reach Devas St, and it was eventually put out of its misery by demolition. At the time of writing a bedraggled but still hopeful notice is offering the site for lease as a drive-in fast-food outlet. So far there are no takers.

> East Ferry Rd 201-207 odd
> Manchester Grove 1-59 odd 2-44 even
> Manchester Rd 15-45 odd
> Glengall Grove 332-206 – 24 houses and 40 flats;
>   332-318 (now 1-15), Yarrow House, Hibbert House,
>   Maudsley House, 268-238, Alexander House.
> St Leonard's St   Twelvetrees House Flats 1-24

* * *

Involvement in public housing in Poplar during the 1920s was an unavoidably political business, due to the revolutionary novelty of the concept and the enthusiastic socialism of the council in power. Soon after Reader's finished their first run of work the entire council, including the mayor, George Lansbury, had been imprisoned for refusing to raise a rate for work outside the borough, which they believed their constituents could not afford. Then after the election of the first Labour Government under Ramsay MacDonald in January 1924, Poplar Council sent a deputation to the Minister of Health asking for various indulgences, again on the grounds of the borough's poverty. The granting of these had set the newspapers shouting dark warnings about "the reds" "showing their hand already", and printing a flurry of letters from Disgusted of Belgrave Square and the Carlton Club. Now, in 1926, actual revolution seemed to be alarmingly near.

From midnight on 3 May 1926, the T.U.C. was to call a General Strike in support of miners threatened with longer hours and less money. Of the trades to be called out, one was building, although with certain exemptions; "All workers engaged on building, except such as are employed definitely on housing and hospital work, together with all workers engaged in the supply of equipment to the building industry, shall cease work."[13]

Despite this apparent permission to carry on as usual, it seemed only wise to approach the local strike committee direct before proceeding to do so, and Richard went up to Dockers' Hall, 1 Newby Place, just off Poplar High Street. The story handed down is that he spoke to Ernest Bevin, president of the Transport and General Workers' Union himself and that he was told in the rather pompous language unfortunately adopted by Union officials that "since the workers need housing, let the building continue." It has not proved possible to check this incident from the records of the Trade Union side, but Reader's went on working, with the unpleasant necessity of a police escort. It is notable, however, that A.P.Gladdish, vice chairman of No.1 Area Strike Committee, wrote to the Poplar Guardians complaining that their staff painters and carpenters were continuing work on the severely run-down St.Andrew's Hospital, Devons Rd, and that the Guardians refused to stop them. The Strike was over in nine days, with no outcome but bitterness which would affect labour relations until the end of the century.

Edith Reader outside 28 Christie Road in the 1920s.

Breakfast time at 28 Christie Road in the 1920s:
Edgar, Richard, Dick & Jack.

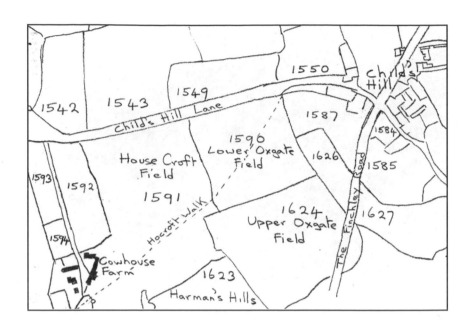

field pattern of Child's Hill with 1840 Tithe Map numbering.

*2 Hocroft Road,
the home of Tom and Annie Reader c.1926-1937.*

4, 6 and 8 Hocroft Road.

2 Hocroft Road in 1929
Luer Koster, Tom Reader, Clayton Reader, Annie Reader, Cecilia
Reader, Mrs. Koster, Martin Koster,
at front: Cissie/Anne Koster.

Clayton Reader with SS1 in front of 9-1 Hocroft Road, c.1932.

Richard, Edith, Annie and Tom Reader at 2 Hocroft Road c.1933.
Edith is in the dress she wore for Edgar's wedding.

OPPOSITE PAGE: *The Kingfield Estate, Isle of Dogs 1923-25:*
infilling at Kingfield, Billson, Parsonage and Stebondale Streets.
The same as the Chapel House Street Estate but 6 inches shorter.

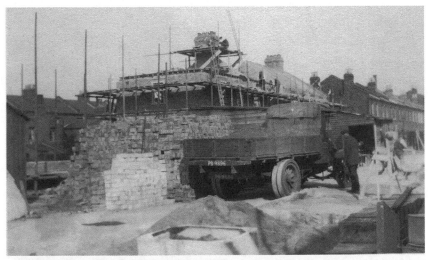

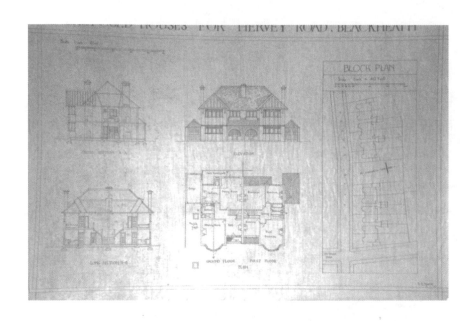

Plan for houses in Hervey Road, Blackheath, 1925.

68 Hervey Road, Blackheath, 1996.

BUILDERS OF REPUTE: THE STORY OF READER BROS.

GLENGALL GROVE, 1926.

LEFT: The ropeworks wheels.

RIGHT: The foundations, possibly flooded to mark the level.

CHAPTER 6 1926 – 1930

Poplar Board of Guardians, Marsh Hill Works, Poplar Housing, Canons Drive Edgware.

On 17 November 1922, Richard's colleague from the Arsenal, Robert Grant had written from Sydney, Australia, with the compliments of the season and a report that "The Iron Trades refuse to go back to the 48 hours week and the seamen object to a reduction in their wages. Unemployment is bad and generally business is putrid." Richard and Tom had themselves had a struggle to get back into business again, and yet the middle to late twenties are the time when Reader photograph albums brim with outings, holidays, get-togethers and people having a thoroughly good time. Given the problems which the strikers and millions of others underwent, these pictures are not, of course, the whole story, even for the Readers, but the steady stream of work from Poplar gave the assurance of regular money coming in, and by 1923 Richard and Edith were taking runs out of South Hackney in a Studebaker. Seaside holidays returned; 1924 saw a party of at least sixteen Readers, relatives and friends crossing rough seas to Jersey and bringing back photographs of cheerful groups, formidable rocks and a seemingly ubiquitous lighthouse.

Richard's three sons had moved their broken voices to the back row of St John of Jerusalem's choir stalls, and for many years the happy custom prevailed of holding a yearly choir dinner at various London restaurants, Dick Reader and friends generally providing the entertainment. Richard was also involved with church affairs, in 1925 mending the clock with his own hands and five years later becoming a church warden. Later, in 1931, the firm was to do extensive work on St John's Rectory, after which the Rector gave Jack an engraved silver cigarette case as a gesture of thanks.

Amateur music flourished once more in South Hackney, and concerts were held in aid of church causes, often including four-part singing by the three Reader boys and fellow chorister Ron Thornicroft. A concert party was taken to a hostel for the homeless in Covent Garden where the speech of thanks to the performers was given by a gentlemanly resident with a cultured voice, a shocking, sobering experience for middle class young people. Edgar's passion for music took him to the Queen's Hall for Promenade Concerts, and he also heard the first performance of Walton's Belshazzar's Feast, Rachmaninov playing his first piano concerto and Elgar conducting his own symphonies. He wrote music himself; a Christmas entertainment called The Bethlehem Tableaux was produced at St Andrew's Hall, Well Street in 1926 and 1927, accompanied by Edgar's specially composed score. Dick developed a useful sideline singing at masonics and as a soloist with amateur choral societies. He became a mason in November 1926, and Edgar did consult an uncle as to whether seeking membership would be advisable from the business angle, but the answer was unexpected; "Believe me, my boy, there's nothing in it." It may have appeared pointless to this particular mason, but it seems unlikely that contacts made would have proved useless. Psychologically, however, all that dressing up and ritual wouldn't have suited Edgar; his sense of humour was not always disciplined and he tended to get the giggles. Even church could produce testing moments.

The South Hackney Orchestral Society was now led by Richard Reader and conducted by Luer Koster the younger from number 19 Christie Road. The son of a carpenter whom Tom employed for a while (he is said to have been good but very slow), Luer had been a conscientious objector and served in the R.A.M.C. during the War, an experience of which he seldom spoke afterwards and never to his children. By 1925 he and Cissie Reader were an item and as she called him Jimmy everyone followed suit, except presumably his parents.

Cissie was married from 2 Hocroft Road Childs Hill in June 1926. The service took place at All Saints' Church, which had looked down over the development of the farmland from its beginning, and although since bombed and rebuilt its door is still the same one through which the unconventional and artistic "Anne", who was trying to discard her old name too, emerged on "Jimmy"'s arm in her emerald green bridal costume. This glaring break with tradition was regarded by older members of the family as not only unfitting but also dangerously unlucky.

Snaps were taken outside the church and Edith photographed groups in the Readers' garden. Annie is large and stately, in a dark, broad-brimmed hat. Tom is in frock-coat and top hat, nearly bald and smoking the eternal cigarette. Richard has put on a lot of weight with new prosperity. Cloche hats rule, except for the seventy-six-year-old Cecilia who sits in ankle-length black silk with a broad, black, velvet bow on her head because she is "getting a bit thin on top, dear." Clayton, Jack and Edgar stand at the back, but there is no sign of Dick. Perhaps he was back in Poplar, minding the shop. The newly-weds moved into half of 55 Prince's Avenue Finchley, still being rented out by Tom.

* * *

It must have been about this time that Cecilia sent the following letter from 2 Hocroft Rd.

> Dear Dick & Edith
>
> I have been over the album to see the best ones to see the past Pictures and hope you will be pleased to see them when I shall be able to meet all my dear friends once again with Best Love to all from our selves
>
> From Mother C.H. Reader

This little brown carte-de-visite album with a brass clasp contains the earliest portraits of the Pailthorpes and Readers, plus the usual few which prove infuriatingly unidentifiable. Even the named Amy Fawcett who "died of want" has not been pinned down, but was probably a girlhood friend. If Cecilia had not taken the trouble to pass this treasure on, the twentieth century Readers would never have known what their Victorian forebears looked like.

* * *

It goes without saying that earning a plentiful amount of money after straitened times relaxes the mind and lightens the heart. It also offers the chance to spend, and one of the things Tom and Richard spent on to the end of their lives was cars; big, expensive, fast cars which carried their owners on touring holidays all over the British Isles. They are in evidence in the wedding photographs, especially Richard's spectacular Peugeot open tourer, and Annie always bought Tom very dark-coloured handkerchiefs, because she knew they would be used for wiping off mud and polishing up brass and chrome. Travelling was not just for summer holidays; bank holiday weekends were spent en famille et en automobile, large groups descending upon healthy seaside and picturesque village. So were many ordinary weekends. It was quite common for Tom to come home from work at Saturday lunchtime and order his family into the car for a night or two at Eastbourne, the family's favourite resort. Their usual destination was Osborne House, but if the party was a large one they spilled over into other hotels on Royal Parade; relatives, friends, neighbours, girlfriends, boyfriends. It must have been overwhelming for quieter guests in smaller groups, as the Readers in strength tended to be cheerful, ebullient and noisy. Was the response always "Oh good, it's the Readers," or sometimes "Oh no, it's them again"?

On the girlfriend side, Dick had a constant succession which he seems to have treated in a cavalier manner; on more than one occasion his brothers had to escort them home because he had forgotten about them and gone out. Jack and Edgar probably had a few as well, but their affections appear to have been fixed fairly early on. Ron Thornicroft had two elder sisters whom the Readers had known from childhood. Their father, Ernest Thornicroft was foreman engineer at Truman's Brewery in Brick Lane Stepney and their mother, née Nina Eliza Adelaide Skeel, was the daughter of a house painter with a drink problem. (Nina and Phyllis were encouraged to sign the pledge quite early on in their lives). Mrs Sophia Skeel may have been expressing longings for a more romantic life when she named her daughters; Mrs Thornicroft's sisters were Phoebe Lydia, Minnie Palmer (after the actress) and Miranda Madeline.

On August Bank Holiday 1926 the pretty Thornicroft girls made their entry into Edith's photograph albums. Nina Madeline was 20, blonde-haired, blue-eyed, lively and talkative, while Phyllis Elsie was 19, dark, dainty and shy. With the attraction of opposites, Jack fell for Nina and Edgar for Phyllis. The girls were at Furzedown Teacher Training College in Streatham, which meant only occasional meetings and a long drive home for the boys during termtime. Both couples were probably engaged before the end of the twenties, but there were to be no weddings yet. Female teachers were not allowed to be married, and the girls wanted to work long enough to pay their parents back for their training.

It seems pointless now to train your daughters for such a short period, particularly as the girls' attractions must have made future marriage a foregone conclusion, but very few respectable middle class women went out to work – their careers were in the home. On reflection, maybe the eventuality Nina and Phyllis were being insured against was early widowhood. Ironically, no money was left for Ron when he won a music and modern languages scholarship to Cambridge, and as he was to be working all his life the priorities seem wrong and desperately unfair; but perhaps he wasn't deliberately deprived, only unfortunate to be the youngest.

He was consigned to the safe embrace of the Midland Bank, which at least had a vigorous operatic society in which to exercise his excellent baritone voice and dramatic talent. He had singing lessons at Trinity College of Music and also from the Italian composer Franco Leoni, who wrote a negro spiritual for him which is now totally unperformable, due to its non-P.C. title. Like Dick, Ron did a steady stream of part-time professional engagements, including work with the B.B.C. in Bristol, and a high spot must have been the Mozart Requiem in the chapel of Christ's College Cambridge on 6 March 1932, when friends from South Hackney came up to listen and the 32-year-old John Barbirolli was in the audience. Edgar was invited to take a walk around the city with this already distinguished young man, and thought he had died and gone to heaven.

* * *

Some time during 1926 or 1927 Florrie and Jessie Gosling, who had years of retail experience between them, bought a fancy goods shop in Windsor, and it first appeared under their names in the 1928 Windsor Directory as Molyneux's. A gang of Reader men were sent down to alter and renovate and it was while supervising this work that Edgar cut the back of his hand with a saw, resulting in a life-long scar; he was extremely fortunate that it wasn't a case of never playing the piano again. 130 Peascod Street had an 18th/19th century brick front but was part of a timber building, the roof of which provided a good uninterrupted run for rats. The sisters reputedly sold occasional gifts to the royal dukes and their children, and played tennis at a local club with the librarian of Windsor Castle and his wife, while the windows above the shop gave relatives a grandstand view when royal occasions brought processions down the street. Jessie was to die in 1936, but the shop remained in Florrie's hands until her own death ten years later. It was then bought by Granville Ltd's Shirt Company and its site was eventually built over by Marks and Spencer's.

* * *

For much of 1927 the Poplar Housing Committee was occupied in considering other possible sites and haggling with owners over price (the owner of Log Hall, Old Ford Rd was described as "idiosyncratic"), but by then Reader's had started on a long series of contracts for Poplar Board of Guardians, mostly at St Andrew's Hospital, Devons Rd, Bromley.[1] It had been built in 1870/71 as the Poplar and Stepney Sick Asylum and gradually extended over the years, but from 1 April 1925 the Poplar Guardians took sole control and set a long programme of improvements in train. The work was to include a garage, an operating theatre, a new Nurses' Home, alterations to the maternity pavilion and a mortuary. The last was in progress by 1929, when a page of Richard's notebook listed items to be ordered including the chilling entry "Panic Bolts". The Guardians had also acquired Langley House, a left-over 1829 mansion at 54 East India Dock Rd in use for some years as a children's home, and Richard's notebook for 1928 lists every room in the house and the cost of work to be done on each. Men were also sent down to do maintenance work, and to build a dormitory and a pair of cottages in Church Lane Dunton for the Laindon Farm Colony, Basildon, Essex, where healthy Poplar paupers worked the land in return for workhouse support.[2]

On 7 January 1928 an unusually high tide spilled the Thames over its walls and banks, flooded the drainage system of London and forced itself into streets and fields. The low-lying, marshy Isle of Dogs was disastrously affected and building brought to a halt, but the hiatus provided a chance for Reader's to start another necessary job.

From the very start the firm's official address had been Tom's and then Richard's home, and the storage of builder's paraphernalia probably took place in site sheds or rented lockups, but with so much work in hand a proper yard with offices attached was now a necessity. The land acquired for this purpose was at the north end of Sidney Rd (from 1938/9 Kenworthy Rd), near the corner where Marsh Hill met Homerton High St and opposite the Hackney workhouse and infirmary. This was the site of Marsh House, demolished in the 1880s, and by 1895 it had been replaced by numbers 1 – 13 Sidney Rd, owned by Mrs Eliza Stevens, cowkeeper of 152 Homerton High Street on the corner of Crozier Terrace.[3] It was still in the possession of the Stevens family in 1919 when a corset factory stood there, but by 1921 the owners were the estate agents Bunch & Duke. Reader's may have rented first, then bought the buildings from them in 1927, and their replacement was to be designed by the 22-year-old Edgar. He had several gos at it. One unbuilt fifty-nine foot frontage with two display windows announced "Building Work of Every Description Anywhere", a claim which recalls the sanguine advertisements of William Reader. Another fully worked-out design had a plain wall and gate onto Sidney Road but handsome Neo-Georgian buildings arranged round a central open space. The final design which accompanied an application to build offices and builder's works to Hackney U.D.C. on 8 December 1927 was a modification of this, put in by Edgar and approved on ll January 1928 by T.Chapman, Mayor.[4]

At that time, the main concern of the planning authorities for such buildings was still drainage and other basic safety matters, for which complete specifications had to be stated; there seems to have been far less interest in what went on above ground unless it was a rainwater gully, a washbasin, a W.C. or a fire exit. Presumably, therefore, once the drains were passed and as long as the stated system was adhered to, any variation in the actual appearance was not all that important. Certainly, the plans passed in 1928 look a great deal more architectural and classy than the buildings which actually materialised. There are a few photographs of Marsh Hill Works, as it was called, though not enough to get a complete view, but the plan's intended rendered and cream-washed walls can be recognised as naked pink flettons, and the offices' pitched, red-tiled roof turned out to be a flat, asphalte one, which was at least useful for stacking things on; there always seemed to be a lavatory pan sitting on top.

This block was on the left as one entered the gate, and contained workmen's W.C., coal store, chief foreman's office, main office with W.C. off, and inner office where the plan chest cum draughtsman's desk stood against the east wall and Richard sat at his desk in the bay window.

The wood store, like an open-sided barn, was to the right of the gate and beyond that stood the L-shaped joinery shop, which came under the jurisdiction of Dick. There was a subtle difference between joinery and carpentry. Joiners made doors, windows, mouldings, fittings etc. for the buildings under construction, and if necessary the work was sent to Young & Marten at Maryland Point for glazing. A lorry was then hired to move it onto the site where carpenters installed it; lighter things went by carrier's horse and cart, which was to be an important part of all commercial life for quite a while yet. At least one present-day Homerton resident remembers collecting sacks of shavings from "the woodyard" for her pet rabbit'a bedding.

The firm's name first appears in the Post Office Directory in 1930, by which time postal problems may have arisen through the presence next door of Freeder Bros, paper decorative goods manufacturers. If the Yard turned out to be a more mundane building than Edgar's design envisaged it was probably through shortage of time, as men were only available to work on it when not wanted at Poplar, but it was to be busy for many years, full of the scream of machinery and the smell of sawdust.

* * *

In March 1928 Richard won contracts for 16 flats in Naval Row near the entrance to the Blackwall Tunnel (Edgar's first big job in complete charge), for 64 flats on the site of the Britannia Rubber Works in River St off Devons Rd Bromley, and in June for six flats in Gale St, three streets away.[5] Once more, he was urged to employ local labour if at all possible and Jack's notebook contains a list of thirty nine names and addresses, two navvies annotated with the words "These two are good – one worked for Mowlems". The Petty Cash section at the end encloses a bill from Millett Bros of Bow for sharpening and tempering 10 pickaxes and repairing two navvy's hammers. A scrap of paper records the hours worked by navvies at River St week ending 2 June 1928 as eight hours a day and four on Saturday. With this rush of work the Readers do appear to have been spreading themselves pretty thin, but they were now employing an enormous workforce spread over many sites; even nightwatchmen were on the permanent payroll.

St Andrew's Nurses' Home received a grand ceremonial opening on Saturday 15 December 1928, accompanied by a commemorative booklet recording the name of R.A.Reader Builder. The large sitting room was to be ornamented with murals and Richard persuaded Edgar to put in a design, as he was a very good amateur painter and why not keep the work in the family? However, the powers that be rejected Edgar's banks of cheerful hydrangeas and commissioned solemn historical figures, which were presumably redolent with symbolism, from an R.A. The Royal Commission's sheet on St Andrew's dates these as 1959, but this must be a misprint for 1929.

A personal friendship grew out of this contract. In one of Edith's many albums is a photograph of two nurses sitting on the sooty roof of the hospital, with St Andrew's Church in the background. These were "Sister Rhoda and Sister Katharine", otherwise Rhoda Whatley and Katharine Bate, and a visit was later made to Little Bullington, 1 Crossbush Rd, Felpham near Bognor, to which the ladies had retired. (Miss Whatley's family came from Bullington in Hampshire.)

The Naval Row flats were finished and tenanted by May 1929. With the redevelopment and gentrification of Docklands towards the end of the century their situation beside the East India Dock and the Blackwall Tunnel became suddenly desirable. They were sold off during the eighties as Naval House, and the balconies which once accommodated the washing of dockers' families have sprouted ornamental ironwork.

Also in May 1929, tenders were at last invited for a long-planned development of a hundred and eight houses at British Street, off West Ferry Rd on the south-west tip of the Isle of Dogs.[6] This was another of the few occasions when Richard was undercut, this time by The Building and Public Works Construction Co.Ltd. of Swindon, but after the Committee received some "confidential letters" about this firm's work elsewhere the contract went to Reader's again. The four-acre site had been difficult to acquire and was to be even more difficult to clear and rebuild. It had been part of the Millwall Ironworks which continued in business across the West Ferry Road, was then occupied by Maconochie's factory which left behind feet of buried, broken, pottery jampots, and the Millwall Cooperage still sat bang in the middle of it because it was too expensive for the Council to buy.

Maconochie's private railway siding would have to be moved, an eight foot wall would have to be built to protect the Chapel House Street Estate from the railway, a footbridge would have to be provided to restore the estate residents' access, and the ground, once the clinker had been removed, was so marshy that the footings would have to rest on reinforced concrete rafts. It was probably during work upon this site that it was decided to remove rubbish by means of Thames barge from a nearby dock. Edgar was asked how many would be required and suggested two, having no idea how much could disappear into the immense holds which regularly carried household and industrial waste downriver to be dumped. The load took up less than half of one vessel.

It had been suggested by the Poplar Housing Committee that photographs should be taken of the site and compared with the completed scheme,[7] but if this was done they have proved impossible to trace.

* * *

A notebook later used by Jack in 1930 and 1931 starts off with weekly lists of men working in Poplar between 1 February and 9 August 1924, probably on the Kingfield Estate. These may record workmen's Unemployment Insurance Fund contributions; one farthing per hour until 5 July, a penny farthing per hour thereafter, and each week is signed H.J.Mills. Henry James Mills was a building inspector in the Central District supervision section of Poplar Borough Council, and had been in service with them since May 1902. Like a great many other unlikely people he had served as a Captain in the First World War, and a fascinating letter home from the Front in April 1918 is preserved at Tower Hamlets Local History Library.[8] Early in 1929 he resigned due to ill health, but the respect with which he was regarded by his employers is revealed by their creating a new designation for him of Chief Clerk of Works, thus allowing him to continue receiving a salary. He died on 23 June in the London Hospital, the General Services Committee regretting the loss of "a thoroughly practical & reliable officer whose services will be missed." Among Jack Reader's possessions was later found a well-thumbed copy of Building Materials by G.A.T.Middleton, published by Batsford in 1905 and bearing Mills's signature on the flyleaf. The two men must have worked together on many Poplar sites, and the book which Mills used throughout his career was almost certainly a farewell gift. It is a comprehensive textbook on the art of traditional building and deeply impressive; presumably much of this knowledge has now been superseded and survives only among specialists.

* * *

At 3 o'clock on Saturday 28 September 1929 the River Street flats, a huge development which had been Jack's first job in complete charge, were opened in the presence of the Mayor of Poplar Charles W.Key J.P., the Chairman of the Special Housing Committee Alderman David M.Adams and the widow of ex-mayor Charles Edwin Sumner, after whom the flats had been named.[9] Not mentioned in the Souvenir Programme but one of the many great and good attending was George Lansbury, by now member of Parliament for Bow and Bromley and First Commissioner of Works in Ramsay MacDonald's government. The Mayor's speech was heckled by a disappointed would-be tenant and Mrs.Sumner's was so inaudible that Mr.Key had to read it again. Lansbury was greeted with cheers but also suffered heckling by the disappointed, for although Poplar Council had built the most housing of any other borough, the problems of East London would still be there for years to come and perhaps for ever.

Lansbury is said to have finished his speech by holding out his arms and inviting the crowd to "Come in, my people!"[10] Edith was employing her ever-busy camera and captured the moment when the people did just that, strolling into the yard of the flats from River Street to inspect what they were or weren't getting. She also took a photograph of Richard and Lansbury together which she captioned "The Builder and the Cabinet Minister." She is most unlikely to have shared his politics but a Minister is a Minister, and the many building schemes put in hand by the Borough of Poplar throughout the 1920s had set the firm of Reader Bros. back on its feet, with a staff of trustworthy tradesmen and a purpose-built Yard able to handle large developments. From 1931 Poplar started to build their estates by direct labour as Heckford had always wanted and the practice continued after his retirement, but by that time both branches of Reader Bros. were busy elsewhere.

St Andrew's Hospital Nurses' Home etc.
Dormitory, pair of cottages etc., Laindon Farm Colony Basildon

Naval Row	Naval House 1-16
Gale St	Sidgwick House 1-6
Harbinger Rd	22-34 even
Hesperus Crescent	1-139 odd 2-62 even
Devons Rd	Sumner House 1-60

* * *

In March 1930, at Woodlands, Shooters Hill Rd, died Cecilia Helen Reader neé Pailthorpe, the last of her generation. Her funeral was arranged by Ras and Florence Buggé, with whom she had been staying, and a few days afterwards a stiff little letter was sent to Tom Reader.

"41 Shooters Hill Rd Blackheath S.E.3

March 10th/30

Dear Tom,

We have just heard of your great loss. Dear Aunt Cissie gone at last. She has had a long life. Our lovely Aunt as we all thought her. Should so much have liked to have known in time, so that some of us could have gone to the funeral or seen it. Edwin wrote & told us, only got his letter this morning. Love to all from all

Yours sincerely

Cousin Flo."

It is strange that the children of Cecilia's brother John Woodyer Pailthorpe should not even have been informed, especially as they lived so near; another mysterious disagreement in the Pailthorpe family, perhaps.

* * *

It is difficult to pin down exactly what Tom Reader had been doing since 1927, when 14 and 16 Lyndale Avenue, Child's Hill were finished. It may have been alterations, decorations and repairs, which are the bread and butter of a builder, he may have been juggling investments, he may have had other sorts of irons in the fire. He has been described as a born dealer always ready to take a gamble,[11] but one hopes and believes it was not on anything illegal, which is more than can be said for a character who lived two centuries before him.

In 1715 James Brydges began to build himself a mansion in keeping with his great position and immense wealth. The first attribute derived from being son and heir of Sir James Brydges, third Lord Chandos of Sudeley, the second from being Paymaster General of Queen Anne's armies during the French Wars. Corruption was a way of life for government ministers and public officials, and a House of Commons committee of inquiry which sat in 1711 discovered that some thirty-five million pounds of public money were missing, of which Brydges certainly received his unfair share.

In consequence of this fortunate windfall he had already started a town house on the north side of Cavendish Square of which only one flanking pavilion remains, and after toying with the idea of Brentford for his country seat he eventually settled on Edgware, on the Roman road from Londinium to Verulamium otherwise known as Watling Street. He had acquired the estate of Canons[12] in 1710 by marrying the heiress Mary Lake, and his new house became one of the most lavishly luxurious ever built. Succeeding his father in 1714 and progressively advanced in rank by the new King George I, the first Duke of Chandos lived as a prince in a palace, where he redeemed himself by a hospitable and munificent way of life and by patronising a wide circle of artists, not the least of whom being George Frederick Handel.

Large amounts of money tend to come and go at the same speed, and by the time the Duke died in 1744 his speculative losses had obliged him to draw in his horns considerably, though he remained at Canons. His son the second Duke made things worse by ignoring financial difficulties altogether and attempting to buy up all land between his two residences, so that he could travel from one to the other without leaving his own property. Inevitably the crash came, and the palace was sold as building materials in 1747 for a mere £11,000. Delectable bits and pieces were carried off to grace other men's properties, and when everything was gone a cabinet maker from Long Acre built himself a villa in the park.

At the beginning of the twentieth century Edgware was still a village of old cottages, with shops and coaching inns stretched out along the main road and the grave of the Harmonious Blacksmith providing a tourist attraction in St Lawrence's churchyard. But plans were in hand for an electric railway to connect it with London, and the building of a tram line in 1904 struck the first blow at its picturesque rurality. The then owner of Canons, Sir Arthur Philip du Cros, sold off the northern part of his park for a golf course and a few scattered developments followed. By 1910 a self-made man of amazing energy was turning his eyes on the area, but even George Cross the hotel entrepreneur had an uphill struggle to get things going until the long-promised electric Underground Railway arrived there from Golders Green in 1924. At last the value of local land rose and profits started to come in.

In 1926 Cross bought 85 acres of Canons Park from a Trust set up by du Cros, and on 17 June a first road and sewers plan was approved by the council. This layout was designed by A.J.Butcher A.R.I.B.A. with a sensitive respect for the beauty and atmosphere of the site; trees were respected and the formal round pond which had punctuated the Duke's stately drive was allowed for by a curve in the road and made to look artistically natural. He also designed a few Tudor-style homes himself to encourage other builders and these set the style for the estate. Sandon's Period Houses followed his example and put up picturesque timbered and brick-nogged houses which bring to mind Snow White and the Seven Dwarfs. They remain to this day in gardens with mature trees and bushes, enormously enjoyable and obviously loved by their owners. Some have suffered replacement doors and windows, but far fewer than might have been feared.

Canons Drive was intended to be an exclusive estate, light years away from the monotonous rows of terraces and semis which mostly characterised suburban development. Like Monkhams twenty years before, names not numbers were the rule at first, few of the properties were under £1,400 and many of them topped £3,000, so a certain slowness in sales was not surprising. Nevertheless, between then and 1939 houses were built by H.A.J. Capps, F.W. Bristow, Sword Daniels and other firms producing one-offs for individual plot buyers.[13]

However doubtful Canons Drive might have appeared as an investment, Tom Reader decided to go for it anyway; he may even have relished the gamble. On 30 October 1930 the Hendon Rural District Council approved an application for six houses between Powell Close and Duke's Avenue to be numbered 42-52, and detailed plans in five different designs were approved during the first half of 1931. The applications were once again under the name of Reader Bros., although Richard seems to have had nothing to do with this speculation and the brothers' business lives were now separate.

The houses were designed in an eye-catching modern style by Tom's 21-year-old son Clayton. Like his cousins and many other builders, he had attended house design classes and they were undoubtedly a young man's bold conception, with semicircular windows, porches and loggias, important chimneys, five bedrooms, three reception rooms, integral garages and large, imposing halls complete with fireplaces. But despite the size of the buildings there was no central heating, which seems inconceivable at this date but was not so at that. In practically every development, coal, gas and electric fires plus lots of fuel storage space were as far as planning for the English winter went, and most Canons Drive buyers would be wealthy enough to have at least one servant to cart coal scuttles and clear away ashes; there were bells in all rooms, with the control box in the cupboard-lined room next to the kitchen.

But this time Tom's gamble didn't pay off. As late as 1937 only two houses were inhabited, though this didn't stop him acquiring an adjacent plot to take numbers 54-68 some time before 1936. They were never to be built.

Despite its slow start, the Canons Drive estate managed to hang on to its exclusive status. Prices rose gradually over the years and building continued after the war though not by Reader's. In 1997 prices advertised for that area in Edgware estate agents' windows ranged between £250,000 and £400,000, and that during a property slump. In 2000 the values stood at £290,000 to £500,000, while those of the six internally modernised Reader houses were said to be in excess of £700,000.[14] The Drive entrance is still dignified by the Duke of Chandos's gateposts, but his majestic lodges have been replaced by blocks of flats – exclusive ones, of course.

Canons Drive Edgware 42-52 even

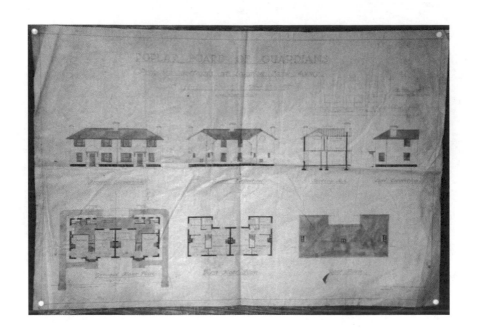

Cottages at the Laindon Farm Colony, Basildon, Essex.

Richard's Hispano Suiza

*Richard Reader by the dormitory built at Laindon, c.1928/9.
Behind is one of the second-hand iron buildings acquired when
the Colony was founded in 1904.*

*Standing: Vic Davis foreman, Edgar Reader, Walter Moore and
Lawrie Moore carpenters, ?, Sam & Tom? Sivier navvies, on ladder:
Thomas Flint carpenter. Seated left: George 'Rasher' Webster scaffolder
& slater (he weighed no more than a rasher of wind). The remaining men have not been identified. The site may be Laindon.*

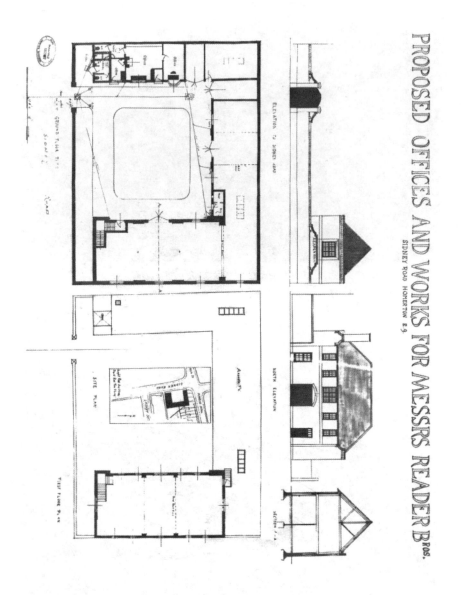

Marsh Hill Works

Design as submitted and approved in 1927.

BUILDERS OF REPUTE: THE STORY OF READER BROS.

The Joinery shop staff, Dick Reader centre front, 1930s.

Marsh Hill Works, 'The Yard'. Dick at the office door c.1937/8.

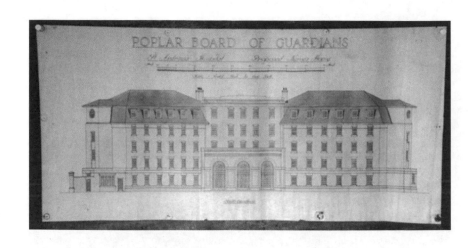

St Andrew's Nurses' Home, Bromley

designed by the Borough Surveyor, Harley Heckford M.I.C.E.

above: Elevation

below: Plan

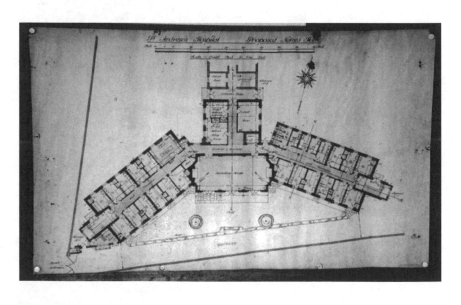

Building the River Street Flats, Bromley.
Left: Devons Road, right: River Street (Maddams Street).

Sumner House, River Street, just before opening. One of several
photos by Jack Reader who supervised the building. View from
Weston Street with All Hallows Devons Road.

SOUVENIR OF THE OFFICIAL OPENING

SUMNER HOUSE HOUSING SCHEME

by

Mrs. A. M. SUMNER

on

SATURDAY, 28th SEPTEMBER, 1929, at 3 o'clock

Councillor CHARLES W. KEY, J.P., Mayor.
Alderman DAVID M. ADAMS, Chairman, Special Housing Committee.

FRONT ELEVATION.

HARLEY HECKFORD, M.Inst. C.E.,
Borough Surveyor.

Brochure for the opening of Sumner House flats,
River Street, 1929.

"The Builder and the Cabinet Minister".

Photograph by Edith Reader.

"Come in, my people!"

Builders of Repute: the Story of Reader Bros.

Canons Drive, Edgware, 1931-5.

Opposite page top to bottom: Nos 44, 46 and 48

Above: Number 50; Below: Number 52 'Pinewood'.

Left: Tom Reader on the building site in Canons Drive, early 1930s, with a local policeman and the keeper of Canons Park.

Below: Annie & Clayton Reader at Pinewood, Canons Drive, 1937.

BUILDERS OF REPUTE: THE STORY OF READER BROS.

CHAPTER 7 1930 – 1939

Chingford, Chislehurst. Death of Tom Reader.

In the middle of the nineteenth century Chingford was a very beautiful place. Travellers on the road through the fields from Walthamstow could see the square thirteenth century tower of its old parish church ahead, near the top of the hill known as Chingford Mount. The road climbed past the church and the ground on the left fell away to give a stunning view of the Lea valley. At Mansfield Hill the road descended to become Low Street and run beside the river to Waltham Abbey, but a right fork known as High Street stayed with the high ground and led to a meeting of four lanes at Chingford Green, around which the largest settlement clustered.

King's Head Hill turned left to cross the valley via Marsh Lane. Bull Lane turned right to wind through forest land to Woodford. Past the handsome new flint church on the Green, a fourth road carried on to where a Tudor Hunting Lodge or Standing stood on the rise overlooking Chingford Plain (at that time enclosed and under cultivation) and frittered itself away into the rides of Epping Forest. Despite the suburbanisation going on elsewhere, the village remained quiet and isolated well into the nineteenth century, because it was on the direct road to nowhere but itself.

In 1870 the Great Eastern Railway reached Hoe Lane Walthamstow and the fields around the station sprouted suburb, much of it of a working class nature which must have alarmed the owners of the area's splendid Georgian mansions. Then in November 1873 the line was extended to Bull Lane, Chingford, where the temporary appearance of the wooden station gave notice that it intended to move on very shortly. In fact the next destination was to be High Beech, a place cherished by those who loved the Essex countryside, and public opinion, now much alarmed by the speed with which such beauty was being destroyed, mobilized into a campaign to preserve what remained of the ancient woodland. After a long struggle the Epping Forest Act was passed in August 1878, and in September the railway line reached its final end at the new Chingford Station within sight of "Queen Elizabeth's" Hunting Lodge. By the time Queen Victoria alighted at that same station on 6 May 1882, drove to the reprieved High Beech and declared the Forest the property of the citizens of London forever, a magnificent mock Tudor hotel stood next door to the Standing and weekend trippers from London were regularly walking up from the railway to enjoy its hospitality. For years to come, the Forest would be the main playground of north-east London, and further trippers' pubs were built around its edges to provide much pleasure and much profit.

Of course, residential development was already starting. Villas popped up on all main roads, and one of the first large estates was begun near the station by the Liberator Building Society, an organization largely kept afloat by fraud which finally sank in 1892, taking the savings of thousands down with it. Their grandiose, eccentric houses look as if they were destined for the Munsters and the Chingford Rise Estate Company continued in the same vein, but unfortunately this highly individual edge to North Chingford is now being elbowed by flats.

By 1920 there was a compact area of development from the Station to the Green, and ribbons of good middle-class houses stretched along the Ridgeway (the old High Street) and down the back route to the forty-year-old cemetery (Heathcote Grove). To the south, a tide of terraced housing was lapping at the bottom of Old Church Hill. But people from built-up areas still came for a day out in the country at Chingford, and many artists painted the picturesque decay of the old church, smothered with ivy and open to the sky. All around was farmland, but much of the open land was already in the hands of people whose plans for it included neither crops nor livestock. The field pattern had changed little since the tithe map of 1843, and it was those centuries-old boundaries which were to determine the shape of development; to a large extent they can still be traced today.[1]

Pursuant to the Town Planning Act of 1925 which belatedly tried to impose some sort of order on suburban development, Chingford Urban District Council produced its own Interim Development Order in 1927, revised into the Chingford Town Planning Scheme in 1933. This detailed document runs to forty-six pages and five schedules, and arouses respect for builders who have to understand and absorb that kind of thing. All road layouts had to be approved by the Council and areas were strictly zoned to prevent unsuitable development. Density of housing was laid down; "the number of building units on the land unit shall not at any time exceed the number obtained by multiplying the number of acres in the land unit by the average per acre specified in the Table below for the density zone in which the land is situate, or where the land unit is situate in more than one density zone, the sum of the numbers obtained by multiplying the number of acres in the land unit within each zone by the average per acre specified in the Table below for that zone." So that was quite clear, then.

Chingford's inevitable future as part of the London sprawl was symbolically recognised in 1929 by the removal of the Council from a shop in Station Rd to a new Trumpton-style Town Hall in the Ridgeway, complete with balcony to wave from. The street map included with Kelly's 1929 Directory shows that a large area to the west of Old Church Hill had already been planned into streets. This had been Cherrydown Farm, now owned by the builders' merchants Good Brothers of Walthamstow,[2] and by 1930 roads and drainage were in hand.[3] The layout can appear irritatingly precious, but Chingford was criss-crossed with footpaths and they had to be assimilated into any plan for building (this may account for the similar complication of the Skinners' Estate, Clerkenwell).

It was not a simple matter to change the route of a right-of-way. A "Certificate or Instrument in writing" had to be lodged with the Clerk of the Peace for the county of Essex and considered by the Justices at the next General Quarter Session. Permission would then be granted in due course, but only subject to the provision of a new highway or footpath to replace the old. So Middleton Avenue took over the function of the ancient path between church and Hall, now in the last few years of its thousand-year life and still a working farm. By 1940 the house was to be engulfed by the Chingford Cork Manufacturing Co. factory and used as offices. Today, if you stand in the unbuilt-up part of Lower Hall Lane, imagine the old waterworks turbine house as the manor mill and the Chingford Industrial Estate as house, garden and outhouses within a moat, you might just about recapture the Manor Hall of Chingford St Paul's. The footpaths of Chingford can still be found snaking round behind back fences and popping up out of nowhere onto roads.

The first house-building at Cherrydown Farm started in the southern part of the estate, mostly by A.Peachey of Walthamstow but also by A.G.Tufton, who had been building on the Chingford Hall Estate the other side of Hall Lane and owned other land in the area.[4] On 2 December 1930 the Chingford Urban District Council approved Reader Bros.' application to build and drain 52 houses on the Cherrydown estate, and in 1932 and 1935 approval was given for the

"Chingford Heights" estate on the northern part of Upper Cherrydown field, abutting onto the churchyard and the Rectory garden. Over the next few years, Reader's built most of Hurst Avenue, all of Priory Avenue and Priory Close, and two houses on the corner with Sewardstone Rd South.[5] To encourage purchase rather than letting, prospective customers were given copies of "How to Own Your Home" published by the Huddersfield Building Society.

It was a mixed development of terraced, semi-detached and detached houses and bungalows, designed by Jack. A common method of dealing with corners was to let the garden of the last house in one street run down the beginning of the other, resulting in a visually boring strip of close-boarded fence, but here Jack created particularly attractive pairs of houses set at an angle so that the building line was not interrupted. The first of these to be built was 13 Priory Avenue and 94 Hurst Avenue, with staggered frontages, louvred shutters, three bedrooms and an integral garage. Few suburban semis were then built with garage attached, but wooden or brick ones were frequently added on request at the end of gardens, access being from a dirt track such as ran between numbers 11 and 13 Priory Avenue to serve Hurst Avenue.

Jack intended to buy 13 Priory Avenue himself, and it was only when it was near completion that Richard announced it was his wedding present. Although his son was naturally overcome with gratitude at such generosity, he couldn't help wishing he had been told at an earlier stage so he could have added personal touches and perhaps spent a bit more. However, his father was given to sudden gestures and the only thing to do was to thank him most sincerely.

Jack and Nina were married on 19 September 1931 at SS. Peter and Paul on Chingford Green. They had wanted to have the ceremony at the romantic old All Saints, which after years of dereliction had just been restored and reopened, but it was not licenced for marriages. The celebratory booklet "The Story of Chingford Old Church" by the Rector the Rev.C.B.H.Knight, was not only full of information, it provided useful advertising space for local businesses, among them estate agents, schools, shopkeepers, undertakers, Edmonds's laundry on the Green, Reader Bros. whose advert carried a photograph of 29 Hurst Avenue, and Albert E.Squire, who was to take the wedding photographs.[6]

The Thornicrofts had bought 81 New Rd[7] when Normanshire Farm was developed a few years before, and the reception took place at the 1906 county junior school directly opposite. Nina wore pale pink and her bridesmaids, sister Phyllis and cousin Mary Ludlow (daughter of Mrs.Thornicroft's sister Minnie) were in cream lace. Dick Reader was best man and the couple "went away", as the phrase was, for a tour of Devon and Cornwall in Jack's Morris Oxford 6.

They furnished their house in the simple, uncluttered style fashionable at the time. A complete reaction had taken place against Victorian and Edwardian taste so that walls were plain and neutral, pictures few, picture rails rare and furniture was becoming lighter coloured. In the hall at 13 Priory Avenue, out of which green-carpeted stairs rose in two flights lit by leaded windows, the brick fireplace held an electric fire, the linoleum looked like large red tiles, and an oak chest just inside the front door bore a brass tray and a dragon-shaped lamp with a chinese shade. The drawing room had blue fitted carpet and blue brocade curtains, the three-piece suite was brown plush and there were orange brocade cushions. As if the house were not a munificent enough gift, Edith had given the couple a black baby grand piano in the style of which Sir Edward Elgar, Messrs Chappell told her, had recently ordered not one but two.

The very large brick fireplace[8] in the dining room may have been individually designed by Jack, though it resembled a Claygate, and there were french windows onto a concrete verandah with glass roof and steps down into the garden. The suite was light oak with emerald sharkskin chairseats, the carpet was a geometric Deco design in shades of beige and dull green, and the floor-length curtains were of brown velvet with a shaped pelmet. The main bedroom had a limed oak suite, a deep petunia carpet, mauve bedspreads and eiderdowns and floral curtains in shades of mauve and green on cream. It also contained a chair in pale green Lloyd Loom, a fashionable item which might conceivably have been found in every new middle class home in the kingdom. The house being situated halfway up the Mount, the view from back windows was extensive enough to include the glow from the burning Crystal Palace five years later, and the field below was empty except for farm buildings.

There was an interesting mixture of occupations and professions among the residents on the Cherrydown and Chingford Heights estates. Jack could watch the Marshalls practicing acrobatics in their Hurst Avenue garden, and next door to him lived a factory owner. Ernest Batten, the firm's secretary moved into 22 Priory Avenue, 21 was bought by Miss Audrey Gains, sister of the boxer Larry and Walter

Moore the carpenter was to move into 106. 10 Hurst Avenue was bought by Dr. St.John Selby, and in 1934 an extension was built on the side containing waiting room, consulting room and dispensary. Richard Reader was now in his fifties and enjoying prosperity, also the fact that he could leave his sons in charge while he and Edith took regular motoring holidays throughout the British Isles. At that time he was running a second-hand Hispano Suiza bought from Jack Barclay's in Hanover Square, and loving every moment of it. It was a preposterous vehicle for Christie Rd, said to be longer than the front-age of the house, and some neighbours tended to look askance at what they saw as outrageous showing off, though Richard at least defused the small boy situation by giving them rides on condition they left the car alone in future. But although he left the planning of estates and houses to his sons he still enjoyed designing the brick garden walls which complemented the architecture and unified the streets so nicely. There are still some of these left, and when the house front remains unmodernised they look very pleasing together; the facing bricks for the Chingford estates were particularly good and included "heather" hand-mades supplied by the Sussex Brick Company.

    Hurst Avenue 1 – 83 10 – 94
    Priory Avenue 1 – 81 2 – 112
    Priory Close 1 – 18
    Sewardstone Rd South 150 – 152 (Waltham Way)

* * *

At the top of Chingford Mount where the road swung round to the right were a farm, an inn, a smithy and some cottages, the whole group surrounded by fields. Behind the idyll, money and specula-tion were already at work and parcels of land had been changing hands in all directions for years. Mann, Crossman and Paulin's bought the Green Man, its land and its cottages in the early 1920s and rebuilt the inn in modern style, while the fields had already been through the hands of more than one builder.

Fields 152 & 153 were sold on 30 Dec 1924 by David Thomas Allen to the Collett Building Co.Ltd, who sold them on in March 1931 to E.R.Boswall,[9] who had already built 133-165 on the other side of Old Church Road. At much the same time Collett also sold land to Arthur George Tufton of Belle Vue, Hale End Rd E17.

A 40 foot wide strip of field 154 was assigned to a tenant as a thoroughfare by the owner G.M.Lowcock in 1923, passed on to the brewers in March 1924, passed to another tenant in January 1925 and to Tufton on 6 June 1930. The Essex County Council had bought field 163 for a new Senior School and by January 1931 Tufton was beginning to make up the thoroughfare into a road which would provide access to both the school and the houses he intended to build on the southern side. But a letter of 22 June informed the County Architect that he was in difficulties, and by 7 September the land was in the hands of Reader Bros.[10]

The final amended plan for Wellington Avenue was approved on 7 February 1933. It is difficult to account for the choice of name, which has no obvious association with the topography or history of Chingford; perhaps Richard was remembering Woolwich Arsenal, whose main thoroughfare is so named. Building had started already, and a sliver of field 163 was bought in order to complete the turning circle at the end. On the north side the road had two terraces, one set back, before the Secondary School, on the south side semi-detached semi-bungalows (2 reception, 1 bedroom, kitchen, bathroom and W.C. on the ground floor, 2 bedrooms and storage space upstairs), and a group at the east end consisting of two bungalows, two semi-detached of a different design and two individually designed detached.

The west end of the plot abutted onto Old Church Road where a terrace of six was built. The two end houses had four bedrooms and an integral garage, and when Dick married in September 1932 he moved into the one on the corner of Wellington Avenue. His wife, Vera Snare was a piano teacher at Trinity College of Music where he had singing lessons and Edgar was to study composition, and his home possessed a feature which no other Reader house could boast; he began to build a small church organ in the back reception room. With the benefit of communicating doors and a grand piano, probably given by Edith, Dick and Vera made music together, joined on occasions by other musical Readers. No stories have come down about complaints from their neighbours, so either they were musical too or the Reader walls were thick. Where house decoration is concerned, modern house-owners tend to go every one to his own way, and the unity of this terrace has now been partly lost. A pair of semis and a detached were added at the north end in 1934.

Edgar and Phyllis had been engaged for some time, and it was while the layout for this development was under discussion that Richard made another of his generous gestures. He indicated the last plot at the end of the road and told his youngest son to "build yourself a house, my boy." Finding himself in the happy position of being fore-warned, unlike Jack, Edgar covered sheets of paper with sketches. An old notebook used during the renovation of premises at Beech St EC2 in 1928 has its unused pages covered with elevations and plans, and it is possible to see the house which was to be number 66 Wellington Avenue gradually emerging. It was in the Old English style, with leaded lights, tile hanging, strapping, a room above the porch genuinely supported by an oak beam, and a front door with a four-centred arch. The pebble-dashed back, however, was flat and rather plain, bringing to mind the criticism of speculative building as "Queen Anne front, Mary Anne back". There is an interesting little square bay window to take the kitchen sink, and a small glass door and loggia out of the dining room, but the back is in no way as imaginative as the front; few house backs are. The continuation of strapping and tile-hanging all round would have added to the house's attractions but also to its cost.

The wedding took place on 10 June 1933 at SS Peter & Paul, with the reception again at New Road School. There had been concern at Cissie Reader marrying in emerald green and it was unconventional for Nina to marry in pink, but Phyllis walked up the aisle in an outfit of such originality that it must have caused a sensation. She was extremely pretty but also shy and reserved, which makes it even more remarkable. Under the headline "Teacher Sisters Wed Brothers", the local paper described her "gown of gold tissue and lace, with a gold net veil held in place by gold leaves" and a spray of dark blue delphiniums on her skirt to match her bouquet. The bridesmaids, schoolfriend Peggy Constantine and again Mary Ludlow, wore blue and mauve and Ron Thornicroft was best man, while the toasts were proposed by Tom Reader and Dick.

Among the guests was Jack & Nina's 5-month-old daughter Nina Jacqueline, as Richard and Edith were now at the beginning of a successful new career as grandparents. Tom already had two grand-sons provided by Cissie and Jimmy Koster, but his son Clayton showed no sign of getting married. He was living a bachelor life of cars, betting on horses and playing clarinet in a jazz trio which did gigs all over north London. His father, who liked a flutter himself and whom he adored, was understanding as long as his son was up in time to get ready for work and make him breakfast. Presumably Annie had hers later.

After a touring honeymoon in North Wales and Torquay, via a Standard which emptied Edgar's bank account, the couple moved into the clean, carpeted, furnished perfection of 66 Wellington Avenue. The hall was distempered in cream, the staircarpet was tomato red, the doorframes were picked out in black, jade green and red and the flush doors were silver grey. A jade green figure holding a glass bowl lit the alcove above a radiator (an unusual feature for the time), and Phyllis had made rugs in fashionable geometric patterns, using the same colours as the paintwork. There were no old-fashioned wooden bannisters; the handrails were supported by plastered brickwork the same colour as the walls. It was an excellent example of fashionable modern decor in the early thirties, and a complete contrast to the Tudor exterior. The drawing room also had distempered walls, and there was a small stained glass window and a Minster stone fireplace. The wedding present Chappell baby grand, (born mahogany but turned fashionably black on Edith's instructions), was draped with a fringed gold shawl, and Edgar's ebonised music cabinet made by a South Hackney neighbour, possibly Annie Reader's brother, was topped by a stupendously colourful Japanese pot-pourri jar. The floorboards were painted black and strewn with rugs.

The dining room at the back, however, was all Tudor, with brick inglenook fireplace and exposed joists in the ceiling. The curtains were at first "floral cretonne" but soon changed for a rich violet velvet. The furniture was oak-veneered and the carpet had a small geometrical pattern in shades of green and brown. A service hatch within the inglenook opened onto the cream-painted kitchen with its solid fuel boiler, gas stove, larder, dresser, and storage for coal and coke in the lobby leading to the side door. If the cream was chipped, bright tomato red showed through, which suggests a first choice quickly thought better of. Upstairs there were four bedrooms, two with small beige-tiled fireplaces, and a black and white bathroom with tiles so shiny they could be used as dark mirrors. The first photographs taken of the completed house show a garden bare except for the layout of concrete paths, but within a few years Edgar, who was a passionate gardener, had turned it into a mass of flowers.

Wellington Avenue 1 – 19 2 – 62   66

Old Church Rd 167 – 183

* * *

In September 1933, Mrs Thornicroft answered a knock on her door and found a pair of sisters seeking accommodation for the younger.

Like many Welsh people at that time of severe unemployment, Rhianon Lloyd Jones had sought work in London and come up from Aberdare to teach at New Road School. The room which had been Nina and Phyllis's was let to her, and within a short time her clergyman father had found Phyllis and Nina Welsh maids to help with the housework. So by 1934 the three younger Reader brothers were living with new brides in new Reader houses within a few minutes walk of each other. Work was just around the corner or twenty minutes drive to Homerton, and business was booming. Afternoon tea was at Priory Avenue on Tuesdays and at Wellington Avenue on Thursdays, and the three families regularly entertained friends and relatives. Altogether, it must have been an enjoyable and heartening time for the whole family until the last weeks of the year, when they were struck by tragedy; Vera Reader's first baby died at birth and she followed it on 20 December.

Vera was buried on Christmas Eve in the churchyard of Bushey Congregational Church,[11] where she had been married just over two years before, and Dick was left with not even a local grave to visit. Her old Nanny, Florence Daniels had already moved in to help with the child, and instead she stayed on to look after Dick. Christmas 1934 was wretched, and for Phyllis, who was expecting her own first baby in the spring, anticipation must have become apprehension. The small bedroom over the porch at 66 had been prepared as a nursery, and she was painting the wall of fitted cupboards with nursery rhyme pictures. It was an immense relief to all the Readers, though of little comfort to Dick, when Josephine was born safely on 7 March 1935 at Glen Lynn Maternity Nursing Home, 96 The Ridgeway, an establishment that had also advertised in the Old Church's booklet.

However, further trouble arrived from another direction. Edith suffered another bout of illness which left her so weakened that it was decided she needed permanent help in the house. Mrs Thornicroft's youngest sister Miranda Skeel, known as Rinda, came to fill the place of housekeeper and companion and remained with her for the rest of Edith's life. She was a small, spry, chirpy woman with a girlish, idiosyncratic laugh and definite opinions, which later led her to shout at television villains. It was Rinda who made it possible for Richard and Edith to remain in their own home to the end, one of the valiant army of maiden aunts which supported the English family.

* * *

At the same time as Edith's illness Tom Reader, still enjoying life to the full, was struck on the leg by a tennis ball and developed thrombosis. As he was a devoted chain-smoker of many years' standing who, on the evidence of the family photograph albums, even played tennis with a fag in his mouth, his physical condition was not of the best and he died on 9 November. The original Reader Brothers partnership was finally ended. Tom had married a beautiful and lovable wife, travelled round Britain in the company of friends and family, smoked, drunk, driven good cars, played games, played the horses, sung, acted and been the family joker. On the whole, he'd had a good time.

As Tom once said, there are people who make wills and people who don't, and it is hardly necessary to say that he belonged to the second category. It took some time to settle his affairs and death duties paid were three and a half thousand pounds on an estate of about thirty two thousand, which doesn't sound bad by today's standards. But it was largely made up of property, in other words, unsold houses. Most were at least let, but sales at the expensive Edgware speculation were hanging fire and Annie and Clayton had the task of sorting everything out.

In 1937 they sold 2 Hocroft Rd and moved into 52 Canons Drive, named Pinewood in acknowledgement of the magnificent giant conifers which still line the road. There is a photograph of Annie and Clayton beside the beige and green tiled fireplace in the back reception room, the Deco style very different from Annie's first Reader-built home at 1 Prince's Avenue Finchley. Cissie and Jimmy Koster left their Buckley house in Pinner and brought their two sons to live with them, so Annie and Clayton moved up to the first floor which was converted into a self-contained flat. Despite Tom's lack of financial foresight they were not badly off but for some reason lived frugally, and only two rooms had carpets. There were rents to live on from Finchley and Child's Hill, and Clayton now spent most of his energies on playing the clarinet while Annie handled business matters.

Downstairs, the integral garage became a bedroom, a bathroom was put in, and part of the large panelled hall became yet another room which appropriated the hall fireplace. The absolutely vital replacement garage was built in the garden. Martin Koster's memories of his childhood encompass his much-loved grandmother, the bachelor lifestyle of his uncle, the garden, Canons Park and brushes with its parkkeeper, and the fact that in winter the big house was freezing cold.

* * *

During the thirties Edgar designed a house for Maude McLachlan's daughter Janet, a charming and graceful woman who had worked as a mannequin or model for the Molyneux fashion house until her marriage to Veere Sherren in July 1931. By 1934 E.O'Sullivan (Kenley) Ltd was putting in planning applications for the site of a house and grounds called Marlings near Orpington in Kent, and that for Janet's house, number 3359, was dated 5 November 1935.[12] The London Borough of Bromley has discarded its early records and the plans have been lost, but a sketch survives in one of Edgar's many drawing books. Little Kingsdale, Orpington Rd, Chislehurst, named after Veere's parents' home Kingsdale in Stanmore, was built on the approximate site of a pair of cottages marked 137 in the 1933 O.S. map, and it is a large attractive house with typical Reader details, such as tile-hanging and large staircase window. The Sherrens were in residence by 1937 and remained there ten years.

* * * *

Even though the Chingford estates had a fully worked out plan, orders were still accepted for specially designed houses, as had been the case at Monkhams. In June 1934 the council approved Reader's plans for a double fronted detached house for a Mr George Rumph at 225 Old Church Road, to be built on part of the garden of Fairview nearly opposite Silverthorn Gardens. On 2 July 1935, however, another plan by architect Raymond J.Ward for the builder C.S.Richardson received approval, but the building doesn't appear in either the Directory or the Electoral Register for 1939, and the bomb dropped outside in October 1940 would have destroyed any half-built structure. A modern house now occupies the site.

An individual bungalow for a Mrs E.J.Wearen was built at 53 The Avenue in 1931, and in 1937 a tile-hung house reminiscent of Edgar's own was designed and built for Mr Herbert Harrison in Forest View overlooking Chingford Plain, on the site of number 39's tennis court. More were to be designed to order on the Dove House Estate, built on fields 114, 115 and the remaining part of 116, which had been bought from James Soper of Low Street Farm by Harold T.Good in 1932.

Due to the steep contours of the land, Dove House Field 115 was an unusual shape, reminiscent of India or South America. It was already named so in 1670, and must once have contained a Dovecot similar to the timbered building which remains in Waltham Forest Council's Depot and Recycling Centre in King's Road on the site of Pimp Hall.

Church Field 116 already had Boswall's houses on its Old Church Road edge, built in 1926 and 1927. Field 114 sloped down to the winding banks of the River Lea, but its western end had been chopped off by a long straight aqueduct bringing the undisciplined Lea water source to heel, and then again by a new road named Sewardstone Road South (now Waltham Way) which was to connect Low Street with the Lea Valley Viaduct. The Dove House Estate used all of these three fields, including the strip left between the aqueduct and Sewardstone Road.

Along the southern edge of the land a footpath led from Old Church Rd down to a bridge across the Lea at Flanders Weir, which had long been a favourite trippers' destination for bathing, fishing and picnicking. In order to make full use of the site this path had to be moved, and the apocalyptic language of the necessary documents is impressive and even reassuring. Reader Bros., they said, desired to divert and turn and utterly stop up a public footway, and once a New Highway was built their desire and proposal was to stop up the Old Highway as useless and unnecessary. Whereupon the Urban District Council of Chingford had held a meeting to consider the said proposal, and resolved that the Old Highway should be diverted and turned and wholly stopped up and the proposed New Highway be made and opened in lieu thereof. Two Justices of the Peace then instructed the Clerk of the Council to put notices in The Chingford Express, at both ends of the footpath itself, and with a Lutheran gesture on the door of the parish church for four Sundays. No-one objecting at the Chelmsford Quarter Sessions in October the measure was allowed, under an "act to consolidate and amend the laws relating to highways in that part of Great Britain called England" passed in the fifth and sixth years of William IV. The process took four months.

On 7 April 1937 two other J.P.s declared that they had examined the new highway (Leadale Avenue) on 2 February and found it in good condition and repair, by which time Our Sovereign Lord Edward VIII's name on the printed part of the document had been unceremoniously typed out and replaced by that of George VI. The road name appears to be filched from the Barclay estate at Clapton Common four miles downstream, both being on high ground sloping down to the River Lea.

The land around the church and rectory was bought by W.P. Render, which must have caused confusion, and Reader's 1935 Proposed Estate plan by T.J.S.Blake of 12 Hall Lane indicates the existence of

Render's Old Rectory Estate to the south and Mortimer's "Dingley Dell" Estate to the north.[13] Reader's house designs were submitted in 1936, 1937 and 1938, and presumably started as soon as approval was received. There was a variety of different types, and individual designs for particular clients included a house with a handsome staircase window and adjoining surgery at 26 Leadale Avenue for Dr Robert & Mrs Hilda Dormer, though they are only recorded in residence during 1936. Number 26 St Catherine's Road was built for Arthur le Boutillier.

Heriot Avenue was probably named from Herriots, the house opposite the Old Church which became Caroline Mount and was finally pulled down by the Abney Park Cemetery Company, but the remaining streetnames seem arbitrary, particularly St Catherine's Rd; no church or house of that name has been traced. It seems that names were chosen for euphony rather than meaning; Priory Avenue, for instance, may have been near a church, but the nearest monastic sites were at Walthamstow and Waltham Abbey.[14]

Reader's had an excellent reputation in Chingford. A few of the original buyers are still in residence, and to paraphrase an unsolicited verbal testimonial from one of them, "they never had a dissatisfied client – except the ones who tried to do alterations and couldn't get through the walls."[15] Their houses were solidly built, and for an estate built on such a steep site remain in remarkably good condition.[16]

>   Leadale Avenue 1 – 91   2 – 76
>
>   Heriot Avenue 1 – 49   2 – 44
>
>   St Catherine's Rd 1 – 25   2 – 46
>
>   Sewardstone Rd South 209 – 265   186 – 222
>
>   Lansdowne Rd 25 – 57
>
>   Dove House Gardens 1 – 19
>
>   The Avenue 53
>
>   Forest View 39a

Field pattern of Chingford with 1843 Tithe Map numbering.

Chingford Mount in the early 20th century showing the Old Church's roofless nave. Centre right, the gatepost of Chingford Cemetery, extreme left, Cherrydown farmhouse.

4 & 2 Priory Avenue with churchyard elms behind, now gone. Note the salt stains on the new garden brickwork.

Builders of Repute: the Story of Reader Bros.

Advertising photographs taken by T.S. Robinson, 185 & 187 Homerton High Street.

Above: 1 - 7 Hurst Avenue, the first houses built at Chingford.

Below: 25 - 31 Hurst Avenue. Written on back: "Group of B1 Houses – price £875 semi-detached, £850 terrace".

*The back view of 94 Hurst Avenue and 13 Priory Avenue July
1934. In the garden of No 13, Phoebe Beardsley (née Skeel), Rinda
Skeel, Rhianon Lloyd Jones, Phyllis Reader, Edgar Reader,
Jacqueline Reader, Nina Thornicroft senior.*

*Jacqueline feeds the milkman's horse.
Behind, 83 Hurst Avenue and 15 Priory Avenue.*

*The dining room,
13 Priory Avenue
c.1931.*

*Jack Reader and Eric
Anderson on the
verandah at
13 Priory Avenue,
1930s.*

167 Old Church Road:
Dick's house.

66 Wellington Avenue, 1933.

The Garden, 66 Wellington Avenue, 1939.

Madeline & Josephine at the gate of 66 Wellington Avenue, 1939.

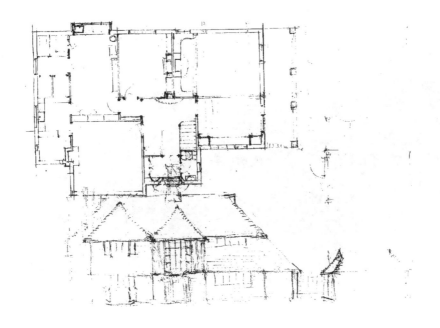

Edgar's sketch for Little Kingsdale, Chislehurst.

Little Kingsdale, 1999.

Builders of Repute: the Story of Reader Bros.

The Dove House estate

Above: Building Leadale Avenue, c.1936.

Below: The same corner, 1998.

ABOVE:

Back of north side of Leadale Avenue c.1936. Beyond, the Lea Valley before the flooding of the William Girling reservoir.

RIGHT:

A page from 'How to own your home' – a brochure from the Huddersfield Building Society, 1938.

HUDDERSFIELD BUILDING SOCIETY

METHODS OF REPAYMENT

The loan may be repaid by lunar monthly payments (i.e., once every four weeks) or calendar monthly payments, as the borrower prefers.

In the following table both lunar and calendar monthly repayments are shown. The equivalent weekly cost has also been given for easy comparison. Repayments being on the annuity principle are inclusive of interest and capital.

For each £100 borrowed.
(Calculated to the nearest penny.)

Term of Loan Years	Calendar Monthly Repayment £ s. d.		Lunar Monthly Repayment £ s. d.		Equivalent Weekly Cost s. d.	
23		11 9		10 11	2	9
22		12 1		11 2	2	10
21		12 5		11 6	2	11
20		12 10		11 10	3	0
19		13 3		12 3	3	1
18		13 8		12 8	3	2
17		14 3		13 2	3	4
16		14 10		13 8	3	5
15		15 6		14 4	3	7
14		16 4		15 1	3	9
13		17 3		15 11	4	0
12		18 3		16 10	4	3
11		19 7		18 0	4	6
10	1	1 1		19 5	4	10
5	1	18 0	1	15 1	8	9

Fractional parts of £100 proportionately.

CHAPTER 8 1933 – 1945

Winchmore Hill, Loughton. War.

William Thomas Paulin, brewer of the Albion Brewery Whitechapel Rd and of Broadfields, Wades Hill, Winchmore Hill Middlesex, died 26 February 1931 in the home which had been built for him when he married in 1877, leaving effects valued at £617,667 16s 4d. He had no son, and his meticulous twenty-eight page will with seven codicils remembered daughters, nephews, brothers, other relatives and his staff at Broadfields. All real estate was to be sold and the money invested by his trustees.

A development plan was quickly drawn up and the estate auctioned at the London Auction Mart 155 Queen Victoria St on Thursday 24 September 1931 by Alfred Savill & Sons, in conjunction with the local firm of E.J.Westoby F.A.I. Lots 2,3,4 and 5 were sold as one to the notable local builder Ingram, who quickly started to develop land on the east side of Wades Hill. The following March Arthur Ingram put in plans to Southgate Urban District Council for the construction of three roads on the site of the mansion and garden, and his suggestion that they should be called Broadfields, Cresswell Way and Paulin Chase was approved, although the first and third were later changed to Broadfields Avenue and Paulin Drive.[1] The road pattern being established, house plots were then auctioned by Chamberlain & Willows of 23 Moorgate E.C.2.

O.R.Davis[2] bought land on the west side of Broadfields Avenue, and Lots 2 and 3, comprising land in all three roads and in Wades Hill, were bought by Reader's who put in their first application for 51 – 61 Cresswell Way in mid-1933, by which time Southgate had become a Municipal Borough. The estate was to be the usual Reader mixture of detached and semi-detached in a variety of styles, designed again by Jack and bearing his trademarks of generous gables, deep eaves and interesting brickwork detail. Occupied houses by both builders first appear in Broadfields Avenue in the 1935 Kelly Directory of Enfield, and the last Reader application, for Paulin Drive, was made in June 1937.

Tom and Annie had between them enjoyed three Reader houses. Sister Florence had spent the first two years of her marriage in 327 Grove Green Road Leyton and a short period in 13 Prince's Avenue

Finchley, while Maude and Ada were still living at Hervey Road Blackheath and Prince's Avenue Finchley respectively. Cousin Janet was at Little Kingsdale Chislehurst. Dick, Jack and Edgar were settled in self-designed Reader houses in Chingford. Richard, Edith and Rinda were still living in a rented terrace house with no bathroom. The reason lay with Edith. It probably seemed a good one when her father and sisters were a few houses down the road, but Frank had been dead for twenty years, Jessie had died in December 1936 and Florrie was at the shop in Peascod Street, Windsor.

Richard had wanted to move for some time. On one occasion he had put a deposit down on a large house in Hollybush Hill, Snaresbrook, but Edith cried all night and he had to go and retrieve his money the next morning. She had acquired a fear of change which was to get worse as she grew older, and to some extent affect other members of the family. There was no argument, just obstinacy unaffected by persuasion or reason, and the only thing to do was ignore it. As Richard walked around the land he had bought at Winchmore Hill he pointed to a clump of trees standing beside the site of Paulin's vanished house. "Don't touch those," he told his sons, "I want them in my garden."

The plot he had chosen was between the back gardens of 13-17 Broadfields Avenue, 3-9 Cresswell Way and the old Memorial Almshouses[3] in Wades Hill. The house had to be exactly right if Edith was to warm to it, and there was probably a lot of plan-scribbling by all members of the family. Three designs reached full-sized paper and survive, but only one is signed. A fine house with a double garage and two bathrooms may owe something to Richard, as the upstairs rooms are labelled Billiards, Guest Room, Rinda's Room and Own Bedroom. Another equally handsome and finished in watercolour, is significantly marked Proposed House for MY MOTHER, and signed J.T.Reader L.I.O.B. A third is approaching the semi-bungalow style and elevation which was ultimately decided upon. On the road plan showing the proposed house's position yet another shape is depicted, with the outline of the final design, by Jack and Edgar in co-operation, pencilled in. The application for the last Reader house on the Broadfields Estate went in on 11 June 1937.

The house faced onto the short road between Wades Hill and Broadfields Avenue, and was one of only two with the address of Paulin Drive; a pretty cottage named Chestnut Lodge left over from Paulin's estate stood on the south side, The Bungalow on the north. The ground floor contained a good-sized hall, two reception rooms, kitchen, scullery and offices, and through a glass door lay three bed-rooms, bathroom, W.C. and a two-flight staircase which led up into the deep roof space. Here were cupboards, another W.C. and a bil-liards and darts room 15 feet by 22 feet 6 inches. There were dormer windows on both sides, the back ones looking out onto Sir William's trees.

The ground sloped away from the back of the house and a brick and concrete verandah ran along behind it, overlooking the garden be-low. Richard's sketch plan of the existing trees and shrubs shows fir, holly, cupressus ("one propped up"), oak, lime, yews, copper beech, magnolia, rhodedendrons and flowering cherry ("nearly dead"). Many of these were incorporated into the new lay-out of winding paths which was full of private corners and surprises. These solid cast con-crete garden paths with a crazy-paving pattern pressed into them would not accord with modern taste, but they were the usual style in the thirties, didn't look too bad when the planting started softening their edges and were extremely practical and hard-wearing.

On 30 November 1937, Richard and Edith went to John Barker and Co.Ltd. in Kensington and chose their carpets. On 2 December their goods were moved from 28 Christie Rd by Thos.Harry & Co. of 21 Upper Clapton Road. On 7 Dec they bought twin beds for the guest bedroom, a four-foot bedroom suite for their own room and a cane seat stool. Carpets were laid on 13 and 21 December. On 12 January 1938, Edith went to Maple's and bought an oak table for £3.10s, prob-ably the gate-leg which always stood just inside the front door.

There must have been tears as Edith drove off in Richard's Packard after thirty three years at 28 Christie Rd, but that year she started a new photograph album for pictures of her new home and captioned them in her usual way. "Our Bungalow." "The Drive." "Dick and Rinda having tea in the lounge." "We have even got a sundial." "The bil-liards room in the roof." "Some of the lupins mixed colours." "Our Scotch Fir." "A view of fruit trees in bloom from scullery window." The house was full of good detail. Oak panelling with a carved cor-nice in the dining room, a plate rack around the hall, an alcove spe-cially built for Richard's magnificent bronze clock, good fireplaces, good joinery, even solid fuel central heating, a very rare luxury at the time.

Phyllis and Edgar had another daughter, Madeline, in 1938, and Stephanie was born to Jack and Nina in 1939, so Richard and Edith's grandchild count was then four. The Bungalow at Winchmore Hill became the centre for family gatherings, where the men gathered in the billiard room and drowned the ticking of watches on Richard's worktable, the children played in the hall, the women talked in every other room of the house and a good tea was served in the dining room or the beautifully planted garden. The Jacobean oak coffer on which Richard remembered standing to be dressed by Cecilia now stood before the oriel window in the entrance hall in the role of toy box; Edith regularly added to its contents, which already included her sons' lead soldiers, vintage First World War and before. Every new hour was announced by clocks of all sizes in every room of the house, and the day was punctuated by outbursts of music-making as Dick, Jack, Edgar and Ron sang, Dick had a go at Rachmaninov Preludes, Florrie Gosling flung herself at The Merry Peasant and Richard and Edith occasionally obliged with a violin and piano duet.

The combined effort to build a house which would please Edith succeeded completely, and she became extremely proud of it.

* * *

A brook with the horror film name of Houndsden or Hounsden Gutter ran along the north edge of the Broadfields Estate, and under the Southgate No 1 Planning Scheme the council had decided to reserve a strip of land on either side of it as a public open space. Imaginative and desirable though this might be, it meant depriving Reader's of the garden ends of numbers 58 to 80 Broadfields Avenue and the entire plot on which they had intended to build 114 Wades Hill. Reader's estimated their possible loss to be £586 10s plus the cost of fencing, but the council considered the figure excessive and threatened to withdraw the reservation, which would surely have suited Reader's very well. However, the correspondence between the firm's solicitor, Arthur Bates[4] and the council was held up by the death in office of two successive Borough Engineers, and it was only in May 1939 that Richard made an appointment to meet Mr R.Chandler the District Valuer on site. If the sheet of paper from a pad advertising Knowles' Killalkali[5] is the one he took to the meeting, it appears he had lowered his claim to £484 and sixpence, and that he actually met another surveyor from the department, a Mr De Bock Porter.[6] The council minutes for July 1939 show his total compensation was £250 and that his legal costs were paid by the council. The Streamside Walk was duly built and remains in use today.

* * *

Outwardly, the Reader houses on the Broadfields Estate are little changed and some not at all, which indicates that their present owners value them. Even the ubiquitous replacement window is to be seen in remarkably few properties, and the house used in Reader's advertisement, 45 Broadfields Avenue, appears to be completely unchanged right down to the Richard-designed brick front wall. The houses are well-kept, as are the gardens. That excellent example of good 1930s suburban building, The Bungalow, Paulin Drive also kept its integrity, at least outwardly. As late as 1997 the only change to its frontage was a new garage door, but a generous plot will inevitably tempt someone to squeeze more money out of it. By April 1999 Richard and Edith's beautiful home had been demolished, and Sir William Paulin's Scotch fir stood amid the devastated garden while the demolisher tried to get planning permission for flats.

Broadfields Avenue	13 – 61	58 – 80
Cresswell Way	1 – 9	2 – 14
Paulin Drive	The Bungalow	
Wades Hill	82 – 112	

* * *

1938 brought a happy occasion, the marriage of Dick to Barbara Birch Tindall. Barbara was a shy woman from a formidable medical family, and worked at Hackney Hospital as a medical secretary. She had met Dick over lunch at a pub in Homerton High Street patronised by the hospital staff, and the girl who had lost her mother early and been taken from her home and family in the north to be brought up by an aunt in Finchley, must have felt enormously supported by having such a strong character for a husband. They were married on 11 June at St Barnabas Church, Woodside Park, but Florence Daniels remained for a while at 167 Old Church Rd, which must have been uncomfortably reminiscent of "Rebecca" and rather daunting. So, perhaps, were the Readers and Thornicrofts, until she got used to them.

* * *

The village of Loughton on the eastern edge of Epping Forest was also growing at this time. Development was mainly to the south and east, and north of St John the Baptist's Church and Church Lane lay a particularly beautiful stretch of countryside in the middle of which the Lord of the Manor, Lieutenant Commander John Francis Whitaker Maitland D.L. J.P. R.N.Ret. was in residence at Loughton Hall. The advowson was also his property so his uncle, the Rev. Peregrine Neave Maitland was installed in the Rectory in St John's Rd.

This feudal manorial situation appeared unchanged for centuries, and yet in reality the Maitland family had been selling off land for building since the 1850s, only 25 years after they inherited the manor from the Whitakers.[7] By 1934 a plan was being discussed for a piece of land between Church Hill, Church Lane and Rectory Lane; a fine, high, sloping site with magnificent views. The intended street names actually meant something; Hill Top was accurately topographical, and Marjorams, Roundmead and The Greens were field names.

In 1937 the laid-out ground was acquired by a Mrs.E.M.Davies and plots began to sell, building applications by Peachey and Ben Horn being passed by the end of the year.[8] Reader Bros received a confirmatory plan of land they had bought (for £16,237) and a copy of the restrictions from Arthur Bates in the last week of September. He was not entirely happy with them.

"On lots 50 to 89 in Roundmead Avenue and Hill Top Close only detached houses may be erected, but these plots only have a front-age of approximately 30 feet." Also, "all plans have to be prepared by Mr R.C.Foster" the vendor's architect "and his fees paid. This seems to me very oppressive and unreasonable, moreover, the plans have also to be approved by Messrs Alfred Savill & Sons",[9] surveyors of the Maitland Settled Estates, "and their fees of £1. 1. 0 for each build-ing has to be paid." A variation was negotiated whereby the plans would be prepared by Christopher V.Cable of Hillcrest, Cuffley, Herts, who had already done the same for C.H.Tysoe's[10] development of 2-20 Roundmead Avenue. Whether he was cheaper than Mr. Foster is not recorded.

 Of course, this didn't mean that Cable designed the houses. Most experienced builders continued to design their own, then send the plans to an architect's office to be copied and submitted. This saved them an enormous amount of work in preparing plans and forms and putting them through the planning process with the council. As building later became more technical and even more legislated upon, the benefits were to increase even further.

The thirty foot plots on the Church Hill Estate were perfectly ad-equate for conventional semi-detached plans, but in most parts of the Reader development they were eventually expanded to accom-modate larger houses; in Hill Top Close 22 houses were built on 30 plots, in Roundmead Avenue 36 houses on 43 plots, in Roundmead Close 28 houses on 32 plots, and in The Greens Close 14 houses on 15 plots, an interesting example of a builder's practice being better than a developer's stipulations. Their first plans were passed on 11 May 1938, including one for a temporary wooden, tiled-roofed estate office which is said to have been brought from the Paulin Estate. It is also said to have been a cabman's shelter, but just where or why is not clear. By the next year they had built 1 – 11 and 21 – 24 Hill Top Close, and 67 – 75 Roundmead Avenue, an attractive variety of detached houses designed again by Jack.

* * *

In late August 1939, Edgar and his family went on holiday to the Prince's Hotel, Torquay. It had been built in 1863 as a holiday home for the Earl of Cork and Orrery and had a superb view over Torbay, which was full of shipping; not just pleasure craft but also grey-painted naval vessels. The children played on the beach in the sunshine and were unaware that their parents and every other adult in the hotel were watching the papers and listening to the wireless news bulletins. Within hours of Chamberlain's speech at 11.15 a.m. on Sunday 3 September, the family was packed up and in the pale green Hudson car, making for South Wales. The children awoke some time later to find themselves being undressed in the kitchen of Rhianon Lloyd Jones's parents' home in Aberdare. Non should still have been there on holiday, but a radio anouncement had summoned teachers back to London to organise the evacuation of their pupils. The New Road School coaches had travelled into Essex that day, following a maternity coach which had to stop regularly so that its passengers could be sick. They were told their final destination at Marks Tey, in Non's case Little Bromley near Colchester, and as the Readers arrived at her home she was settling herself into the Georgian Rectory, having seen the children into their billets for the night.

Jack had driven his family down from London and taken their maid Joyce home to Mountain Ash on the way, up a road so steep that he had to remain in the driving seat hanging onto the handbrake while she got out; a failure in gentlemanly behaviour which was very unlike Jack. Edgar and Phyllis's Jessie had already been seen off from Paddington some days before. Once the two mothers and four children were settled into Arosfa, Tanybryn St, the fathers returned home.

Building was brought up short, not least because unsold houses were requisitioned for Government use including those at the Roundmead Estate Loughton, although plans for numbers 1 – 18 The Greens Close were officially passed eleven days after the outbreak of War. They were not to be built for fifteen years. The Building Societies stopped making loans, and a young couple who had put a deposit on a house in Roundmead Avenue were touched and grateful when Richard, once again with the sweeping gesture, told them he would be their building society. He was, and they finally paid him off after the war ended. Arthur Bates drew up a new agreement for the renting of houses, for who would buy a house when it might be destroyed at any moment?

The mechanism for war was largely in place. Shelter trenches had been prepared. Civil Defence had been organised. Gas masks had been issued. Now evacuation had taken place and Air Raid Precautions brought into being months before swung into action. The building of surface air raid shelters was put in hand, and on 4 October Reader Bros. heard from Messrs Young & Co. consulting engineers of 6 Queen Anne's Gate SW1 regarding those to be erected for Hackney Council in Hertford and Culford Roads, De Beauvoir Town. The works were to be on a "Cost plus Profit Basis" set out as "Materials: Wages to tradesmen, labourers, foreman and extra pay for charge hands (plus Employers' Liability and Third Party Insurances at the rate of 1¼ per cent): Employers' Contributions for Health and Unemployment Insurances: District Surveyors' Fees (if any): Water for Works. Add 5 per cent for establishment charges, supervision and plant, and to this total add 7½ per cent for profit." In Poplar, the firm converted deserted infant schools into emergency gas decontamination posts and mortuaries.

Jack and Edgar kept each other company by sharing 66 Wellington Avenue and 13 Priory Avenue in turn, probably to avoid requisition, and by October they had found a rented furnished house out of London for their families and drove up to Aberdare to fetch them. With no motorways and few arterials, London to Aberdare and Aberdare to Surrey were long, slow journeys, involving narrow roads, blackout and removed signposts. Stopping to ask for directions was not necessarily helpful, as paranoia about spies and fifth columnists had taken hold. It is obvious why the brothers chose Surrey; since their childhood in the first war they must have associated the area with safety, and St Lawrence, 2 Heathfield Drive, Earlswood was only a couple of miles from Doods Rd Reigate. The children settled well enough, despite a certain unhappiness with the Japanese Samurai armour in the hall, and the two eldest would start Fridays by singing "It's a Lovely Day Tomorrow" and Saturday with "It's a Hap-Hap-Happy Day", because that was when Jack and Edgar came down for the weekend; again the same pattern as Richard and family in the first war.

A leather-covered pocket diary[11] stamped with the words "Arthur Sanderson & Sons send you greetings 1940" contains almost nothing but notes regarding Dick's effort to obtain highly necessary petrol coupons. "21 January Ration Book from L.C.C. Room 91 County Hall. 22 January Applied for extra petrol. Dis.Pet.Officer Bromyard Av.Acton W.3. 9 July Waiting for Ration Book. 21 October 1940 Applied for Ration Book L.C.C. Room 91 SE1..." Amongst this tedium two other occasions are recorded; one a meeting of the Bouverie Masonic Lodge, the other a booking to sing Maunder's "Olivet to Calvary" on Palm Sunday at the Central Baptist Church Orford Rd E17; some activities still continued undisturbed.

The perennial arguments between builder and client continued too. The draft of a letter to Hackney Borough Council re air raid shelters was scribbled by Dick on five pages of a Watteau-decorated notebook which might well have come from Barbara's dressing table:

"...The prices generally may appear high to you, but we would point out that other architects who have audited our a/cs have declared them not only satisfactory but considerably cheaper than some other firms...You particularly mention the case of No.178 Dalston Lane costing £38-7-11 as against No.216 Ridley Rd costing £33-0-0. All materials for Ridley Rd could be dropped from the lorry outside in the street, concrete mixed in the street & wheeled in barrows straight down running planks via the side entrance to the job – as against 178 Dalston Lane, where there was no room for stacking outside or inside, all flettons had to be delivered in small loads as required & carried by hand down a staircase into the garden ...nos 5 & 7 Cecilia Rd was a case of under estimation in a rather desperate attempt to keep key men going pending another contract, which fortunately we have now got in hand". What he nearly said but wisely changed was "..to keep special men engaged pending a contract for some hundreds of these shelters in another boro, which fortunately we have now commenced." Options had to be kept open.

* * *

Christmas 1939, when Jacqueline received her first bicycle, was spent down at Earlswood and the two families were still there for Josephine's fifth birthday on 7 March, when she received a green child-sized tea trolley, for good toys had not yet disappeared from the shops.

On 5 January 1940, when the war was still phoney but normal life for nearly every family in the country had been disrupted, the Huddersfield Building Society sent a roneoed letter to Reader Bros concerning property on the Chingford estates, with added name and reference number at its head.

"Dear Sirs, The above, whose Mortgage to the Society is guaranteed by you, has applied for a reduction in the amount of his monthly subscription payable in respect of the Mortgage owing to his income being reduced as a result of the war. I am instructed to inform you as a matter of courtesy that the Directors propose to permit him to reduce the monthly subscription of £6. 0. 4d now payable by him to £4. 0. 0. until such time as they consider circumstances call for a revision and on the understanding that he informs the Society of any improvement in his income."

Over the next eighteen months the firm received at least fifty of these letters, the monetary sums varying with each case, and they must have been well aware that should any of the mortgagors default the cost of repayment would fall on them.

Some houses had been bought as investments for renting out. The owner of 2 Leadale Avenue and 1 Priory Avenue, for instance, had "been suffering various reverses through empty properties, and tenants who have not paid their rents." He had now "obtained a job and hopes in a few months to straighten out his affairs," which suggests that his income up till then had come entirely from property. By December 1940 the owner of a house in Hurst Avenue had suffered loss due to bombing. "Considerable damage has been done to his property and tenants have had to leave. Previous to this he had some unsatisfactory tenants who left owing £17 in rent", the equivalent of several hundred pounds today. This unhappy venture into property as investment was made by "a clerk with a small income".

Like most other evacuees who had left London in September 1939, the two Reader families returned from Surrey when the threat of immediate bombing proved groundless. The hot summer of 1940 was enjoyed in their gardens and interrupted by the occasional incident, but then in September the London Blitz proper started. The three brothers had naturally provided themselves with air raid shelters. Jack's was on the east side of the house, between the side gate and the children's play house built by the Yard joinery shop. Edgar had bricked up the porch which led from his dining room into the garden. Dick had a brick and cast concrete, freestanding shelter between 167 Old Church Rd and the fence onto Wellington Avenue. Richard had put his in at the back of his garage and moved the front doors several feet forwards. It was shared by sister Maude, now widowed, who moved into the Bungalow and declared it "the most comfortable time of my life." With central heating, it probably was. Richard now had a picture of Churchill wearing a siren suit[12] beside his chair in the dining room, and Edith had used the alcove on the other side of the fireplace for family photographs – <u>drawing-pinned</u> to the oak panelling. For those without a builder in the family, pre-fabricated Anderson and Morrison shelters had been widely provided and Mrs Doris Kircher, the dressmaker at 104 Priory Avenue who made a lot of clothes for Nina's family, found the Morrison in her back room ideal for cutting out on.

On the night of Friday 27/Saturday 28 September 1940, Jack and Nina heard a loud explosion nearby, and a short while later answered a knock on their door to find Dick and Barbara in their dressing gowns. A 1,000 kilo high explosive bomb had fallen at the junction of Wellington Avenue and Old Church Road and shattered both their own house and many others around. At the time of the explosion Barbara was in the shelter and Dick had just brought in a tray of tea, which naturally went everywhere. The whole shelter moved an inch on its foundations but remained in one piece and Barbara, who was pregnant, received only a splinter in her shoulder. It was after this that Ernest Thornicroft, Phyllis and Nina's father, asked Reader's to build an identical shelter in his dining room. Floorboards were removed and the shelter, containing four fold-down bunks, was built directly onto the house foundations.

A tenant had done a flit from 51 Priory Avenue, so Dick was able to move in there with what he could salvage from his gutted house. The just completed organ was gathered up and removed to the Yard, where in the fullness of time he reassembled it and occasionally had a tune. Barbara's baby, Richard Anthony, was born on 17 January 1941 at Whatton Hall, Loughborough, one of three stately homes now accommodating the bombed City of London Maternity Hospital. He received a prompt visit from his aunt Ethelwyn Tindall, who as Assistant Matron drove constantly from mansion to mansion while Matron Edith E.Greaves stayed on duty in the remains of 102 City Rd EC1. Some years after the War, Ethelwyn was to unearth three cardboard boxes of unused petrol coupons while preparing to move, and to ask Dick, far too late, if he could use them.

On the last night of the Blitz, 10/11 May 1941, Arthur Bates's office was destroyed along with the whole south side of Pancras Lane; the north side had gone the previous December. A possible relic is a vellum deed melted into a solid lump of no practical use except as a paperweight, and many early Reader Bros papers must have been destroyed.

At the outbreak of war, Mornington School on Chingford Green (now Mornington Hall) had been taken over as an Air Raid Precautions post, as it was expected that all children would be sent to the country for some time. The failure of this expectation to materialise meant that its pupils, including Jacqueline and Josephine Reader, had to be taught first at home and then in the canteen of Edmonds's Chingford Laundry next door. A short period back in the school's own premises terminated when the building was again requisitioned as a British Restaurant, and by 1942 the school had closed down. The Reader girls changed their blue and gold school berets for green cloche-shaped hats and Miss Ethel Hummerstone's Melford House School at 49 The Ridgeway. Extra-curricular activities continued; dancing classes with Miss Eileen Pyne at 63 The Ridgeway and piano lessons with Mrs Dorothy Cook at 72 Mansfield Hill. Mrs Cook's son Colin was a called-up, red-haired commercial artist who spent his leaves chain-smoking and playing the violin in the kitchen, where the girls sat and talked to him while awaiting their turn at the piano.

Ron Thornicroft went into the Navy, and he and Non Lloyd Jones were married at SS Peter and Paul Chingford Green on 16 December 1943, during a leave. But although the three tall, strapping Reader brothers were given medicals ready for call-up, to their great surprise they were all rejected due to poor eyesight. Jack tried to get into the Royal Engineers, explaining to the interviewing officer that he was a builder and therefore knew how to construct and extemporise construction in emergencies, but was interrupted by a warrior bursting with martial zeal. "We don't construct," he retorted, "we destroy!" So much for all those Bailey bridges.

But construction was just as useful at home, particularly when things were regularly being knocked down, and in addition to Jack's service as a firewatcher, Edgar's with the Home Guard and Dick's with the Auxiliary Fire Service, the brothers and staff took turns to firewatch on the roof of the Yard office, surrounded by paint, paper and wood. It is said that Richard Reader had no use for insurance companies, regarding them as leeches who took money but were reluctant to pay out. If he really acted as he believed, this risky practice could have been catastrophic during the War, though there would at least have been War Damage payments – eventually. Everywhere, finding labour for emergency war damage repair work was a problem. Reader's new Register of Employees started in 1943 reveals that nearly all men were over 40, and a large proportion of those in their 50s and

60s; three labourers were over 70. But all firms were in the same boat and labour shortages were to be even more acute on one job.

Some time during the winter of 1943-44, Reader's were contracted along with many other London builders for a construction project at the East India Dock, under the control of Sir Malcolm McAlpine and the Sir Cyril Kirkpatrick Group of engineers. They were part of a force comprising some 550 firms and 25,000 men countrywide, and like all the rest had no idea what they were building. The plans given them were for an immense cast concrete structure which might possibly have been prefabricated emergency housing had it had doors and windows, but no-one was given drawings of the complete scheme and the secret was kept. The East India Dock had been drained to provide a large enough area, with the result that the dock wall collapsed in two places. However, work was only temporarily interrupted and when the 200ft by 60ft Thing was complete the dock was reflooded and it was floated out and towed away. In June the builders found out what they had been building; caissons for Mulberry Harbour B, assembled on the French coast at Arromanches for the Operation Overlord landings.[13] Edgar composed a stirring ballad entitled "At Six on the Sixth of the Sixth" and sent it off to the B.B.C for Peter Dawson, but with no luck.

In the second half of 1944 younger men drafted in from the North start to appear in Reader's Employees Register; their home addresses were in Leeds, Bradford, Doncaster, Rochdale, Liverpool, Cheshire, Nottinghamshire, Durham and Glasgow, but also in Worcester, Sherborne, Birmingham, Herefordshire and Wales. Most of this emergency labour had moved on by early 1945 and the workforce was once again drawn mainly from the east London area. With demobilisation, new workers were starting with the firm by the second half of 1945.

Nina had a son Howard John on 13 January 1944 and Edgar Nicholas was born to Phyllis on 18 March. Barbara gave birth to Francis Joseph (Frank) on 24 November in the same year. It was hardly the best of times for coping with childbirth and new babies, and the advent of the V2s in September 1944 sent Jack's and Edgar's families out of London again, this time to Harborough Grove, Sale, Cheshire, where Edgar's former next-door neighbours from 62 Wellington Avenue,[14] Frank and Elsye Ballard, had invited them to share their large Victorian house. Jack and Edgar arrived via crowded trains for occasional weekends through the coldest, whitest winter for years, but all were back south in plenty of time for Tuesday 8 May, VE day, on which Jacqueline went off to Woodford County High School and the others to Richmond House in the Ridgeway (red and grey), where they were given a personal Union Jack for waving and sent home again.

A few days later the family gathered rations-in-hand for a celebration party at The Bungalow, where Richard had draped bunting across the frontage and Rinda was wearing a Union Jack apron.

Sale of plots on the Broadfields Estate 1932/3 by Arthur Ingram. Reader's bought Lots 2 & 3, and the proposed Streamside Walk was to run along the top.

*Newspaper advertisement for the estate
showing 45 Broadfields Avenue.*

78 and 80 Broadfields Avenue, 1999.

102-106 Wades Hill 1999.
Inset: design for No 106.

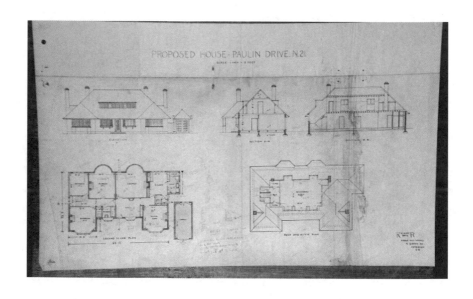

Jack's design for The Bungalow, Paulin Drive.

The Bungalow with Rinda Skeel at the door.

The hall. Richard was a clock and watch enthusiast.

The garden.

*The verandah, which eventually developed
settlement problems due to the steep slope.
Behind, the Memorial Almshouses, since rebuilt.*

The billiard room.

Richard in the panelled dining room.

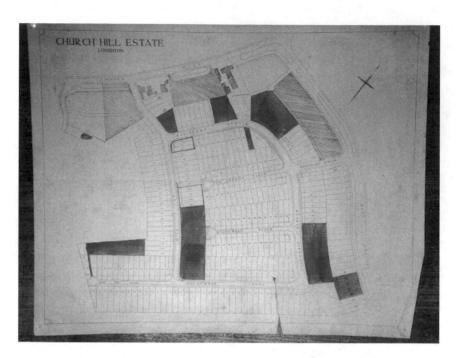

Plan for Church Hill Estate, Loughton,
as drawn up by the Maitland Estate.

71, 72 and 73 Roundmead Avenue,
just before the outbreak of war.

Josephine on the north-west side of Roundmead Avenue, c.1939. The LCC Debden Estate was to be built beyond the houses which mark Rectory Lane.

Dick in Auxiliary Fire Service uniform.

Beyond the lower lefthand corner, the crater of the bomb which destroyed houses in Wellington Avenue and Old Church Road Chingford, including Dick's. To the right, the Reader shelter stands firm.

Left: VE Day: Richard prepares to hoist the Union Jack.

Below: The Bungalow's garage, extended to make room for the Air Raid shelter.

The Victory party. The blurred picture may denote emotion.

*Nick, Edgar, Rinda, Non, Jack, Frank, Howard,
Nina, Barbara, Ron.*

The bungalow site 1999.

CHAPTER 9 1945 – 1959

Post-war repair and reconstruction. Death of Richard Reader. Loughton.

War not only demands courage, endurance, suffering and the deaths of millions, it also requires an enormous bureaucracy to run it. Practically no aspect of life remained free from official control, and this situation continued for many years after 1945 as the country slowly and painfully cleared up the mess. Everywhere, requisitioned suburban houses held those who had lost their own or were in use as offices for ministries and organizations, and people spent hours of their lives in them, queuing for pieces of paper. Edgar received an economical little unbleached sheaf of them in May 1945, consisting of Leaflet UFD/6 (Revised) about utility furniture and household furnishings, an offer of £41 7s 6d in compensation for curtains shredded by windows blown out on 18 February, and a Brown Docket for curtain material. Had be been granted a Green Docket, the footnote would have been dispiriting; "Green utility furniture units cannot be used yet. The Board of Trade will make an announcement about them later, but it may be several months before they can be used."

The housing situation was desperate, and was to get even worse when the demobilised servicemen started to return. There was an urgent need for building skills, but once again skilled men had been killed or maimed. Nissen huts became council houses as the military moved out, and prefabrication had already been introduced as an emergency building method by 1944; Reader's were doing work in connection with the "erection of hutted dwellings" for Poplar Council by March 1945, possibly the construction of concrete bases. The cleverly designed "prefabs" brought in complete sections from the factory and bolted together on site, were meant to last ten years but can still be seen today in parts of the country. They are often regarded with affection by their inhabitants and some have even been listed. They are said to have been cold in winter, but for most of their occupants that was nothing new – central heating was a long way off yet. During the famously bad winter of 1947, fuel was short, coats, hats and gloves were worn indoors at home and at school, and a wretched Canadian exchange teacher at Woodford High School crept about muffled up to the ears and the picture of misery, incredulous that such conditions had not closed the schools.

After the channelling of all resources into war for six years, everything was in short supply and there was no way that permanent homes could be provided until there were enough bricks, tiles and timber with which to do it. To eke such things out, the building trade was controlled by licences: every job costing more than £10 needed one, and only £100 per year could be spent on one job. War damage grants had to be claimed for from the War Damage Commission and permission could take months to come through, as paper crawled from desk to desk and from department to department. Everywhere was battered and dingy, but decoration of houses which hadn't seen a lick of paint since 1939 was allowed only under strict conditions; "The painting must be restricted to priming and one coat and only applied where necessary to prevent serious deterioration as laid down in the instructions of the Ministry of Works. No building trade labour other than tradesmen painters must be engaged on the work."[1] Like every other business, Reader Bros spent a lot of time filling in forms and struggling with ministries, while directives arrived regularly on their desks and new legislation demanded time-consuming practices.

The rebuilding needed in mainland Europe was even more extensive. In 1947 Jack went to study reconstruction in Holland with other members of the London Federation of Master Builders, as guests of the Rotterdam Master Builders. There he made friendships which lasted the rest of his life, and within a short time became fluent in Dutch.

It would be impossible to trace and tedious to read a complete list of work carried out during this difficult period, but a selection from surviving correspondence and plans for the years 1945 – 1950 will give an overview of the kind of things that came the firm's way, and the difficulties they involved. The greatest source was war damage repair for both local authorities and private individuals. Builders had been dealing with it on an emergency basis throughout the War, but an enormous backlog remained. In January 1946 the Metropolitan Borough of Poplar sent Reader's (mis spelt) a £4 rate demand for land at 26 Hewlett Rd, Roman Rd, Bow. This house had been destroyed by fire on the night of 19 March 1941 due to the A.F.S. running out of water, and it seems likely that the firm was using the ground for a site shed while repairing surrounding bomb damage. The house had been rebuilt by 1956, but the entire east side of the road was later redeveloped for council housing.

Licences for repairs were not necessarily forthcoming. Numbers 22 and 23 Hill Top Close Loughton had been forced to jump on their foundations like Dick's air raid shelter, but being much larger had cracked. A plan was made for rebuilding them by June 1946, but the work was not completely finished with until 1950. Permission for £190 worth of repairs to the National Provincial Bank 351 Wick Rd E9 was refused in November 1946 because "Licences are now being granted only on empty dwellings, and to meet statutory notices." A rather plaintive request from a Homerton timber yard – "Could you possibly get the wall outside our office rebuilt, it looks so untidy" – almost certainly received the answer "not yet."

One of the earliest repair jobs done by Reader Bros. was for Messrs R.Lazarus Ltd 11 Kenworthy Rd, directly behind the Yard and reached by a drive on its southern side. This was a "nursery shoe" factory which had been damaged by high explosive blast, and the Specification of Works provided in June 1946 by the surveyor, Howard Sharp F.A.I. of Whetstone, covers ten pages and includes the thorough overhaul and repair of displaced roofs. Reader's estimated the immediate cost at £900, and quoted the controlled materials (i.e. those requiring a licence) as 0.133 standard of softwood, 1000 bricks (common), 400 slates, and 600 feet of super building board (laminated). This work was done by 1948, but they were still renovating the factory until 1956.

St John of Jerusalem's Rectory in Church Crescent E9, where the Readers and Thornicrofts had attended many church functions and garden parties in the past, was in bad condition after years of bomb damage and neglect. The Schedule of necessary repairs was drawn up under the Ecclesiastical Dilapidations Measure 1923-1929 by an ecclesiastical surveyor, W.Chas.Waymouth F.R.I.B.A. of High Holborn, on 27 November 1946. On 9 May 1947 Reader's sent their first estimate for £125. It was not until 2 February 1948 that the licence (Ministry of Works, Control of Civil Building, Defence (General) Regulations, 1939, Regulation 56A) was sent to the Rev. Parsons by the borough engineer, and it was for repairs to the roof and gutters only, total cost not to exceed £15 7s 6d. Others must have followed because Reader's sent two invoices to the Rector on 22 November 1948 "amounting to £94 7s 0d" and "within the £100 licence free limit for the year 1948", and proposing to leave the rest until January 1949 "when one may assume permission to use another £100 free limit." On 3 August 1949 they also quoted £280 for the fitting of galvanized wire guards to the church windows, presumably because of vandalism. Work continued until 1954.

At the Star Shoe Co. 72 Chrisp St E14, the first account for war damage repairs and dilapidations was sent to the architect in December 1946, and a further licence for £75 worth of work was issued a year later, on condition that labour was not transferred from residential property and that slates smaller then 16" x 8" should be used where possible. However this sounded it was not exactly a go-ahead, as Reader's were requested to "please make application for permits for controlled materials, in connection with which I am sending you Ministry of Works modification notification regarding plasterboard, and obtain the materials but NOT start the work until you hear again from me. Messrs Wm Clarkson & Partners[2] are negotiating with the War Damage Commission and the work should not proceed until a technical officer has visited the property." Payment for this job was eventually made via five certificates of satisfaction which had to be sent to the Star Shoe Company for payment. The last was in February 1949, but Reader's had to send reminders before it was honoured. Times were hard for everyone.

The draft specification for Frank Windsor, cabinet maker, 228/32 Cambridge Heath Rd E2, was sent from Adams Smith, son & Walker[3] architects on 24 October 1946. A lantern light was to be made by George Hennings-Hamer (windows) Ltd,[4] who said that steelwork would take 12 to 16 weeks and glass 6 to 7 months (the glass position was "very difficult"). There were delays over licences, shortages, estimates and payments by the War Damage Commission, the cheque finally being paid by Frank Windsor 7 November 1949.

The correspondence concerning War Damage repairs to Fairways Ltd. building materials merchants of Lollar Wharf, 102 West Ferry Rd, Millwall E14, starts with the essential licence forwarded to Kenworthy Rd on 10 April 1947 by the new Borough Engineer of Poplar, Mr. William John Rankin, who was by then living in a Reader house in Chingford. The licence was for repairs to the caretaker's flat and came tidily within the permitted limit at £88 14s 8d. On 4 July Mr.Herbert Spooner of Hooper Cushen & Co.[5] informed Reader's that he had received Ministry of Works licence No. C15/BI/120639/2 authorising work to be put in hand on three damaged crane piers. The time sheet for August to October shows four men employed on the flat; a labourer, 2 slaters and a general foreman. Several more licences were required and there was a problem with the reinstatement of a damaged pier before the installation of an electric crane. An argument followed with Messrs Butters[6] of Trafalgar House about whose fault it was that it wasn't level, Reader's having assumed the previous pier had been correct and neither having checked with the remaining piers. With the exception of the licences, this sort of aggravation is probably still par for the course in building, and the final payment from Fairway's Ltd only appears in the Sales Ledger in March 1956.

Secondhand machinery had been bought from F.H.Marshall & Co.Ltd[7] a Hackney furniture maker, and joinery was provided for many other builders. There was much rebuilding and repair work throughout the City and West End, including Constable & Co.'s premises at 10 Orange St WC2, where Michael Sadleir gave Edgar a copy of Forlorn Sunset, unfortunately not signed. Other jobs were a garage for a doctor at 153 East India Dock Rd,[8] joinery for Monger's Cottages to the north of South Hackney Church, repairs to the Norris Almshouses at 145 Victoria Park Rd, extensive works to Nevill's Bakery, Harrow Rd Ell, repairs to Taylor & Petters, mica merchants of 3-11 Westland Place N1 and alterations and renovations to several office suites in the magnificent Deco office block Plantation House,[9] Fenchurch St, where parking vehicles was a nightmare. Edgar's desperate protestation to a policeman that he was working for "a peer of the realm" (Lord Bessborough) cut no ice at all. Private homes worked on included that of F.K. Bromley of Russell and Bromley, who told his American wife she made Edgar sound like an Admiral of the German navy. Another was the Pelham Crescent house of Sir Leopold Savile, and work was also done for his firm Sir Alexander Gibb & Partners, Queen Anne's Lodge, Westminster.

Life was full of frustrations; "Unfortunately, we have had to repaint the outside of a block of 69 flats due to poor quality paint, and in order to get our money, which, as you may imagine has considerably delayed our programme." Ironically, even with so much needing to be done, government limitations could make work hard to get, and like all building firms, Reader's sometimes wrote round trying to drum it up because "we are very quiet at present". In 1949 they wrote to the architects Tooley & Foster of Buckhurst Hill Essex offering their services; "– we have executed between the wars for the borough of Poplar alone, housing schemes to the value of half a million pounds, whilst the speculative side of our business built and sold some two thousand houses[10] at Chingford, Winchmore Hill, Loughton, Cricklewood and Edgware, between the years 1932-1939. . . we still retain about sixty of our regular employees." At other times they had to refuse offers because "it just so happens that we have a contract requiring our full attention for the next few months." Another source of work was the conversion of larger properties into flats, widely undertaken in response to the chronic housing shortage.

* * *

In about 1946 Edgar and Phyllis decided to move out of 66 Wellington Avenue into a larger house and garden. It seems likely that the initial idea came from Phyllis – one cannot imagine Edgar abandoning the house he had designed for himself, his bride and later his three children without a strong pang of regret. But a certain amount of noise and disturbance had invaded Wellington Avenue with the opening of an evening Youth Club in the school building, and the removal of railings from the park next door had resulted in vandalism and an occasional stone through the tempting staircase window. (A later owner has dealt with the problem via protective mesh). A large, roomy, Edwardian house with a third of an acre of garden was eventually found.

The first reaction of the head of the family was disapproval. The reason doesn't appear immediately obvious at this distance in time; perhaps distrust of change, unease at the abandonment of a Reader house as if they were marrying out of a religion, or perhaps it was a feeling of insecurity at a member of a close family going it alone on such an important decision; it has to be remembered that none of the three sons had ever done that before. But for Richard the strongest reason was an emotional one, for the house was on the Monkhams Estate Woodford Green. He couldn't understand how Edgar could even contemplate living in a place which had given him so much trouble and so many bitter memories.

75 Monkhams Avenue was not built by Reader's, but was only four houses up the road from those which were. It had been designed in 1906 by D.Millner Knight of 35 Bancroft Rd E1, and in 1922 the empty plot 73 was acquired to accommodate a motor garage with loft. A flat was added behind it in 1929 to house a chauffeur, and this was later turned into a doctor's surgery.[11]

By 1947 the property was run-down, like all post-war houses, and the decor and furnishings left by people who had gone abroad rather quickly were going to be fairly rowdy to live with until the necessary quietening-down licence could be obtained. But it had enormous potential as a family home, as estate agents say, and Edgar and Phyllis went ahead with the purchase, which must have taken some strength of mind when facing profound disapproval from a father and a boss. The lady in green satin pyjamas who occupied the flat soon moved out, and throughout the summer family cleaning-up parties worked on the house and picnicked in the pile of hay which had been harvested from the neglected lawn. The necessarily minimal repairs and decoration included wiping out royal blue walls and life-sized Disney figures from a bedroom, for there are limits to what one can live with, and the drawing room was also redecorated pretty quickly. Out came the Edwardian fireplace and overmantel, in went a cream and brown tile slab, and the colour scheme of the finished room was the fashionable brown and porridge.

The family moved in during the school summer holidays and Edgar immediately joined the choir of All Saints Woodford Wells and the Woodford Choral Society, which came to provide useful outlets for the performance of his music. Richard gradually got used to visiting, but on one occasion a remark was passed about people moving into a Reader house down the road. "Someone would have to have moved out first, wouldn't they?" he said sharply. It was irrational, but the wounds still hurt.

75 Monkhams Avenue became a comfortable home with a beautiful garden, complete with grass tennis court dug out single-handedly by Sam Sivier the navvy. Countless family parties were held there and since the 1990 sale its eventful life has continued, in the form of two complete renovations.

* * *

When the Army finished with 70 Roundmead Avenue Loughton it handed the property to the Ministry of Health. Forseeing a further long period during which the house would remain requisitioned for homeless families or council offices or a day nursery or a clinic, or whatever need the Ministry felt should be met in Loughton at that particular moment, Dick quickly claimed prior right, on the principle that he himself had been bombed out, was in temporary rented accommodation and needed a permanent home. This was granted on condition that he stayed there for twelve months, and a Priority Distribution of Building Materials and Components Priority Certificate (officialdom has no fear of tautology) was granted in July 1946 to put it into decent condition. The determination displayed by Jack's military interviewer to make a virtue of destruction, was in evidence among most Service personnel in requisitioned property, witness the cavalier way they treated the Stately Homes of England. At number 70 the materials needed to repair damage caused by both sides in the conflict were 1,000 facing bricks, 4 tiled fireplaces, 8 gallons of paint, 4 gallons of distemper, 3 ceiling blocks, 3 ceiling roses, 1 electric fire, 3 lamp holders, 6 plugs & sockets, 6 switches, 1 gas washboiler, 1 gas waterheater, 4 feet of flexible tube, 1 ball valve, 2 taps, 1 W.C.pan, 1 water waste preventor, 2 W.C.seats, 3 open fire grates, 1 independent boiler, 1 manhole, twelve feet of rainwater pipe, and door and casement fittings for the entire house. When you consider that at least this amount was needed for countless thousands of houses throughout the country, the need for careful licencing becomes obvious.

Barbara's sister Enid Tindall had been in China since 1925 working for the Church Missionary Society. Having sat out the Japanese occupation, she was forced to leave the country when the Communist Revolution broke out and arrived home in time to deliver Bernard William,[12] Richard and Edith's ninth and last grandchild, at 70 Roundmead Avenue on 29 March 1947, before the C.M.S. sent her off again to Malaya. Reader's undeveloped field opposite the house later came in handy for November firework parties.

The Ministry of Works licence to rebuild Dick's bombed house at 167 Old Church Rd was sent to the architects White & Mileson of 147 High Rd Loughton by the Chingford borough engineer on 13 June 1947. By 24 July the rebuilding was under way, and they were continuing negotiations with the War Damage Commission for compensation. The house was being completely reinstated with the exception of the garden, though vanished fences had been replaced by a brick wall. Dick asked Arthur Bates, now at 54/56 Coleman St after a few years at 22/23 Lawrence Pountney Lane, to act for him in the sale.

The price was to be £4,500, and the Canning Town buyer paid his £450 deposit on 28 August 1948. Contracts were exchanged on 21 October and the sale was completed on 11 January 1949. On the same day a letter arrived from the buyer, expressing appreciation for the quality of the attention and workmanship, and asking for a photo or rough sketch of the garden to assist his claim for war damage restitution. According to the letter of reply, Dick and Barbara made a "diligent search" for photos, but could only offer coloured moving picture film, which must surely have been regarded as a bonus. However, providing copies in triplicate for the benefit of officialdom was going to be a problem. Dick suggested that "if a War Damage Commission representative could be induced to sit through a film show at my house, complete with whiskey and soda, no doubt results could be obtained – anyway, I'm willing." Whether an offical was so induced is not recorded, but the still extant film in question would have shown that the exploded garden was a real loss, and worthy of a reasonable sum in compensation.

In September 1948 the statutory year was up and Dick ready to move to a permanent address, looking at property of the small-holding type in Hertfordshire, Essex and even as far away as Buckinghamshire. By August 1949 he had settled on Paslow Cottage, Nine Ashes, a house with a large piece of ground in rural Essex. This quiet hamlet near Chipping Ongar was at the meeting of B roads to Norton Heath, Blackmore and Stondon Massey and contained a sprinkling of period houses, including the Georgian-fronted Larkin's Farm and two delightful cottages, Ivy Lodge and Box Cottage. Paslow Cottage was built some time after 1896, probably for the curate in charge of the Church Room or the teacher of the school, and Dick's family moved in on 30 November 1949.

* * *

The widespread destruction of buildings must surely have been regarded by the moralists of architecture as a wonderful opportunity. They had still been at it in 1939, when the tone of "Houses we Live In" published by the Ministry of Health was kind but firm. For garages "decoration is inappropriate, and is out of keeping with the trim and businesslike lines of the modern car." Housewives "who try to save labour by having doors and windows painted in a dark colour, do so at the expense of enjoyment and cheerfulness." A front door should not look "eccentric or pushful", and "freshness and gaiety can be secured by the correct proportions of window to wall." This last is illustrated by a brick wall bearing two rows of flat glass sheets. The house is blank with despair and gaiety a nonstarter.

The books and magazines about building brought out during and after the War again looked forward to making all things new, either pouring scorn on the past or using the subtle approach of "you don't really want to keep all that old stuff, do you?" It is surely not accidental that the final photograph in Penguin's "Living in Cities" by Ralph Tibbs is of two men demolishing a building with Gothic windows. "Human Factors in Housing"[13] published in 1948 made the usual digs at speculative builders, but also good points about the necessity for central heating and sound proofing, and the unrealism of planners who expected neighbourhoods to flourish in unwieldy units of ten thousand people. The Daily Mail Ideal Home Book 1948-9, produced for the returning yearly exhibition, was surprisingly moderate, showing homes with modern furniture but a classical feel. For some reason a central section was devoted to Thomas Rowlandson, as "Old prints look well on walls. They provide that touch of romance without which no home can be truly welcoming." There must have been many young architects tearing their hair out at such backward thinking. The battle between the two schools would soon be joined, and won at least temporarily by the modernists. However, as their mid-century efforts are now being increasingly derided, it might be wise for all A.R.I.B.A.s and all speculative builders, to remember that whatever they build will one day be regarded by someone as pretty dreadful. It may even be swept away.

* * *

There was as yet no sign of being allowed to start building again, and although hopeful enquiries were beginning to come into the office, nothing could be done without the inescapable Licence. In November 1948 Reader's answered one letter with the information that "If we can get six people with licences, we shall build in Greens Close, Roundmead Avenue, Loughton. We have two customers who have managed to procure licences from the Chigwell Council, and if you are fortunate with your application we could then show you the drawings of the proposed six houses, after which you may be sufficiently interested to make our third customer. You will appreciate that the government limitations make it impossible for us to build less than six at a time with any hope of making a profit."

At about the same time they answered questions from Arthur Bates about the possible sale of 5 Hill Top Close. "The above property has not been de-requisitioned, the council have been paying us the large sum of £50 per annum in quarterly amounts of £12.10.0" The following year, sale of another house in this road was held up due to difficulty in finding Mrs E.M.Davies, who had to be informed. This was another complication which bedevilled business at that period; a large proportion of the population had moved home and could not be traced. Yet another was dealing with people exasperated by years of government interference in their lives, and ready to stand up smartly for their rights as soon as they suspected they had been infringed. A man whose house had had to be virtually rebuilt after bomb damage, was told in 1950 "We thank you for your letter of the 10th inst., and note your intentions to proceed against us through your Solicitor. We would however, inform you that you have been misinformed as Firstly, we have received no payment from the War Damage

Commission for reinstatement of fences, Secondly, there were no fences in existence at the time of the bomb incident."

On 21 May 1949 Chigwell Council granted Reader's permission for 17 houses and garages in The Greens Close, to be invalid if not substantially commenced within three years. They included "four copies of form L.R.D.1," so that "we may apply to the Minister of Town and Country Planning for a Dead Ripe Certificate." This renewed the permission granted ten years before, ready for when restrictions were sufficiently lifted. The stipulations for the estate came up again in August 1950, when Arthur Bates wrote to Mrs Davies' solicitor.

"These stipulations were, I believe, imposed for the protection of the remaining part of the Maitland Estate. I understand, however, that the remaining part of that Estate has been sold to the London County Council and the general character of the neighbourhood has been lowered, and my Clients consider that it would be un-economical to erect detached houses only, and moreover, the stipulation as to the plans being prepared by Mr.Cable and to the approval by Mr.Maitland's surveyers will add to the expense. My clients, as you no doubt know, are builders of repute, and are capable of preparing the plans without the assistance of an architect. My clients would like if possible for the stipulations to be modified so as to enable them to erect detached or semi-detached houses and also that the stipulation as to the preparation of the plans and of their approval by Mrs Davies's surveyers should be entirely released."

But Mrs. Davies didn't agree that the tone of the neighbourhood had been lowered, and said that all owners on the estate would have to be consulted if any change were to be made in the stipulations. She also asked for the qualifications of the architect Reader's would propose to instruct. Reader's proposed to instruct White and Mileson, who duly renewed the Dead Ripe Certificate in June 1952. The final plan for The Greens Close was not to be submitted to the council until December 1953.

* * *

Richard Reader had been in failing health for some time. Like his brother Tom he was a life-long smoker, progressing to cigars when success arrived. He now had severe emphysema and his visits to the Yard or the building sites were rare. He remained in the comfort of the Bungalow, cared for by Edith and Rinda, and died there 28 August 1950.

He was buried in Southgate New Cemetery, Waterfall Hill and among the flowers was a representation of half-open Pearly Gates with a card inscribed "Beloved Guv. The Boys." Quite a number of Richard's earliest employees were still in the firm, and their affection for him was strong. Arthur Bates, at that time bombed into 22 Laurence Pountney Lane, had drawn up Richard's will in October 1942; it could have been an update, a replacement for one destroyed in the Blitz, or even the first time he had got round to it. Richard left legacies to some of his longest-serving men, including Ted Courts carpenter, Vic Davis foreman, Walter Moore carpenter, Jack Mead painter, Ernest Batten clerk, Ted White foreman, and Samuel Webb ganger navvy. In addition, all employees who had been with the firm for 5 years or more received £5.

To "my dear wife and sweetheart Edith Jane Reader absolutely in happy remembrance of our long life together with all its joys and sweet companionship and for which I have always been most grateful" he left The Bungalow, all personal and household goods, shares in Erith & Co.Ltd,[14] Defence Bonds, War Savings Certificates and all money in his account at the Stamford Hill Branch of Barclays Bank, presumably opened before the first World War when he was managing for D.S.Barclay.[15]

Other legacies went to his three daughters-in-law, three sisters, nine grandchildren and to Rinda Skeel "in appreciation of all her care and attention given by her to my wife and myself during the many years she has been with us." The firm was not mentioned. All these legacies were bequeathed free of duty so that the whole burden of taxation fell upon the business. Inheritance Tax had increased enormously since the end of the war, and his trustee sons were faced with financial crisis.

It seems remarkable now that the three Reader brothers managed to keep going at all, but the changes necessary in order to pay death duties led to a complete re-organization of the firm. As part of this a legal partnership agreement was drawn up between the brothers, an arrangement which had almost certainly never existed before between Tom and Richard, or between Richard and his sons. However, the length of time it took to straighten everything out is revealed by the fact that the grandchildren's legacies were not paid until ten years later.

* * *

The Chingford Council's decision to build flats on the open land behind 13 Priory Avenue persuaded Jack and Nina that it was time to move. The particulars circulated by Campbell's of 26 Old Church Rd described the house as "built by Messrs Reader Bros. in 1931 for the personal occupation of Mr. J.T.Reader," and "situate in an imposing and sought after position on the corner of Hurst Avenue and Priory Avenue ... having an attractive front elevation of cream washed walls, green shutters and leaded windows." The massive air-raid shelter beside the house was dubbed a "brick tool shed". Other good points stressed were "large front gardens ... beautifully laid out with rockeries, crazy pavings etc., and among the features of the accommodation are spacious and well lighted rooms, all quarry tiled window sills and open outlook from the rear." On the final point, unfortunately, evidence to the contrary was obvious from the back windows in the form of ground-clearing and foundation-digging, and meant that the asking price of £4,500 eventually had to be lowered. Jack and Nina found a charming historic house with a barn and plenty of garden at the top of Church Hill Loughton. Some worries were expressed by others about the age of the building, but Jack pointed out that Meads had stood up for several hundred years and wasn't going to fall down now just because Jack Reader had bought it. They moved in on 14 February 1952 surrounded by thick snow, too late to show it to Nina Eliza Adelaide Thornicroft who had died of bronchitis a few weeks before. She was buried with her husband in St John's churchyard, just across Church Lane.

* * *

It had always been a bonus for family members that bespoke joinery could be obtained to order. Over the years the Yard had provided them with children's playhouses, needlework and rug-making boxes, tables, shelves and cupboards. At Meads, a modern fitted storage unit was made for Howard's bedroom (though the maid's bell remained in the corner), and the drawing room fireplace was designed by Jack and built by Jimmy Tagg and Sam Sivier. It was brick with fitted mantel and shelves wrapped around the chimney breast, the wood being old pews salvaged from St John of Jerusalem South Hackney. Jimmy forecast that on winter evenings they would sit around the fire and say "Old Jim done that", and of course they did. But the most individual item was made at Loughton by Wally White the machinist in 1960. Edgar's sixteen-year-old son Nick played with the Essex Youth Orchestra and was due to take a hired Boosey & Hawkes contrabassoon on a four day tour of Amsterdam and Germany. Its case was completely inadequate for such a perilous expedition so the instrument was taken along to Wally, who produced a strong, perfectly fitting wooden box. It was last glimpsed about twenty-five years ago, in a rat-infested orchestral store under Blackfriars Bridge.

* * *

Repair and rebuilding continued slowly and often painfully as paper continued to shower from above upon those undertaking the task. There was plenty to be done in Hackney, which had been heavily bombed. Extensive reconstruction was carried out for Walter Gould & Sons sawmills and timber merchants at Homerton Bridge, Marechal Ruchon briar pipe makers of 154 Homerton High St, and nearly £15,000 worth for the British Steel Frame Co. Ltd 193 Cambridge Heath Rd.

In the early fifties Reader's did nearly £40,000 worth of work for Leyton Borough Council, starting with what their Sales Ledger describes as an extension to the Town Hall in High Rd E10, although the council's 1951 minutes refer to it as alterations, conversion of rooms and decorations. Before the council could put any work out to tender, the consent for money to be borrowed had to be sought from the Ministry of Local Government and Planning, including that for architect's and surveyor's fees and the clerk of works' wages. Reader's won the initial contract with a tender of £2460, and smaller subsequent ones were granted to them direct to save time.

Also undertaken for Leyton B.C. was the building of council housing on bomb sites. Between late 1953 and July 1955, Reader's filled in gaps at 14-18 and 63-67 Crownfield Rd E15, and built "3-storey flatted houses" in those at 48-50 Barclay Rd E11 and 607-615 High Rd E11, while a meek little two-bedroomed pair was put on the site of 68-74 Vernon Rd E11, looking shy and uncomfortable among their Victorian elders and betters.

The Isle of Dogs Housing Society Ltd employed them on their block of flats, St Hubert's House Janet St E14,[16] to the tune of nearly £18,000, Kearley & Tonge of EC3[17] to nearly £3000. To give further examples in round figures, nearly £600 was earned for work at the Arsenal Stadium in Highbury, £1800 from Fison's Ltd of Sackville House Fenchurch St and £1500 from Gee Walker Slater 100 Park Lane W1. In the public area, they earned £4000 from Poplar Borough Council, £2000 from the Borough of St Pancras, £400 from St Thomas's Hospital and £3100 from the War Damage Commission. The sum of £59 15s 4d due from the Ministry of Works was written off as a bad debt.

> 14-16 65-67 Crownfield Rd E15
>
> 48-50 Barclay Rd E11
>
> 609-615 High Rd E11 The righthand half was built later.
>
> 68 & 70 Vernon Rd E11

* * *

In February 1954 the Yard was sold to Sidney Lyons & Co. Ltd furniture makers of Shoreditch, and Reader's bought a twenty-one-year lease on a much smaller office and yard at Blenheim House, Blenheim Rd, Leyton.[18] Here Jack dealt with paperwork, quantities and estimates, and made up the men's wagepackets for Edgar to take round each Thursday. Meanwhile Dick was here, there and everywhere, dealing with officials and drumming up work. The plan chest, crammed with old drawings and documents, was moved into the flat behind the 75 Monkhams Avenue garage, although about a foot had to be sawn off its top in order to get it in. Although a nucleus of the pre-war work force remained, the Register of Employees shows that from now on men living near the sites were employed on a temporary basis, while younger ones tended to depart quickly for National Service. Mrs Ivy Pattrick of Stratford, who had worked at Homerton as a clerk since 1947, didn't follow the firm to Leyton but Ernie Batten stayed on until 1959, when he retired.

The Ministry of Health brought out a hopeful, forward-looking report on housing in 1953, and it contains one statement which seems to demolish a myth; non-traditional building methods were more expensive, at least at that time. Whether or not this situation changed, the future was largely to lie with industrialised building, though traditional methods hung obstinately on. Books of new house designs had been appearing ready for when permission came and at last "Designs for the Smaller Home", brought out by The Builder, started its introduction with the news that "The licensing restrictions which prevented many prospective owners from building the houses they had planned, were abolished by the Government in November, 1954, after being in operation (in various degrees of severity) for 14 years."

The site office at Loughton had been opened and refurbished, the sale of existing houses was going ahead and new building had started. Although plans sent in to councils now bore the names of White & Mileson, the first drawings were Edgar's and he was to initiate all post-war designs for the completion of the estate and for other Reader houses. The plans for Roundmead Close had already been passed; semis with an optional garage and fourth bedroom over it, finished with white rendering. In The Greens Close the design approved pre-war was abandoned and the same plan as Roundmead Close used with a brick-faced ground floor. Numbers 17 and 18 The Greens Close, a one-off pair with tile-hanging and oriel windows reminiscent of 58/60 Wellington Avenue, were sold in October 1955. The rest of the close had been developed with semis before the war by Ben Horn. For Hill Top Close and Roundmead Avenue, Edgar produced at least six new houses with individual variations to suit the buyers. The building line was slightly staggered as before and the effect very pleasing, even more so once trees, shrubs and gardens had reached maturity. Hill Top Close and Roundmead Avenue are one of the least changed and best kept of Reader streetscapes, and even with the LCC Estate, which was sensitively done, views from the upper windows are still excellent.

The Sales Day Book records the first post-war sale, 28 Roundmead Close, as 25 March 1953 and the last, 1 Roundmead Avenue, as 9 July 1958, although 29 was built later on the site of the Estate Office and sold in June 1959 for £4375.

Hill Top Close	1-11 14-24 cons.
Roundmead Ave	1-29 odd 55-75 cons.
Roundmead Close	1-30 cons.
The Greens Close	1-14 cons. 17 & 18

"Three-storey flatted houses." 48-50 Barclay Road, E11, 2000.

Blenheim House, Blenheim Road E15, 2000.

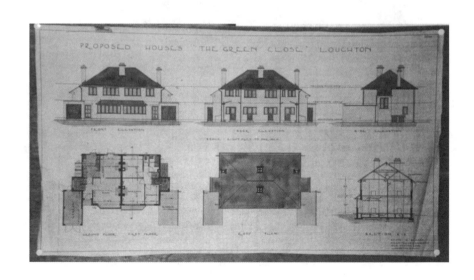

The Greens Close, Loughton. Postwar design.

57-63 Roundmead Avenue Loughton, 1950s.

5 & 3 Roundmead Ave, 1950s.

CHAPTER 10 1949-1967

Deaths of Annie & Clayton Reader. Alterations & Extensions. Chipping Ongar, Nine Ashes, Moreton. Reader Brothers Ltd. Death of Edith Reader

Like his three cousins, Clayton Reader was rejected for active service because of weak eyesight and he spent the war in the Shetlands designing aircraft hangers. Soon after his return the Koster family moved out of Pinewood, Canons Drive and went down to Brighton, where Cissie/Anne embarked upon an enterprise worthy of her father by doing up neglected Regency property, converting into flats and renting out. As a result of this she acquired a beautiful home at 19 Lewes Crescent and had the heart-stopping experience of opening the door to her girlhood idol, Jack Buchanan, when he came to view the basement flat. Clayton remained at Pinewood looking after his mother, whose sight was failing, and handling the renting of his father's property.

Annie Reader died intestate in 1949, fondly remembered by her children and grandchildren (though they could have done without another administration to sort out), and Clayton was alone in the house. In 1952 he went down to a dance in Brighton given by the music club to which the Kosters belonged. Here he met Mary Argent, a cousin of Jimmy's, and started a friendship which gradually became a romance. Mary was married from 19 Lewes Crescent at St Mark's Kent Town on 30 May 1953 and the couple remained in residence at Pinewood.

The adjacent piece of land bought by Tom was now sold except for plot 54, where they intended to erect a smaller house for themselves. The upstairs kitchen had become Clayton's workroom where he did carpentry and made models, and a design for this house now joined them. Pinewood still had no central heating, but there were heaters in all rooms and the boiler in the breakfast room made it a cosy place to eat, beneath the bell control box which had never called a servant in its twenty-year life. The couple's daughter Pauline was born on 21 December 1957 at Edgware General Hospital.

Clayton died suddenly of a heart attack on 8 August 1964 aged 58, another Reader victim of heavy smoking. The three Reader brothers were much saddened at the loss of a lifelong friend, and his sister was appalled to find out that he, too, had neglected to make a will, assuming that everything he owned would automatically go to his wife. Alas, the laws of inheritance are nothing like so simple.

* * *

Dick's move into rural Essex meant that the three Reader families now rarely all met together. He had always been a bit of a loner, unlike the close relationship of Jack and Edgar, and the traumatic destruction of his first marriage probably increased this tendency. He and Barbara had made a new life and circle of friends, and Richard, Frank and Bernard attended The Gatehouse preparatory school in Ingatestone, where the signalman allowed a few train-mad boys like Richard to eat their sandwiches in the signalbox at the end of the garden. A fellow pupil was local boy the future Lord Petre of Ingatestone. Dick had become deeply involved in local affairs and government, a commitment which lasted until the end of his life. When he was made chairman of the Epping and Ongar District Council in 1956, Jack and Edgar gave him a brotherly send-up on the lines of "Why on earth you?", to which he answered "Because I've got a loud voice." Thanks to the singing lessons he took in the twenties and subsequent semi-professional engagements doing oratorio, masonics, etc., he had acquired a bass boom which could have silenced the House of Commons, let alone a committee.

From 1947 Ethelwyn Tindall became matron of the City of London Maternity Hospital and its other department at 76a Liverpool Rd N1, now largely used for geriatric nursing. For some years she lived in a flat on the top floor in City Rd, very handy for babysitting when Dick and Barbara went to shows or masonics, but by January 1952 she had bought the timbered Hardings Farm, Nine Ashes which had by then lost most of its land. Reader's renovated the house and from there she travelled to work by motorscooter.

Dick's local contacts helped him to find work in the form of decorations, repairs and alterations, but also to snap up available plots of building land. As early as April 1953 a layout plan was produced by White & Mileson for a proposed estate at Cooper's Hill, Marden Ash at the southern end of Chipping Ongar, which at that time was the terminus for the London Underground Central Line and therefore commuter country.

It used to be a surreal experience to leave the tube at Epping, cross the footbridge, board a wooden carriage pulled by a long-funnelled steam engine, trundle peacefully through fields and woods along a single track, stop at the minute Victorian stations of North Weald and Blake Hall and finish up in a country town, whose church contained Roman brick and which was overlooked by the remains of a motte and bailey castle. This quaint stretch of line had been completed in 1865 by the great railway builder Thomas Brassey,[1] and was not to be electrified until the end of 1957. For connoisseurs of the eccentric it was never the same after that.

However, Marden Ash was not totally unchanged. A road called The Chase, constructed around the east end of a footpath, had been there since St James's Church and its priest's house were built in 1884. The 1920 Ordnance Survey map of Ongar in the Reader archive also shows Cloverley Road, built on field 28 in about 1903, pushing north from the beginning of Brentwood Road and advancing hopefully on the allotments down by the Cripsey Brook. The remainder of the western side of Coopers Hill as far as the Greensted road turning contained three large houses and ten late Victorian semis called Eyke Cottages. The field pattern behind as shown on the map had since been considerably changed by piecemeal purchases. Much of it had come through the hands of a builder and brickmaker, a coal merchant & contractor, and a sawmill owner, and when Reader's decided to purchase, a fair number of Land Searches, Deeds and Transfers had to pass through the hands of Arthur Bates and Raggett Wakefield, solicitors of Ongar, before the transaction was complete. Despite the 1953 date of White & Mileson's road plan, the main parcel wasn't transferred into Reader's hands until November 1955, another until November 1956, and 1 Eyke Cottages and its garden, the property of Miss Mabel Florence Hadler spinster of Coopers House, only became theirs on 28 February 1958.

In the meantime the Loughton estate was still in progress, and between the end of 1957 and November 1959 extensive renovations and alterations were taken in hand at Dyers, a former brewery house with a Georgian front on the east side of Coopers Hill. The drawings in the Reader archive by L.D.Tomlinson & Partners of Quadrant Arcade Romford, involved the part demolition of the rear wing and the building of a flat-roofed kitchen with no pretensions about fitting in with the rest of the house, a practice which was automatic then but which would be much harder to get past a planning officer now, or English Heritage. The council copies no longer exist, so it is difficult to tell whether this was the scheme actually carried out.[2] The owner changed his mind more than once during the work, with the result that costs went up and the presentation of the final bill resulted in a full and frank exchange of views. Despite these extensive works, the house was advertised for sale in the early 70s as "in need of modernisation", though this may only have referred to the outhouses and coach-house which have since been converted into homes.

Another alteration and renovation job was undertaken at 17 Palace Gardens Buckhurst Hill, a small, late-Victorian, semi-detached cottage which had been bought by Edgar's daughter Josephine and her fiancé Michael Robert Boyle. Josephine was the first Reader of her generation to marry, and the couple were touched by Edgar's regret that the firm was not in a position to give them a new house for a wedding present, as Richard had his sons; needless to say, they had had no expectation of any such thing. Times and situations had changed for ever over the last twenty-four years and they were only too grateful to receive all work done free instead. This was still in progress when the wedding took place at All Saints' Woodford Wells on 21 September 1957, and they moved in two weeks later.

The roads and sewers for the Coopers Hill Estate were built by W.C.French of Buckhurst Hill who had done the same for the Monkhams Estate in 1904, and Dick's eldest son Richard, who was studying civil engineering at Imperial College London, helped with the setting out.[3] As soon as the last piece of land was in Reader's possession, fencing was ordered from W.A.Skinner & Co.Ltd of Long Ditton Surrey for the office and workshop area; the former was to be 36 Coopers Hill, once 1 Eyke Cottages, and the latter a temporary building erected in its garden. Reader's first order for bricks went in to Erith & Co. 455 Old Ford Rd E3 in February 1958 (plain flettons were 117s 6d per 1000, facing bricks 295s 6d per 1000).

In July, the Eastern Gas Board quoted for the provision of gas, offering "7½% commission on the sale of gas appliances (5% on refrigerators) which result following a list of the names and addresses of the customers who are purchasing your houses, being sent to us." Within days this had been raised to 10%. The Herts and Essex Water Company expressed themselves willing to install mains once "the necessary financial details have been determined", but meanwhile the standpipe installed for Messrs French could be used subject to their agreement. The Marley Tile Company of South Ockendon quoted for the supply and fitting of concrete roofing tiles, which indicates that Reader's no longer had tilers permanently on the strength.

In August sand and ballast were ordered from S.J.Bird & Partners of Ongar, and samples of facing bricks were requested from the London Brick Company, also a quotation for metal windows from Crittall's of Chelmsford.

In September Post Office Telephones for the Cambridge area prepared to install a service to the estate, windows were ordered from Henry Hope & Sons Ltd (also of Chelmsford and presumably cheaper), and an order was sent to the London Brick Company. In October more sand and ballast were ordered from Peters & Barham Ltd of Romford.

By February 1959 a resident of The Greens Close Loughton was looking forward to moving into another Reader house; "I do hope you will very soon be commencing the building.....We still like the Ash trees and the Horse near No.16 so please preserve for us." He had suffered a lightning strike the previous year and was "very anxious to make the change before thunder storms and the lightning risk is with us again." It was not surprising; he had had the same alarming experience at a previous house. Unfortunately, on finding that the new road had Green in its name as well, he decided this would be pushing his luck and withdrew from the purchase.

In March Pilkington's Asphalte Co.Ltd of Commercial Rd E14 was ready to supply and lay floor tiles "as you require the Show house to be ready for Easter." By 2 June deposits had been put down on numbers 1, 2, and 3 Green Walk and by August sales were moving well, with buyers largely drawn from south west Essex but also Birmingham and Highgate.

On 5 April 1960, Edgar had a barrel set up on site to celebrate the birth the previous day of his first grandchild and Edith's first great-grandchild, Malcolm Charles Boyle, but also in April the house prices went up by £100 or more due to a recent pay award for labour. Other things were going up too, so that Arthur Bates worried "I hope the sales will not fall through on account of the coming rise in railway fares." Towards the end of 1960 Skinner's the fencers also put up their prices, citing the aforementioned increase in labour costs but also rises in materials. The following year the Marley Tile Co. were to put up prices because of the increase in purchase tax and labour rates.

In June 1960 Reader Bros asked the Water Company for permanent connections to Nos 21 & 23 Green Walk. Edgar's daughter Madeline was married at All Saints' Woodford Wells in September, and she and her husband Peter John Langham moved into 21. The Epping-Ongar tube extension was still in operation, but fares had gone up and anyway Peter preferred to shorten his journey time into London by driving to Woodford and boarding the Central Line there. It was a time when extensive car-ownership was coming in and railways were going out, and many other commuters were doing the same thing. This led during the sixties to the destruction of a large part of the British rail network and the subsequent construction of the motorway system instead. From then on, passenger numbers on the Epping-Ongar line gradually dwindled, although complete closure was held off for more than thirty years.

* * *

At the end of the 1950s building fashion was moving away from the politely modern style of postwar development, dedicated yet again to the ideal of a clean, bright, cheerful, healthy environment, and starting to slide downhill into puritanical architecture which would combine mean-spiritedness with aggression and at its worst, of which there was to be a very great deal, make a virtue of ugliness. For the Architecturally Correct, ornament, homeliness and prettiness were out, almost immoral; squareness and plainness were in. Windows should not twinkle but stare, and red bricks and tiles were far too warm; they must be white or grey and preferably have a close relationship with concrete. Some christened the movement Brutalism, and it is likely that many of its proponents didn't see the name as at all pejorative.

Under the pressure to clear bomb sites and slums and build anew, many savable houses were destroyed merely because they were old, and the quickly-built, factory-made tower block took their place. Industrialised housing had to be assembled by its makers, and for the first time since its introduction in 1890[4] standing order number 225, requiring competitive tendering, was suspended by the L.C.C. so that specialist prefabrication firms could be approached direct. The majority of traditional builders probably looked at these rearing novelties, drew a sharp breath through their teeth and said "They're going to have trouble with those." The Readers certainly did, and who can say they were wrong? As the century ends the A.C. towers are gradually being demolished, while the despised Victorian houses surviving in their shadow are in the process of repair and restoration, because that's the sort of place people who have the privilege of choice like to live in.

A few years ago, an eminent architect in a radio discussion referred slightingly to the "pitched roof mentality", whereupon another eminent architect pointed out that a pitched roof was the only kind which worked. It can be argued that few public buildings put up in the 1960s and '70s have worn well; blocks have had to be painted in bright colours, clad in polychrome brick or blown up, and the National Theatre and its sinister environs are due for a humanising makeover. The very boring Paternoster Square development beside St Paul's Cathedral is on its way down, and it would be nice to see it followed by the Barbican fortress, which seems designed to keep those outside from getting in and those inside from getting out, and could well contain a nuclear shelter for important people somewhere within its deep basements. The strange thing is, so does the Chipping Ongar area.

In 1952 the Air Ministry demanded nearly fifty acres of land from Mr J.A.J.Parrish of Pump House Farm, Kelvedon Hatch, and proceeded to construct a massive three-storey nuclear bunker beneath the undulating fields. To hide the entrance they built an "ordinary farm cottage" in the centre of Highash Wood, though it is very hard to believe that any intruder who got as far as that would have been deceived, even without the guards, barbed wire and military vehicles parked outside; stylistically, it has War Department written all over it. However, for the fitting out of this rural dwelling local labour was called upon, and one of the firms is said to have been Reader Bros. Of course, the whole thing was top secret, and despite all the RAF personnel and the number of vehicles coming and going, few locals realised what was actually being built, not even the firms working up on top. Among the Readers the story only surfaced recently, when the bunker was sold back to the Parrishes and opened to the public. It is well worth a visit, if your suspension can cope with the long, winding road in.[5]

* * *

Like every other builder, Reader's now built their houses in the modern style; it would have raised a laugh from architects, planners and buyers alike if they hadn't. There were four types of home on the Ongar estate; Type A, a two-bedroomed L-shaped bungalow with integral garage; Type B, a two-bedroomed double-fronted bungalow with optional garage at the side; Type C, a double-fronted house with living room, kitchen-diner, three bedrooms and integral garage; and Type D, a larger version of C with two reception rooms. All these might be modified according to the buyer's taste, especially the last, which could be built with three, four or five bedrooms. The survival of early pencil drawings suggests that the initial conception took place in Edgar's brain, but Dick and Jack would have combined on estimating costs and suggesting modifications. For instance, a semi-detached bungalow with a steep, hipped roof became modified into Type A, which had a shallower, less expensive roof and a fashionable wood-clad gable. The plans and elevations were therefore a three-way co-operation, and further alterations would have been worked out with the architects before they finally went to the Council.

The Coopers Hill Estate was clean, unfussy and as thoroughly "contemporary" as the illustrations in the Ideal Home plan books, but Edgar managed to get in a few little details of a backward-looking and appealing character. The type B bungalows, for instance were plain except for porches which curiously harked back to suburban Tudor, and Type D houses had tilehung fronts and porches with brick or trellised pillars to support a climbing plant. It says much about the style of building in vogue at the time that this was a very rare feature indeed, almost odd. Metal poles were the A.C. way of doing the job, and anyway, why mess up a nice clean living unit with plants?

The first houses in Green Walk were sold in April 1959 and the last to sell was number 9 on l February 1962. By this time an adjoining piece of ground had been acquired for Spring Gardens, leading from Green Walk into Kettlebury Way, but which was eventually built as a cul-de-sac named The Spinney. The first house in this road was sold in the same month as the last in Green Walk. The land was bought from Mrs Alice Sawkins, newsagent of Ongar High St who had used it for grazing, and the agreement included the erection of a bungalow for her free of charge, as her shop with flat over was to be demolished for a Midland Bank branch which now appears a perfect example of 1960s style. Mrs Sawkins' horse Dolly, possibly the one which the intending buyer of 16 Green Walk found so picturesque, not only remained while the houses went up around it, but was occasionally found on doorsteps late at night when residents put out milkbottles. Additional entertainment was provided by a bricklayer answering the call of the local part-time fire brigade, and being cheered off site by the rest of the work force.

* * *

At the same time as the development at Coopers Hill, other work was going on at Nine Ashes.[6] Two Type B bungalows named The Hawthorns and White Walls (now Maltings) were built in 1958 on

O.S. land parcel 376, next to the pair Avila and Hope Cottage. A third with a hobbies room addition and named Fairholme was approved in January 1959, on parcel 414 at Paslow Wood Common.

In 1961 plans for improvements to the old wooden Rose Cottage in King St, which was badly in need of them, were drawn up by E.J.Thurston A.R.I.C.S. of Chigwell. It had already been derelict in 1955, when the three Reader boys had no problem in obtaining access to the upper floor in order to watch the emergency services dealing with an aeroplane crash in the field behind. It was later bought by Mr. & Mrs Percy Radcliffe, licensees of the Black Bull in Fyfield and the Red Lion at High Ongar, with the object of retirement. Various plans survive, some for repair and extension and two by Edgar for complete rebuilding, but the plans eventually prepared by White & Mileson and approved by Epping & Ongar R.D.C. in May 1962 were for a two bedroom, through-living-room house, with garage one end, conservatory at the other and a porch slightly like the Type B bungalows. It was completed by August.

A four-bedroom detached house for Mr and Mrs Norman Gernat was approved early in 1963. It was to be built on land between Ivy Lodge and Hardings and featured an interesting long staircase window at the front. The site contained a large pond which had to be drained and the house, first drawn by Edgar but of course re-drawn and submitted to the Epping Rural District Council by White & Mileson, was finished in December 1963 and satisfactorily named Old Pond House.

In 1959 Ethelwyn Tindall retired from the City of London Maternity Hospital, but being only sixty and not the retiring type found work with the Civil Defence Organization taking exhibitions around in a large lorry. At the height of the Cold War a nuclear holocaust was not just a depressing thought but a definite possibility, and the Government organised a countrywide campaign to tell the general public how to cope in the event of attack and to persuade them that it would be possible to survive it. That they believed this propoganda themselves seems most unlikely, particularly once you have seen round the Kelvedon Hatch Nuclear Bunker. Presumably Ethelwyn did believe it, and those who saw the exhibitions were possibly better served by illusion than they would have been by the stark truth.

Barbara and Ethelwyn's sister Enid also reached retirement age in 1961 and returned from Malaya, while their aunt Mrs Constance Hazlehurst was now in her eighties and in need of companionship. It was therefore decided to build a home for all three of them on land next to Paslow Cottage and plans were drawn up by Edgar, who was likely to be the most patient with three mildly eccentric ladies. The house, called "The Birches", was finished in 1964. For some reason no plans or papers survive, either in the Reader archive or in the Epping Forest Council planning department, but it was probably similar in style to the Type B bungalows only with two floors, and alterations have taken place there since.

Although rural developments such as these were happening fairly regularly now, the County of Essex Development Plan 1964 studied the whole picture and endeavoured to take control. Its intentions included providing for "a limited increase in population at specified villages", with the desirable number of houses stated and infilling regarded as the least destructive way of achieving it. The filling in of Nine Ashes was therefore continued by other builders, and there are now very few gaps left between Nine Ashes Farm and the Black Horse pub. The hamlet is still surrounded by fields, however, which was the object of the County Council's exercise.

* * *

Arthur Bates died aged 86 on 11 June 1960, after sixty-four years in practice and at least thirty years handling Reader's legal business. His firm was absorbed into Candler, Stannard & Co. of 8 Breams Buildings, Fetter Lane, but by the middle sixties Reader Bros.' affairs were being handled by Raggett, Wakefield & Co. in Castle Street, Chipping Ongar.

* * *

The winter of 1962/63 was one of the worst on record, with building and practically everything else at a standstill, but at the beginning of February 1963 a kind message of comfort and reassurance was sent to Edgar by a resident of Hill Top Close, Loughton. "Now that the cold spell seems to be over you might be interested to know that by taking only elementary precautions we stayed clear of all trouble. I don't think anybody along here had any serious difficulty and considering the thousands who suffered frozen tanks and mains and burst pipes this is another tribute to your standards of design and construction. In fact, only central heating could have improved our comfort! I expect the weather has given you plenty of headaches and hope things will be better now."[7]

While it was not unusual for houses still to be built without central heating in the 1950s, it is worthy of remark that it was often absent in the sixties, too. Number 21 Green Walk, for instance, only had one small radiator in the kitchen dining recess and one in the lounge.

It also has to be said that Reader's general good standing and frequent good relations with satisfied customers didn't completely preclude the problems that bedevil builders and wind up buyers; undisciplined children who rioted through show houses, chipping paint and scratching floors; complaining residents, sometimes about nothing but occasionally for good reason; cracks in plasterwork, boilers or fires which didn't draw, paint which deteriorated, even paint which turned out to look different from the way the buyer had expected it to and which must be done all over again. The best of builders have their off days and there was some disadvantage in living on one's own estate, in that any dissatisfied neighbour could get hold of you twenty-four hours a day. Back in the Chingford days, a particularly persistent lady made the trip to the end of Wellington Avenue so often that the exasperated Edgar accused her of wearing out his doorknocker. It was she who, having got him into her house to investigate yet another problem, opened the door of the bathroom in passing and remarked "Look, it's beautiful; it's never been used."

The last house to sell in The Spinney was number 15 on 13 June 1963, and two houses numbered 32 & 34 Coopers Hill, built on the garden of 36 where the joinery shop had been, were sold in September. A few houses on single plots were also built in the area for specific clients. At Queen St, Fyfield, two individually designed detached on land behind the post office were sold in December 1964 and named Beaumont and Riverdale by their owners. A Type D at 18 St James's Avenue Marden Ash between St James's Lodge (the priest's house) and the Old School, was sold for £6300 on 13 May 1964.

On the east side of Coopers Hill, a pair of cottages which in 1904 belonged to Mr Thomas Bretton were demolished by order of the Epping and Ongar R.D.C. in November 1962; some bricks and tiles went to patch up Meads. Reader's made enquiries about the land in June 1963, acquired it in August from Mrs B.J.Bretton and squeezed a pair of thoroughly sixties maisonettes numbered 49 and 51 onto the site in 1964. Another Type D at 12 St James's Avenue was sold for £7500 in July 1965.

At Moreton, a house to be called Aldeburgh Dale was planned for Mr. George W.Prentice on a vegetable garden, part of land parcel 134. The White & Mileson plan, similar to Type D with dark brown tiles, purple facing bricks, interlinked lounge and dining room, 3 bedrooms and a balcony over the protruding garage and porch, was passed on 4 May 1965, and an extension was applied for by Mr & Mrs

A.J.Clark in 1973. Its subsequent history casts an interesting light on the unpredictability of planning decisions. A 1981 application for a bedroom over the rear extension provoked comment from a county planner to the effect that with a house like that nothing much mattered (not verbatim). An application for a bedroom over the garage and a new porch in December 1987 was criticised by an assistant county planner; the proposed tile-hanging was not correct for Essex, and the "farcical" proposed timbers on the gable bore "no relation whatsoever to the modern building." Rendering was suggested as the correct finish. Finally (so far), in 1995 there seems to have been no difficulty whatever in obtaining permission for another back extension which matched already installed replacement windows and exterior cladding made of white UPVC, which has to be game, set and match to the owner. The original house peeps round the later accretions, and now stands just outside the boundary of a conservation area and next door to a listed building.

As the Coopers Hill estate neared completion, Reader Bros asked White & Mileson to add their name to the list of those tendering for other work, as once their joinery works and office had moved to a new site they would be in a position to take on other small contracts. It was time to move on again.

* * *

Things were not getting any easier for small building firms. The soaring price of everything, especially land and labour, meant that you needed to be big in order to afford the financial outlay, and to have large reserves to fall back on when payment was slow in coming in. Apart from all the usual hazards, Reader's had recently found themselves in a situation which must have been unique for them; the settlement of one of their houses because of an unnoticed, long-filled-in drainage ditch. The public perception of building contractors is that they are well off and well insured, and that in such a situation insurers would pay out promptly for underpinning and/or rebuilding, that being the kind of event they were insuring against. But the claim was disputed, hanging out the business for a long, expensive time and saddling both sides with legal bills. In this case at least, Richard Reader's opinion seems to have been justified.

One way of preparing for such disasters was to become a private limited company. The Readers approached Alfred Neill & Co. enquiring how this could be done, and their accountants sent a summary of their situation and advice on how the company/ies could be set up in October 1963. It also covered the mitigation of death duties, with which the brothers must heartily have agreed, being severely once bitten. Reader Brothers (Builders) Ltd was to handle the business of building and Reader Brothers (Investments) Ltd the renting and sale of property,[8] and the two companies were incorporated on 26 February 1964 with the three brothers as the only directors and shareholders. The cost of the whole exercise was estimated beforehand at about 70 guineas, which sounds a very small amount now but was probably not the final figure; so many individual expenses are involved in such changes, not the least being new stationery and a new collection of rubber stamps.

The first meetings of the companies were held at 36 Coopers Hill on 19 March with Mr J.C.Greengross in attendance on behalf of Alfred Neill & Co. Dick was appointed Chairman and Jack Secretary, and the two new companies duly took over from Reader Bros. on 6 April. The papers surviving from this big step reveal that it was not an easy get-out but a very complicated business, not least because of the many people and organizations who had to be informed in time, and the number of official bodies which had to be dealt with in the correct manner. Licencing of the firm's vehicles, for instance, had to be applied for all over again, but the change enabled the firm to remain in business for another nine years.

* * *

Unfortunately, it was not possible to talk Edith into the avoidance of death duties. In vain her sons encouraged her to move capital into more sensible places, or at least to spend more of it on herself; a new fur coat, for instance, to replace the tired garment which had probably been with her since the prosperity of the twenties. "I won't have anything to leave you, dears," she protested. Any comeback to the effect that the government would see to that made her alarmed, tearful and hurt, and the attempt was given up. It is not easy to decide just how naive about money and business Edith really was, as she had been allowed little knowledge of either since her marriage; she said herself that she had never been told how much her husband was earning. This could have made her over-anxious during bad times and over-extravagant during good, but after years of being shielded from such men's matters she probably just didn't want to be bothered now.

She died on 1 March 1967, aged 91 and was buried with Richard. Her will made in 1951 after his death held no surprises; £1,460 of bequests free of duty, everything else to her three sons, "everything" consisting largely of cash and the Erith shares which her husband left her. Money she had put into the firm would be liable for tax. The gross sum sworn was £61,464, the duty demanded £22,349.

As is often done, the inheritance tax was paid quickly via a bank loan and the realisation of the assets went ahead as soon as possible. The Bungalow was cleared and the three families met there to divide furnishings and discover forgotten items in drawers and cupboards. It was sold by December at a slightly lower price than expected, which at least meant a welcome refund in estate duty. The Erith shares were divided in three and gradually sold over the next few years.

Rinda Skeel, with no home, employment or raison d'être left, expressed the wish to live with one of her nieces. Nina and Phyllis took it in turns to have her, but the absence of responsibility and a household to look after didn't suit her, and dementia became an increasing problem. She might have been better off in a flat where she could be her own woman at last, but she was 78 and had never lived alone in her life; she had devoted herself to the Skeel, Thornicroft and Reader families. Strong though her opinions and feelings were, Rinda never wanted independence.

Coopers Hill Estate, Chipping Ongar

Green Walk	1-39 odd	2-32 even
The Spinney	1-16 cons.	
St James's Avenue	12 & 18	
Coopers Hill	49 & 51, 32 & 34	

Nine Ashes

    The Hawthorns, White Walls, Fairholme,
    Rose Cottage, Old Pond House, The Birches,
    Chigwell (chapter 11)

Moreton   Aldeburgh Dale

Fyfield   Beaumont & Riverdale

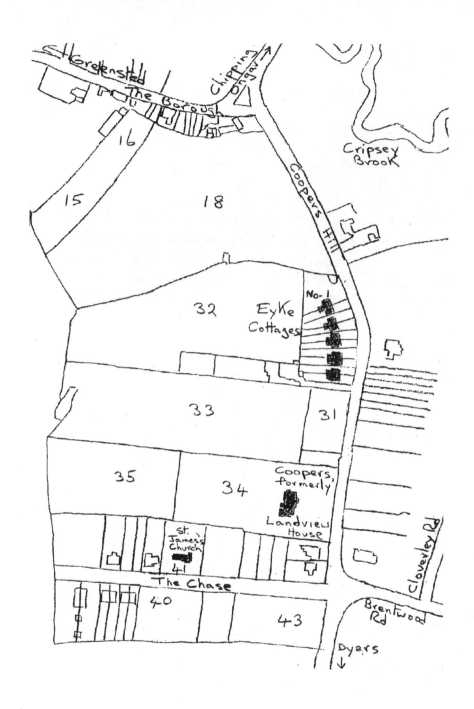

Field pattern of Marden Ash, Chipping Ongar,
with O.S. numbering,

Builders of Repute: the Story of Reader Bros.

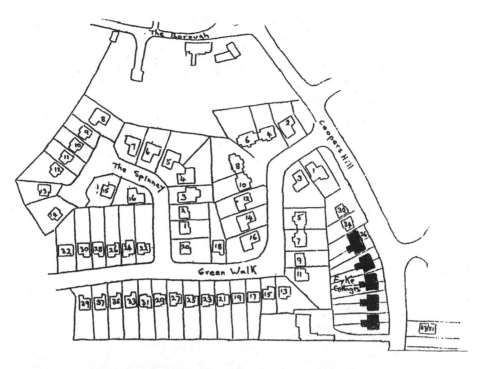

Coopers Hill Estate, Marden Ash

The garden of 21 Green Walk, 1966 with backs of C-types 29-23 behind. Madeline, Paul, Edgar, Zeba, Phyllis, Stephanie.

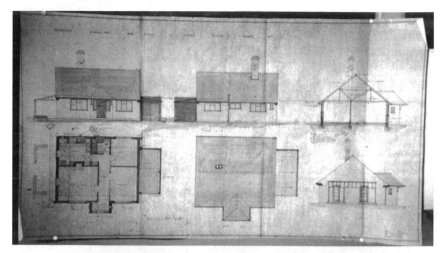

Coopers Hill Estate: Type B double-fronted bungalow.

*View of Castle Hill Ongar from Green Walk, 1999
with A-type bungalow no. 2.*

Type C houses in The Spinney, 1999.

BUILDERS OF REPUTE: THE STORY OF READER BROS.

*Old Pond House,
Nine Ashes, 1963.*

*Reader-built pram shed at
17 Palace Gardens,
Buckhurst Hill, 1963, and
Douglas Bruce Boyle.*

CHAPTER 11 1963 – 1977

Chelmsford. Woolmongers, Stondon Massey. Work for Essex County Council. Extensions, renovations etc. House at Nine Ashes. The firm is wound up. Deaths of Dick, Jack and Edgar Reader.

The spread of greater London was inhibited by the Green Belt Act of 1959 but not ended. New satellite towns continued to swallow land which had never remotely expected to become a mere adjunct of the capital, and beyond the rescued fields commuter suburbs appeared in country towns and villages. The building which had once followed railways now followed motorways and the price of land shot up in the whole of the south-east. The first housing estate worked on by T.J. and R.A.Reader in the 1890s was in Leyton, not much more than a mile and a half from their Hackney homes; the last built by R.F., J.T. and E.C.Reader in the 1960s was in Chelmsford, the county town of Essex and 32 miles from central London.

In November 1963 a Chelmsford estate agent was handling the sale of new houses with integral garage, central heating, plastic gutters and pipes, and ceilings finished with Artex plastic, a substance which was to prove remarkably difficult to dislodge once its day had passed. The existence of a copy of these particulars in the Reader archive, and of numerous leaflets from the 1963 Ideal Home Exhibition, shows that the brothers were studying the next fashion; the three-storey "town house" which was economical with land because of its narrow frontage, and which took care of the street-parking problem without the old, messy solution of back lane and afterthought garages.

The Broomfield Road runs due north out of Chelmsford, crosses the River Chelmer at Little Waltham and then runs straight north-north-east to Braintree, which was where its Roman builders were making for. By 1874 a curve to the west had developed between Broomfield Pottery and Broomfield Hall, and the whole stretch of road back to Chelmsford was edged with eminently desirable villas in spacious grounds; even now their cedars and other specimen trees stand like tombstones for the departed. At the Patching Hall Lane turning lay Newbarn Farm, part of the Broomfield Hall Estate, and by 1921 houses had been built along the edge of its land in both roads. On 24 June 1927 the farm and Broomfield Hall itself were sold at the Chelmsford Corn Exchange by order of Samuel Metson's executors,[1] but over thirty years later Newbarn still survived.

Some time before 1964 Reader's bought 229 Broomfield Rd, next door to the farm. Barnfield was a "well-built detached residence built in 1913" as Harrods' estate agency had described it in 1932,[2] with a usefully large garden. Four Copeland fireplace panels hand-painted with flowers were salvaged during demolition and taken home by Jack, but if he intended to install them in his own house it never happened. They did, however, prove an investment, eventually making £510 at auction. The firm also acquired a humbler property, 17 Patching Hall Lane, as direct egress into the busy Broomfield Road was not feasible, particularly so close to a cross-roads, and the cottage's long thin plot would provide access.

The site being so far from Loughton, Reader's employed a local chartered architect, Derek Walden, with knowledge of the ins, outs and idiosyncracies of the local planning system, and a site layout and two house designs were sent to the Chelmsford Building and Town Planning Committee early in 1965. Permission to develop was given in March, and in August a lay-by was approved to separate any parking associated with the development from the main road. All the proposed homes had integral garages, but visitors had to be catered for and the era of the two-car family was beginning.

In November the council approved the name of Barnfield Mews. The nearest thing the site had seen to a mews was probably a cowshed, but Mews was a fashionable address at the time and all the smartest people lived in them, though not necessarily in Chelmsford.

There has been some difficulty in pinning down the history of this development. At least some of the fashionable town houses were originally envisaged, but for some reason they were abandoned, and Edgar's initial sketch of the layout allowed for three more houses than the one drawn up by Derek Walden. The latter also incorporated steps down into the parking bay on the Broomfield Road, and it is not clear from council minutes whose idea this was, or why numbers 6-20 became eight terraced dwellings instead of nine town houses. The architect has been unable to check his own records as in 1982 he suffered the irreparable loss of his life's work, when his office at 136 New London Rd went up in flames.

The houses eventually built were of two storeys with some of the front kitchen windows given privacy by white slatted boarding, a widespread architectural device of the time. The first sold was number 38 in August 1966, and the last number 6 in August 1968. Prices ranged from £4895 to £5250. Today the estate is well-kept and remarkably unchanged, with only one case of replacement windows, so the architecture is able to speak for itself and for its date appears almost endearing.

There seems to have been friction with the firm developing the adjacent corner plot, where the farmhouse and its buildings had stood. A copy of a solicitor's letter survives dated 23 August 1968, but as it is in the form of a fairly primitive photostat which has had tea or coffee spilt on it, the details of the contention are not clear. Possibly it concerned access or damage by vehicles, as the other firm was then building 1 – 15 Barnfield Mews. It seems the Chelmsford development was not without problems, and it was also a very long drive from home.

17 – 19, 6 – 40 Barnfield Mews Broomfield Rd Chelmsford.

* * * *

In February 1968, Peter and Madeline Langham moved out of 21 Green Walk, Marden Ash. They now had two children, wanted more room and more garden, and had found what they were looking for in Woolmongers, Woolmongers Lane, Stondon Massey, a mile down the Stondon Road from Nine Ashes. It was a small timbered house previously known as Woolmongers Farm and had been modernised and extended by the previous owner who had sadly not lived long enough to move in, although he had come to sit outside in his car and look at it during his last weeks. It had two reception rooms, another flat-roofed sixties kitchen stuck on the back and three bedrooms. The pigsties were opposite the front door and the garden was still a sloping field. Reader's demolished the pigsties and built a double garage with loft over, and by the end of 1970 the Langhams were ready to extend the house.

Edgar's design, dated December 1970, nearly doubled its size, adding music room, larger kitchen, lobby and cloakroom downstairs, and walk-in airing cupboard, two bathrooms, box room and fourth bedroom upstairs. The finished result was a gracious house with the tile-cladding Edgar was so fond of, fitting comfortably into its developing garden and the rural backdrop. A further plan was drawn up a few years later for the addition of games room and swimming pool off the lounge, but was never built.

At much the same time and for the same reason, Edgar's other daughter moved from 17 Palace Gardens, Buckhurst Hill. Edgar and Phyllis were delighted that Michael and Josephine would be living just down the road from them in Monkhams Avenue, but Edgar was additionally pleased because it was a Reader house, one of those on which his father and uncle had expended so much care, hope, worry and disillusionment. Very little had been done in the way of modernisation during the previous years of its life; it retained much of its original brown or grained paintwork, but one grate and one complete fireplace had been removed, the scullery had a "new" porcelain sink and had lost its copper, the range had been replaced by a small solid-fuel boiler and there was a newish bath and wash-basin.

Of course, Reader Bros. moved in; the skip appeared outside, the sound of banging and men's voices resounded throughout and the worm-eaten floorboards from the main bedroom came sailing out of the window. When the hall wallpaper was stripped, instructions for the original decorations were found scrawled on the wall above the stairs – probably in Tom or Richard's writing. In a back bedroom, the end of a gas bracket still stuck out of the chimney breast. The renovation which followed was perhaps a little more enthusiastic than would be considered conservationally correct now. The cracked white tiling with green, pink and white art nouveau patterned borders was hacked-out of scullery and bathroom. A double stainless steel sink unit was put in the scullery and the red quarry tiles were covered by plywood and vinyl. The larder was blocked up and turned into a coat cupboard in the hall; had it been larger it would have become a cloakroom. Cast iron fireplaces were removed from all bedrooms except the master, one being reinstalled in the dining room, and the original pull chain and cistern were taken out of the upstairs W.C. But the kitchen dresser and cupboards weren't touched and the house kept its character, even under the vivid assault of 1970s decor. The original wooden gate was still there, but had to be replaced by a replica a few years later. It was one of the last to survive, which means that the original names of the early Monkhams Estate houses are now, with very few exceptions, forgotten.

* * *

On 10 October 1969 the firm sold off its renovated secondary office, 36 Coopers Hill, for £7000 and functioned again from temporary site offices and Blenheim House, where Jack now had to spend much of his working life alone. This didn't suit his personality at all. At lunchtime he would drive down to Wanstead Flats to eat his sandwiches and indulge his passion for birdwatching, but it cannot have been a time he greatly enjoyed. Much of the joinery machinery was out on site, and the building's contents were now largely of a might-come-in-useful character, such as vast numbers of half-used tins of paint.

The van which brought some of the work force out from east London was kept there for a while, but this was later parked outside the driver's house.

As the next decade started, the ninth and final one in which Reader Bros. was in existence, Dick Reader reached his 67th birthday, Jack his 66th and Edgar his 65th. They had four daughters and five sons between them, but none wanted to go into the building trade. The firm would therefore have to be wound down so that the three brothers could retire.

For the time being there was still work in hand. From 1969 the firm did work for the Essex County Council, especially a long contract at Wansfell Adult College, Piercing Hill, Theydon Bois and its Woodberry Annexe next door, where they had a temporary site office for some time. Other E.C.C. work included Epping Health Clinic, Buckhurst Hill Community Centre and numerous schools.

Extensions for Barberry Cottages near Woolmongers were finished in January 1970, and another at All Saints Cottage Harlow Common in September. A house named Chigwell (where he had previously lived; a common naming practice for those who buy new houses) was built for Walter Arthur Nichols J.P. between The Birches and Paslow Cottage, and finished in September 1971. High Ongar Village Hall was refurbished 1970-72, and extended at the front with utilities and a new porch. In 1972/3, Reader's completed an extension to "Catons" and repairs etc. to "The Rookery", both at Norton Heath, Nine Ashes, and an extension was built onto High House, Fingrith Hall Lane, Blackmore. And of course the regular routine of decoration, repair and renovation continued over a wide area of Essex.

Enid Tindall died in September 1971, the last of the three women living at The Birches, Nine Ashes. She received an obituary in the Daily Telegraph to which Dick and Barbara responded, and a long letter arrived from its writer containing a full account of Enid's distinguished and valuable war record in China, about which she had never spoken a word. The firm renovated and decorated her house throughout at the expense of the executors (Dick and Barbara) and it was sold to Mr.P.E.Jackson by December 1972.

In his regular moving-on to the next project, usually a dam or reservoir, Dick's engineer son Richard bought The Willows, Barton St, Barrow-upon-Humber Lincolnshire and proceeded to do it up himself. Lawrie Moore the carpenter (son of Walter) went up there in June 1972 to help him with the enlargement and fitting of the kitchen, and the two slept on camp beds amid the chaos. Moore's time sheet states that he worked for twelve hours each day for twelve days, which must have earned him a good sum.

* * *

Had the firm continued for a little longer Edgar would have been able to oversee a building job by walking a few yards instead of driving miles. 75 Monkhams Avenue was built on a double plot, and an area at the side planted with fruit trees (known rather grandly as The Orchard by the family) was large enough to accommodate a small house and garden without encroaching on the tennis court. With retirement nearing Edgar decided to release some useful capital. Of course, it wasn't a straightforward matter. Apart from the usual lengthy planning procedures, a Monkhams Residential Precinct Policy[3] had been drawn up which stipulated "discernible" gaps between all houses. It certainly would be a tight fit, but the removal of the garage flat's bay window, which was beginning to leave of its own accord anyway, would allow a plot 136 feet long and 30 feet wide, narrowing to 27 at the end. Towards the end of 1972 he approached an architect to discuss the development, for some reason not White and Mileson.

It was still the era of brutalism; it seemed that nobody in the architectural profession dared design in any other style, and the preliminary sketches provided were what might have been expected from an architect of the time, indeed the first impression on looking at the drawing of 71 and 75 with the proposed 73 between it, is that the aliens have landed. Edgar sent back his own, of a more traditional house which would fit in with its neighbours, and the architect replied with a brutalist house wearing a pitched roof, claiming it thus reflected surrounding Edwardian style. Edgar considered he was mistaken in this opinion.

By March 1973 the two sides had worked out a compromise, although Edgar saw problems ahead for the users of the downstairs W.C.; "I would not care for a W.C. that was a "passage room" with two doors. … I should go in constant fear of being "out-flanked" at a delicate moment," he wrote. It would also be possible to lock someone else out in the garden. With this problem seen to, the application went to Redbridge Council on 14 March and particulars of sale of the land with planning permission had been drawn up by the middle of July.

The site was already subject to restrictions agreed in 1904 between James Robert Twentyman and the first buyer, Henry Albert Summers, but Edgar added special conditions of sale of his own, in particular for the preservation of a Deodar and a Cupressus Lawsoniana which had once been in his garden, and for any alteration in the plan to be subject to his own approval. It was sold on 25 September 1973 at Ambrose & Son's Auction Rooms, 149 High Rd Loughton, to the Woodford firm of A.R.Sheppard Ltd.[4], whose relatives, Sheppard Bros., had been building on the Monkhams estate at the same time as Tom and Richard Reader. Number 73 Monkhams Avenue was completed and sold in 1974. It is more neo-Regency in style than Edwardian, but the classical dentil ornament along the bay is similar to Edmondson's decoration on 3 – 17 Monkhams Avenue, and the use of eclectic detail is very Edwardian indeed.

In February 1973 the firm received its last payment from the Essex County Council Divisional Building Surveyor, and the last four employees were paid off on 29 March. They were Wilfred G. Essex bricklayer, the third generation of his family to work for Reader's; Lawrence W.Moore carpenter, the second of his; William H. Joselin carpenter who had been with them for at least thirty years (born 1907 employed by 1944) and T.W.Bostwick labourer of Shelley, Essex.

The contents of a brown folder labelled Blenheim Rd begin with notes and figures scribbled on the back of a Wages Return sheet. "A Builders Yard with joinery works in Leytonstone complete with machinery, scaffolding etc. for disposal (firm closing down) short lease, renewable by agreement. Planning permission for continued use as builders yard until 1976. Details from Mr Reader."

On 15 June 1973 Dick wrote to their landlord in Bexhill.

"Dear Mrs Hyde,

We three brothers are contemplating retirement from business, as we are all either approaching or past the age of seventy. Our lease of Blenheim House and yard will complete the twenty-one years in February 1975. The planning permission will complete the present five year period in January 1976. There is, therefore, a little time to spare. However another firm of builders are interested in the yard and office, and the plant and machinery. They would like to take over the short remaining period, with your permission of course, either on a sub-letting basis to us, or directly to you on new and agreed terms. Obviously, before we can give any answer to this builder, we would welcome your ideas on the subject. Otherwise, we had intended to sell off the plant and complete our trading at the expiry of the lease in February, 1975."

Mrs Hyde was agreeable and another builder, Mr E.R.Wing of Clayhall, proved willing to take on the remainder of the lease, negotiate a further one and buy the plant and machinery. The draft of Dick's letter informing her of this goes on "I was most interested in the last paragraph of your letter of June 1973 re your parents [in law?] in Monkhams Drive. My brother Edgar lives in Monkhams Avenue, and his married daughter in one of the houses built by my father and his brother, also in Monkhams Avenue. We carried out some alterations a couple of years ago, and it was most interesting to examine the tremendously generous specification which was considered quite ordinary in those days – of course wood was £9 per standard – it is now £250/300 per standard."

The hand-written inventory of items to be left at Blenheim House lists all the builders's equipment, especially the wood-working machinery. For the last few years most of the joinery had been bought in, but the joinery shop had once been Dick's pride and joy and it nearly broke his heart to part with it; Edgar's son Nick took a load of wood down to his house in Manor Rd, Farnborough, Hampshire, where he was doing alterations. The furnishings of the office, where Jack worked alone for several years, are listed as 1 set of keys, 1 table desk, 3 chairs, 1 steel cabinet & key, and 1 mahogany & glass book case; it sounds like a hermitage.

Contracts were exchanged on 15 February 1974, and Reader Bros. vacated the premises on Saturday 16 February, although the completion date was not until 4 March. On 7 March Raggett wrote that he had completed the assignment of the lease and enclosed cheque for £1,853.86 and his receipted account.

* * *

Edgar had not quite finished his career yet; Dick's second son Frank bought a cottage next door to his own in Stilton near Peterborough, and in June 1974 sent drawings (engineer's not builder's, he apologised) and information to his uncle regarding his proposed amalgamation of the two. Edgar duly went up to view the place and then sent a drawing and three pages of notes elucidating his proposals with great clarity. These, Frank said in his letter of thanks, "were able to harden our rather vague ideas into a plan which incorporates all our wishes and more besides." Frank prepared the copies sent in for planning permission with little deviation from Edgar's ideas and carried out most of the work himself, as had his brothers in their homes.

Another family conversion job also came Edgar's way. Just before Christmas 1974, his son Nick and family moved from

Farnborough to Fielder's Cottage, South Town Road, Medstead, Hampshire. It was an early nineteenth century agricultural worker's cottage surrounded by a large piece of land, but in poor condition, in fact Edgar considered it to be a poor house altogether. On the family's arrival it proved impossible to live in, largely due to the total removal of the rotten lounge floor by a treatment firm which still hadn't finished the dampcourse, and the digging by three men of a trench in the drive for mains waterpipes, on the orders of the Abbey National.

 Nick's wife Barbara and their three children went to stay with Edgar and Phyllis for Christmas, and back in Medstead the grand piano stood on end in the little dining room, the downstairs furniture sat in the dilapidated lean-to and Nick and Terry, Barbara's brother-in-law, attacked the fabric. Edgar, who was a man who needed order in his surroundings, was horrified by the state of the building and couldn't understand why his son should have bought it. But by the summer of 1975 the floor was renewed, the front door had been moved, a new Selborne brick fireplace designed by Edgar had been built in the living room by a local craftsman and the house was habitable. Barbara's father, John Collins, had also helped with the emergency work over Christmas, but had been taken ill soon afterwards and died in May. By October, Nick and Barbara were contemplating an extension to accommodate her mother.

Edgar drew up plans to enlarge the small house of two rooms, kitchen, bathroom and three bedrooms by the addition of large kitchen, lobby and W.C. downstairs, fourth bedroom and bathroom upstairs and a ground floor flat for Mrs Collins. Nick put the applications in in March 1976, the footings for extension and double garage were started in May and local bricklayer Harry Martin built the walls. Meanwhile, Mrs Collins lived in a caravan in the garden. It was the year of the Great Drought and the catchment well beside the house became indispensible; the whole area was scattered with them as there was no natural watercourse for miles. Clouds finally started to gather in October while Terry and Nick were putting the last slates on the roof, and they just made it.

The end result of all this upheaval and work was a charming family home with a pretty garden and plenty of room in which Nick and Barbara could fulfil their dream of a small-holding. To house some of the cows, goats, pigs and hens a large shed was acquired from farther up South Town Road, and brought down to Fielder's Cottage one glorious summer afternoon in 1977 by Nick and fellow members of the Royal Philharmonic Orchestra. A barrel had been brought in, and it is said to have been one of those occasions which stick in the memory.

* * *

Unfortunately, Jack didn't live long to enjoy his retirement. He had an emergency operation in 1974 from which he never fully recovered and died in July 1976. He was buried in St John's churchyard nearly opposite his home, in fact the mourners walked behind the hearse in country style. The occasion was made even more poignant by Rinda asking who all the flowers were for, and Josephine's son Malcolm remained at Meads to look after her during the service.

Dick died on 18 March 1978 at Paslow Cottage, thirteen days before his 75th birthday and after months of increasing ill-health and an exploratory operation. His funeral service at Blackmore was attended by representatives of local councils, committees and organizations, and by children from local schools. A memorial concert was held in July at Ongar Comprehensive School, of which he was Chairman of the Governors, and a plaque was put up in St Lawrence's church.[5]

Only now did his sons learn from their mother that Dick had been married before; he had insisted that the existence of Vera should never be mentioned, part of the process of denial by which he had dealt with his loss. They were astonished, although Richard had occasionally had suspicions; all those pieces of sheet music with a name erased from the top, Edgar's throwaway line at his Silver Wedding party about following his brothers' example in getting married, why the eldest should have married so many years after his brothers. The rest of the family were equally amazed that the secret had been kept so long, considering that none of them had realised there was a secret to keep. It is just possible it was the wish to do so that sent Dick out into Essex.

Edgar lived until 1994, painting, composing, keeping up the beautiful garden of 75 Monkhams Avenue until it became too much for him and dying just before his 89th birthday. The biggest disadvantage of a long life is that you outlive your contemporaries, and by the time he died only Nina and Non were left. He missed them all, but particularly Jack, Ron Thornicroft and of course, Phyllis; their ashes are buried together just inside the wall of St John's churchyard Buckhurst Hill. His musical compositions are not entirely forgotten; Roger Fisher, organist of Chester Cathedral and once a choirboy at

All Saints' Woodford Wells, sometimes plays his splendid Prelude and Fugue for organ at recitals, and the Benedicite and chants were sung at All Saints until a few years ago. The manuscripts are in the music cabinet that was made him for a wedding present and his paintings hang in the homes of his descendants. He always regretted that his work was never published, but the achievement of designing and building good houses which people still enjoy living in is not a small one, and this the Readers did.

Running a building firm is a hard, frustrating, worrying and exasperating business, particularly if you try to do it well. Every member of the Reader firm had his full share of difficulties, particularly in its last years, but from this distance in time their lives appear to contain a fair degree of fulfilment and their work to have great value and usefulness.

* * *

Reader Brothers, Builders and Contractors are still discussed when descendants get together, and the old anecdotes are retold and bent a bit further. Papers, photographs and objects are widely scattered; the brass and mahogany letter scales from the Yard sit on an occasional table; Ernie Batten's bentwood chair lives in a cottage and has acquired a canvaswork seat; a treadle wood lathe is in Suffolk.[6] A rusting 22 yard measuring chain sits in the corner of an outhouse, its metal pegs retaining twists of brown 1958 newsprint advertising housing developments. The plan chest with all contents, including countless scraps of paper scribbled with drawings of houses, has been squeezed into a back bedroom. There are no more professional builders in the family, but among other occupations Tom and Richard have three assorted engineers, an estate agent and nine musicians to their credit, many of them able to turn their hands to do-it-yourself building.

Estate agents have not forgotten Reader's, either, and in Chingford the name tends to be invoked to indicate quality in a property, occasionally when a Reader never went near it. This must be galling for the builder who did, and it is a great pity that the names of those who created the surroundings we live in should be forgotten. In the process of practicing their trade and earning their living, builders shape the way we live and provide us with the scenery we look upon, and we should remember who deserves the praise or the blame.

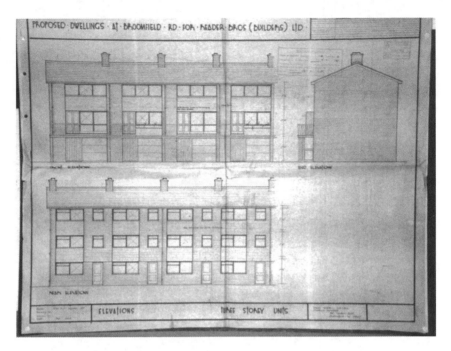

Proposed town houses for Barnfield Mews, Chelmsford, 1965

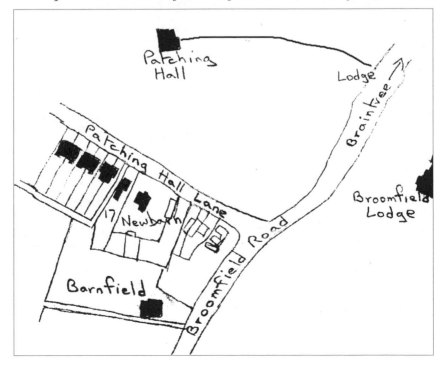

Position of Barnfield and Newbarn before demolition.

22-12 Barnfield Mews, 1999

40-30 Barnfield Mews, 1999

AFTERWORD

Suburban housing has been much abused, both verbally and physically, for like everything else building is subject to fashion, and its value usually judged by conformity with the present one, hence the continual modernising which has gone on ever since man decided a cave was old hat. It has almost always been sneered at by architectural experts, (with the exception of any designed by themselves), but its styles are as valid as, and no more pastiche than a Roman terrace with sash windows built by Nash, or any other tries at Classical made since the fall of the Roman Empire.

Most people know nothing about architectural style or period; for them a house is modern or old-fashioned, and the latter must either be pulled down or changed, as an out of date house is such a pitiable thing that it needs to be saved from itself by transformation into a modern one. But of course it cannot be done; a house of one period cannot be made into a house of another. A Victorian house with "Georgian" features stuck on will never look like a real eighteenth century one because it has neither the plan, the structure, the proportions nor the building materials of the eighteenth century, and a Georgian house with double-glazed plastic window frames and a frosted-glass front door will never look like a real modern house for the same reason. The two styles can only rub along together in a sometimes enjoyable botch.

But the introduction of D.I.Y. and Home Improvement from the 1950s onwards has been so widespread, wiping out local as well as period style, that the percentage of houses still totally themselves is small and getting smaller all the time. It must now be hard to find the enthusiasm to design and build a house with care and finish, good materials and fine workmanship, artistry and concern for the setting, when you know that someone, sometime is certainly going to make a dog's breakfast of it.

Many a buyer's relationship with their new home seems like asking someone to marry you and then insisting they undergo plastic surgery; if they didn't like it why did they buy it, and why spend enormous sums of money on alterations when they could have had an architect-designed, custom-built house for the same outlay? Doors and windows are a house's features and their style is its identity, dating it as clearly to the informed eye as a date on the gable, so why not enjoy them, particularly now that "a wealth of original features" is a good selling point and authentic wooden replicas can be made for much the same price as ready-made PVC? It is tempting to say do what you like to a 1960s house, but here again, even these will one day be recognised as period pieces; they may even produce sheets of jade or orange plastic for those wishing to restore them.

Then there is the matter of additions, and whether they should blend with the original house or be built bang up to date. It is surely much wiser to go with the style and materials of a house than against them, or the addition will belong to the sore thumb school. There used to be an argument to silence those who protested about intrusive modern extensions. In the great mediaeval cathedrals, it said, they always used the latest fashions in building, and it worked wonderfully. Yes, they did, and a lot of the time no, it didn't. The effect is always architecturally and historically interesting, but from the artistic point of view the building would look much better all of a piece. A Perpendicular clerestory over a Norman nave doesn't have the power and integrity of the original one, and one of the main reasons for the effectiveness of Westminster Abbey is that a nave completed two hundred years after the chancel is built in the same style, while later Tudor filigree can be enjoyed all by itself in the lady chapel.

Of course, many old detached houses had Georgian fronts stuck onto them with which the owners could impress the neighbours, and there is no doubt that these now look very appealing, but suburban villas are usually designed as part of a larger whole, and their effect depends on their remaining so. The whole point of a West End terrace is that the eye slides easily down its uniform length and receives an impression of grandeur, and the humble terrace was built with the same intention, to give dignity to a humble street. Suburban builders turning out rows and rows of identical houses like those in Leyton High Road, adorning them with stone carvings and labelling them Hughenden Terrace, Claremont Terrace and of course Rayner Terrace, obviously didn't envisage them being chopped up into a bag of individual all-sorts; imagine a Regent's Park terrace with its stucco walls painted in different colours, occasional statues removed by tenants who thought they were old-fashioned, and replacement doors and windows set between corinthian columns whose surface has been rendered flat and disguised with plastic trellis. Had they been under individual ownership during their nadir, it would have happened.

All man-made objects have to survive the forty or so years in which they are laughable before they can be seen clearly as period pieces, and before their style, ornament and right to exist comes to be respected. The small proportion which do is what gives antiques their value, and to a certain extent the same is true of houses – although there is no building so perfectly unspoiled an example of its type that it will not remain in danger of destruction, listed or no; vide the spiteful treatment of St Pancras Station's Midland Grand Hotel by the arrogant sixties, and the destruction of the Firestone Tyre factory, Great West Rd and Mappin and Webb's in Poultry.

With knowledge, a house can be dated to its decade, and the detail occasionally identified almost to the year and traced to its very begetter. Who started putting those nice red or blue glass strips around 19th century doors and windows? Why did stucco start going out of fashion about 1870 and the scornfully discarded timber return, albeit only as strapping stuck onto brick? When and why did suns start to rise and galleons start to sail in suburban stained glass between the wars? Why was an approximately Georgian fanlight stuck into the middle of front doors in the 1970s, and why did the latest conception of Tudor doors blossom into rows of large carved roses? Find the answer to these questions (not necessarily easy) and you learn what a period house means, and what was happening when it was built. For the answer to the last, one would hazard a guess that it was a yearning to get back to cosy tradition after the cold 60s, combined with architectural ignorance produced by the same period.

House history is as significant as family, national or world history and we should not obliterate it but allow it to tell us its story. And to those who have kept at least the frontage of their Reader house intact, a personal thank you.

Eastbourne, 1926.

APPENDIX A
HOUSES AND FLATS BUILT AND/OR DESIGNED
BY READER BROS. not including extensions, alterations etc.
Chronological order

Spratt Hall Estate Wanstead
    Dangan Rd   16-66 even
    Spratt Hall Rd   22-25 cons.

Grove Green Rd Leytonstone 325-359 odd

Prince's Avenue, Ballards Lane, Finchley 1-65 odd (13 & 15 dem)

Monkhams Estate Woodford Green
    Monkhams Avenue   39-65 odd
                             2-4 8-30 76 even
    Monkhams Drive   3-15 23-25 odd
                             2-28 even (28 dem)
    King's Avenue   3-13 odd
                             2-10 even
Clapton Common
    Ashtead Rd   12 – 44 even
    Craven Walk   44 – 58 even
    Leadale Road   1 – 69 odd 2 – 46 even
    Lingwood Rd   51 – 69 odd and maybe 1-49 odd 10-36 even

Housing for the Borough of Hackney
    Gunton Rd   65-95 odd 66-96 even
    Cleveleys Rd   69-83 odd 70-78 even
    Casimir Rd   5-37 71-105 odd

Housing for the Borough of Poplar, Bromley and Bow
    Baldock St   1-11 odd
    Ridgedale St   41-55 odd
    St Leonard's Road Flats nos.1-9 between Chadbourn St
                        and Clutton St
    Grundy St   Heckford House 45A-F

Avenue Farm Estate Child's Hill
    Cricklewood Lane   270-308 even (278-282 dem)
    Lyndale Avenue   1-15 odd 2-16 even
    Hocroft Rd   1-9 odd 2-22 even

Housing for Borough of Poplar Bromley and Bow

    Kingfield St   1-27 odd 2-28 even

    Billson St   18-26 even

    Parsonage St   13-39 odd 18-32 even (13, 15, 33-39 rebuilt,

                          18-24 dem)

    Stebondale St   40-50 even

Harvey Rd Blackheath   68-78   82-92 even

Housing for Borough of Poplar Bromley and Bow

    East Ferry Rd   201-207 odd (201-203 rebuilt)

    Manchester Grove 1-59 odd 2-44 even (33-39 rebuilt)

    Manchester Rd   15-45 odd

    Tiller Rd (Glengall Grove 332-206, being 24 houses & 40 flats)

        1-15 formerly 332-318, Yarrow House (bombed), Hibbert

        House, Maudsley House (bombed), 268-238 (bombed),

        Alexander House.

    St Leonard's St   Twelvetrees House 1-24 (dem)

    Naval Row   Naval House 1-16

    Gale St   Sidgwick House 1-6

    Harbinger Rd   22-34 even

    Hesperus Crescent 1-139 odd 2-62 even (1-13 rebuilt as 1-11)

    Devons Rd   Sumner House 1-60

Canons Drive Edgware 42-52 even

Chingford

    Hurst Ave   1-83 odd 10-94 even

    Priory Ave   1-81 odd 2-112 even

    Priory Close   1-18 cons.

    Waltham Way (formerly Sewardstone Rd South) 150-152 even

    Wellington Ave   1-19 odd 2-62 66 even

                       (some bombed and rebuilt)

    Old Church Rd   167-183 odd (some bombed and rebuilt)

Little Kingsdale Orpington Rd Chislehurst

Chingford

    53 Chingford Ave (formerly The Avenue) (dem)

    39a Forest View

    Leadale Ave   1-91 odd 2-76 even

Heriot Avenue	1-49 odd 2-44 even
St Catherine's Rd	1-25 odd 2-46 even
Sewardstone Rd South	209-265 odd 186-222 even
Lansdowne Rd	25-57 odd
Dove House Gardens	1-19 odd

Broadfields Estate Winchmore Hill

Broadfields Avenue	13-61 odd 58-80 even
Cresswell Way	1-9 odd 2-14 even
Wades Hill	82-112 even
Paulin Drive	The Bungalow (dem)

Church Hill Estate Loughton

Hill Top Close	1-11 cons. 14-24 cons. (22 & 23 bombed & rebuilt)
Roundmead Avenue	1-29 odd 55-75 cons.
Roundmead Close	1-30 cons.
The Greens Close	1-14 cons. 17 & 18

Housing for Borough of Leyton
14-16   65-67 Crownfield Rd E15
48-50 Barclay Rd E11
609-615 High Rd E11 left hand block
68 & 70 Vernon Rd E11

Coopers Hill Estate Chipping Ongar
Green Walk 1-39 odd 2-32 even
The Spinney 1-16 cons.
St James's Avenue 12 & 18
Coopers Hill 49 & 51 32 & 34
Nine Ashes Essex
The Hawthorns, White Walls (Maltings), Fairholme,
Rose Cottage, Old Pond House, The Birches, Chigwell

| Moreton Essex | Aldeburgh Dale |

Fyfield Essex
| Queen St | Beaumont & Riverdale |

Newbarn Estate, Broomfield Rd, Chelmsford
Barnfield Mews   17-19 odd   6-40 even

APPENDIX B
THE READER ARCHIVE

The Plan Chest built by the joinery shop at Marsh Hill Works, Homerton about 1929 was moved to Edgar Reader's home in 1954 and to that of Josephine Boyle in 1990. The contents were removed and labelled before its second dismantling and the contents of each drawer recorded. Some items were of no relevance and were discarded, but the remainder of the archive was sorted, listed and replaced in the drawers in chronological order. In addition to items listed elsewhere, it contained the following.

Grey, elephant-sized folder labelled "Reeves & Son Ltd. manufacturers of artists' materials, London", containing plans for Finchley, Woodford, Clapton, Blackheath & Child's Hill. Also Jack's academic exercises, 2 proposed designs for the Yard and 3 proposed designs for The Bungalow Winchmore Hill.

Numerous plans, loose drawings, drawing books, notebooks, diaries, letters, bills.
Deeds, Documents, Tithe Redemption Certs., Land Certs.
Blank drawing paper, roll waxed map linen, tracing paper, roll of plastic film.
Carborundum, blotting paper, carbon paper, quarto flimsy typing paper, sealing wax, dip pen, glass inkwell, black and blue bottles of Quink, white ink, white poster colour, box coloured chalks, paper bag of white chalks, drum of tape, two old paintboxes, paintbrush, blotter, drawing instruments, brown envelope containing pen-nibs, paper of 1½" pins, elastic bands.
Various paper and map weights.
Various trade and business cards.
Price sheet for Marconi valves.
Samples of cork and plywood from Cork Manufacturing Company, Chingford.
Draft sale and letting agreements 1939.
Stanley knife, spirit level, hornrimmed glasses in case.
Building licences for garages from Chingford U.D.C. 1930s.
Cheques 1930s.
Stationery for 36 Coopers Hill & Blenheim House Leyton.
Forms for The Commissioners of His Majesty's Works and Public Buildings and for the Borough of Chingford War Damage Department.

Change of address label to Roundmead Ave Loughton.
Packet of unopened De La Rue playing cards with advertisement for Hadfields paint manufacturer on the back.
London Passenger Transport Board workman's ticket
Gold Watch.
Medal with Prince of Wales's head; reverse Church Lad's Brigade Review 18th June 1927 Present on Parade.
Recruitment classification cert. R.A.Reader 14th October 1916.
Is That Lamp Going Out?   Hodder & Stoughton 1910
Burton of the Flying Corps   Herbert Strang 1920
Hugo's Dutch Without a Master.
Hugo's French in 3 Months.
2 unmatched cricket bails.
Part of canvas camera case for Box Brownie.
Disintegrating King James Bible.
Black leather wallet/purse containing trade card for T.J. & R.A.Reader., Builders & Contractors 1 Princes Avenue, Church End, Finchley, N. George V halfpenny.
Tin of Rinstead Pastilles.
"Altoid" peppermint box containing black tailor's chalk.
Photographs by T.S.Robinson 185/187 High St Homerton of houses in Hurst Ave Chingford.
Air Raid Precautions Handbook No 1 (2nd edition) Personal Protection against Gas.
Paper Union Jack on pin (for lapel).
Guide to Chingford Old Church.
Guide to Greensted Church.
A Smuggler's Song by Rudyard Kipling in Edgar's handwriting [to be set to music?]
Manual for Suffolk Punch Motor Mower bought 4 June 1954.
Blotter presented by White's Garage of Ongar.
Plans for flats in Rotterdam by Johan van Bokkum November 1955.
Goods Vehicle Fuel Rationing Coupons 1957; mint condition.
Box labelled Le Soir Handbag Style No 7203 Colour Gold containing; coloured pencils, felt tip pen, band from Anchor tapisserie 0144, drawing ink, bottle opener, piece of chain, tailor's chalk, screws, paperclips, nibs, keys, drawing pins, razor blade etc.
O.S. maps of Buckhurst Hill 1920, Ongar 1920, Hackney Marsh 1951, Farnborough Hants 1964, Aldershot & Guildford 1974, 2 of Loughton, 3 of Hampshire, maps of Shanklin and Fyfield.
Papers re Ongar Council and Essex Education Committee 1950s.
Holiday brochures 1970s. Etc., etc.,…

Other items came from an overflow box and from Jack's home at Meads, Loughton, while a file labelled "Joinery Estimates" contained various personal bills and papers from 1902 to 1950. Several black bagsfull, including ledgers and postwar correspondence, were salvaged from the High Ongar garage of Dick's widow, Barbara, and more items still occasionally trickle in from various branches of the family.

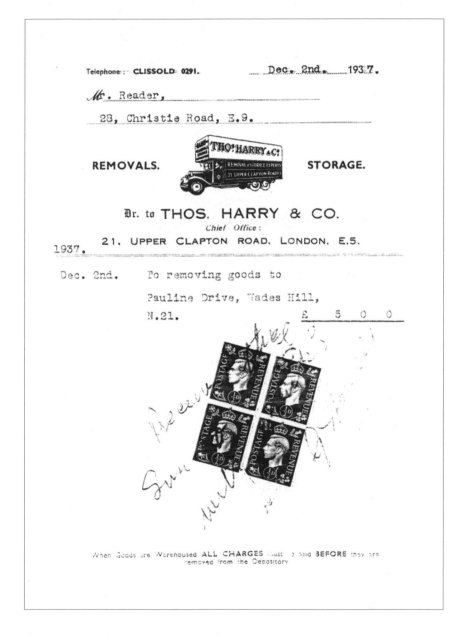

APPENDIX C
BOOKS AND MAGAZINES FROM READER BROTHERS'
OFFICES & HOMES

BUILDING MATERIALS THEIR NATURE, PROPERTIES AND MANU-
FACTURE
A text-book for students and others by G.A.T.Middleton A.R.I.B.A.
author of "Stresses and Thrusts" "The Drainage of Town and Country
Houses," "Surveying and Surveying Instruments," "The Principles of
Architectural Perspective," etc. Illustrated with 197 Diagrams and 12
plates from photographs. London B.T.Batsford, 94 High Holborn 1905
[Flyleaf signed H.Mills; clerk of works to Poplar Council]

THE IDEAL HOUSE a series of Designs for Ideal Homes by W.Rupert
Davison architect 6 Duke St Adelphi W.C. (copyright)
Published by William J.Baker 6 Duke St., Adelphi, W.C.
To Her Royal Highness The Princess Christian of Schleswig-Holstein
This Work is by permission Dedicated.
[From the Ideal Home Exhibition, Olympia, 1910]

HACKNEY GAZETTE DIAMOND JUBILEE SOUVENIR 1924 price 3d.
[The Casimir Rd Council Estate is included in the list of "Municipal
Landmarks."]

HOW TO ESTIMATE BEING THE ANALYSIS OF BUILDERS' PRICES
giving full details of estimating for every class of building work, with
thousands of prices, and much useful memoranda
by John T.Rea architect and surveyor.
Fourth edition, revised and enlarged with over 400 illustrations.
Published 1925 by B.T.Batsford Ltd., 94 High Holborn.
Made and printed in Great Britain by the Whitefriars Press Ltd., London and Tonbridge.

BUNGALOWS AND SMALL COUNTRY HOUSES 2/6
Edited & Published by The Architect Imperial Buildings Ludgate Cir-
cus EC4. 1925?

MODERN HOUSES AND BUNGALOWS Plans, Sketches & Photographs of Houses by Many Architects with Notes & an Introduction
by Hugh B.Philpott (Editor of the "Illustrated Carpenter and Builder")

Office, 8 Temple Avenue, EC4
Printed by the National Co-operative Publishing Society Ltd., 22 Long Millgate, Manchester. 1925?

THE LONDON BUILDING ACTS 1894 – 1926 and other acts relating to buildings in London with standing orders, by-laws and regulations and an introduction and annotation of the acts by
T.J.Kelly of The Inner Temple Barrister-at-Law. 1928.
Issued as a supplement to Laxton's and Lockwood's Builders' Price Book. Published by Kelly's Directories Ltd established 1799, 186 Strand, London, W.C.2. Also a list of the Metropolitan District Surveyors, with the boundaries of their districts, and a list of the Metropolitan Borough Surveyors.

THE SMALLER HOUSE OF TO-DAY by Gordon Allen Chartered Architect late Royal Engineers, Fellow of the Royal Institute of British Architects. Author of "The Cheap Cottage and Small House." London B.T.Batsford Ltd., 94 High Holborn. 1926

ARCHITECTURE a magazine of architecture and the allied arts and crafts Vol.VII No.41 Nov-Dec 1929
published by The Builder Ltd Catherine St & York St Aldwych WC2

THE SMALL HOUSE POINTS & PITFALLS by David Evelyn Nye A.I.A.A. The Guardian Press 183 High St E17 6d 1920s?

SMALL HOUSES AND BUNGALOWS
Edited by Frederick Chatterton F.R.I.B.A.
Published 1932 by The Architectural Press, 9 Queen Anne's Gate, Westminster, S.W.

TOWN AND COUNTRY PLANNING
Patrick Abercrombie M.A. F.R.I.B.A. Professor of Town Planning, University College London.
published by Oxford University Press 1933 second edition 1943

I WANT A HOUSE OF MY OWN
published by The Huddersfield Building Society 1935

MODERN SMALL COUNTRY HOUSES
Edited by Roger Smithells

Published 1936 by Country Life Ltd, London
Printed in Great Britain by Hazell, Watson & Viney Ltd., London & Aylesbury.

THE MODERN HOUSE IN ENGLAND by F.R.S.Yorke, A.R.I.B.A.
published 1937 by The Architectural Press, 9 Queen Anne's Gate, S.W.1.

SMALL HOUSES £500 – £2,500
Edited by H.Myles Wright M.A., A.R.I.B.A.
Published 1937 by The Architectural Press, 9 Queen Anne's Gate, Westminster
Printed in Great Britain by Billing and Sons Ltd., Guildford and Esher.
[Contains advertising leaflet for four of Laing's ten estates. Flyleaf inscribed "To Dear Daddy From Jacqueline and Stephanie. Christmas 1940"]

HOW TO OWN YOUR HOME A concise explanation of how the Building Society provides the most economical and convenient method of achieving home ownership. 1938
Huddersfield Building Society Established 1864
Head Office: Britannia Buildings, Huddersfield

PERSONAL PROTECTION AGAINST GAS Air Raid Precautions Handbook No. 1 (2nd Edition) Price 6d net 1938
Printed and Published by His Majesty's Stationery Office

HOUSES WE LIVE IN Ministry of Health 1 shilling
Published by His Majesty's Stationery Office 1939

ARCHITECTURE ILLUSTRATED Vol.19 No.111 August 1939 one shilling net. Editorial, advertising and publishing offices 44 Doughty Street, London, W.C.1

TOWN PLANNING by Thomas Sharp Penguin Books Ltd 1940

AN INTRODUCTION TO MODERN ARCHITECTURE
by J.M.Richards Penguin Books Ltd 1940

LIVING IN CITIES by Ralph Tubbs
Penguin Books Harmondsworth Middlesex 1942

SPONS' ARCHITECTS' AND BUILDERS' POCKET PRICE BOOK 1943
edited by Clyde Young, F.R.I.B.A. 70th edition
London E. & F.N.Spon, Limited, 57 Haymarket, S.W.1

THE INSTITUTE OF BUILDERS: RULES OF THE LICENTIATE DIS-
CUSSION CLUB & RECORD AND NEWS of Club December 1943

MINISTRY OF HEALTH MINISTRY OF WORKS HOUSING MANUAL
1944
London His Majesty's Stationery Office two shillings net

DICTIONARY OF MATHEMATICAL DATA
333 Precise Definitions W.Millington B.Sc.
Bernards (Publishers) Ltd. London W.6 Copyright 1944

STANDARDS REVIEW 1945 No. 1
Period Review of the British Standards Institution
Issued quarterly

TOMORROW'S HOUSE a complete guide for the home-builder
by George Nelson, Consultant Editor Architectural Forum, &
Henry Wright, managing editor Architectural Forum.
Published 1945 by The Architectural Press London, and Simon and
Schuster New York. Price fifteen shillings.
[three sheets of notes by Jack enclosed, one on Reader Bros
Roundmead Avenue Loughton writing paper.]

HOUSES FOR MODERATE MEANS
by R.Randal Phillips, Hon.A.R.I.B.A.
Published 1936 by Country Life Ltd. 2-10 Tavistock St, Covent Garden W.C.2 Third printing of second edition 1946. Printed in Great
Britain by Billing and Sons Ltd., Guildford and Esher

IDEAL HOME MAGAZINE May 1948 one shilling and sixpence
Published by Ideal Home Magazine, 57, Long Acre, W.C.2

DAILY MAIL IDEAL HOME BOOK 1948-9
A Daily Mail Ideal Home Exhibition Publication
Editor Margaret Sherman
Published by Associated Newspapers Ltd., Carmelite House, Lon-
don E.C.4

MINISTRY OF HEALTH HOUSING MANUAL 1949
Printed in Great Britain under the authority of His Majesty's Stationery Office by The Campfield Press, St Albans
Price 3s 6d net

THE LAW SOCIETY'S GAZETTE December 1951
[Containing article on Free Conveyances]

HOUSES FOR MODERATE MEANS by R.Randal Phillips
Hon.A.R.I.B.A.
4th edition 1952

THE NEW SMALL HOUSE
by F.R.S.Yorke F.R.I.B.A. and Penelope Whiting A.R.I.B.A.
Published 1953 by The Architectural Press, London
Printed in Great Britain by Willmer Brothers & Co.Ltd., Birkenhead.

ANNUAL REPORT OF THE MEDICAL OFFICER OF HEALTH for the year ending 31st December 1953 for combined districts of Epping U.D., Epping R.D. and Ongar R.D. [R.F.Reader then serving on the Public Health Committee for Ongar.]

NEW HOMES AND PLANS FOR BUILDING
A Fawcett How-to Book 75c
Fawcett Publications Inc. Greenwich, Connecticut 1955

IDEAL HOME BOOK OF PLANS 1955 Edition 5/-
published by the proprietors of "Ideal Home" magazine
Odhams Press Ltd., Long Acre, W.C.2

DAILY MAIL BOOK OF HOUSE PLANS
New designs for Houses and Bungalows including those exhibited at the Daily Mail Ideal Home Exhibition, 1955.
Edited by Trevor Smith L.R.I.B.A.
Published by Associated Newspapers Ltd., Northcliffe House, London, E.C.4

DESIGNS FOR THE SMALLER HOME five shillings
The Builder architectural series.
[Plans and photographs of architect designed small houses and bungalows. 1955?]

RURAL DISTRICT COUNCILS ASSOCIATION
Minutes of the Annual Conference held at The Winter Gardens Eastbourne on 21 – 24 June 1955

FIFTY MODERN BUNGALOWS edited Felix Walter F.R.I.B.A.
pub. The Architectural Press London 1955, revised 1957
18s 6d.

IDEAL HOME BOOK OF PLANS 1956 Edition 5 shillings
40 New Homes including designs by seven women architects
published by the proprietors of "Ideal Home" magazine
Odhams Press Ltd., Long Acre, W.C.2

DAILY MAIL BOOK OF HOUSE PLANS 1956 2/6
Published by Associated Newspapers Ltd Northcliffe House EC4

BUNGALOW & HOUSE DESIGNS FOR EVERYONE a selection of
plans and elevations by Francis W.Julian, J.W.Stephenson, R.E.Paylor,
C.P.Christie
An illustrated Carpenter and Builder publication 1956?

DAILY MAIL BOOK OF HOUSE PLANS
New designs including exhibits at the 1957 Daily Mail Ideal Home
Exhibition Price 2/6 [two shillings and sixpence]
Edited by Trevor Smith, L.R.I.B.A.
Published by Associated Newspapers Ltd., Northcliffe House, Lon-
don, E.C.4

IDEAL HOME MAGAZINE BOOK OF PLANS 1957 Edition
Price five shillings
Published by the Proprietors of "Ideal Home" Magazine.
Printed in Great Britain and published by the Proprietors, Odhams
Press Ltd., Long Acre, London W.C.2

DAILY MAIL BOOK OF HOUSE PLANS
including exhibits at the 1958 Daily Mail Ideal Home Exhibition and
the Brighter Homes Exhibition, Manchester. Price 3/6.
Edited by Trevor Smith, L.R.I.B.A.
Published by Associated Newspapers Limited, London.
Printed in Great Britain by Waterlow & Sons Limited, London and
Dunstable.

IDEAL HOME MAGAZINE BOOK OF PLANS 1958 Edition five shillings
Published by the Proprietors of Ideal Home Magazine
Odhams Press Ltd., Long Acre, London W.C.2

DAILY MAIL BOOK OF BUNGALOW PLANS 1961 3/6
Published by Associated Newspapers London EC4
[article re house costs Daily Sketch 6.9.1961 enclosed]

PLANAHOME BOOK OF HOUSE PLANS 1962 Ninth edition
Price twenty shillings
Published by Planahome, Lloyds Bank Chambers, King St, Richmond, Surrey. Director H.M.R.Finn.
Printed by J.H.Broad & Co.Ltd., 8 King St, Richmond, Surrey.
"The publishers reserve the copyright of all the designs, photographs and printed matter shown in this book (with the exception of advertisers' material). The publishers reserve the right to withdraw any or all of the designs shown in this book without notice. The publishers reserve the right to refuse to supply building plans or documents offered in this book either on initial or subsequent orders should they so desire."

DAILY MAIL IDEAL HOME EXHIBITION 1963 Catalogue & Guide 2/6

DAILY MAIL BOOK OF HOUSE PLANS 1963
Published by Associated Newspapers Limited London E.C.4
Printed in Great Britain by Cox and Wyman Ltd., London, Reading and Fakenham. Price 3/6 [three shillings and sixpence]

COUNTRY LIFE BOOK OF HOUSES FOR TODAY H.Dalton Clifford pub. 1963 by Country Life Ltd Tower House Southampton St WC2, reprinted 1966.

DAILY MAIL BOOK OF HOUSE PLANS 1964
Published by Associated Newspapers Limited, London E.C.4 & Printed in Great Britain by Cox and Wyman Ltd., London, Reading and Fakenham.
Foreword by Sir Robert Matthew C.B.E.,, A.R.S.A., President R.I.B.A.

DAILY MAIL BOOK OF BUNGALOW PLANS 1964-5 3/6
Published by Associated Newspapers Ltd London and printed by Cox and Wyman London & Reading.

THE CLAY TILE BULLETIN Vol.1 No.12, no date
Pub.by The National Federation of Clay Industries Drayton House,
30 Gordon St WC1 printed by Merritt & Hatcher Ltd., Blackheath Rd
SE10

CATALOGUE Sale by tender of land adjacent to The Mansion, Tring
Park Herts. closing date noon 29 September 1972
Edward Erdman 6 Grosvenor St W1X OAD

APPENDIX D
BUILDING TRADE ADVERTISING LEAFLETS ETC.

General Constructional & Engineering Co (Bedford & Son) Ltd. 97 West Ferry Rd E14 architectural metalworkers no date.
[At this address c1938-1973. 1955 Dir Entry; constructional engineers, fireproof doors & shutters, iron & steel doors etc makers, and at Hutchings St E14]

IN FOLDER MARKED PAMPHLETS: ELECTRIC WATER HEATING
Advertisements torn from The Architects' Journal; Sadia 22 July 1948, 9 December 1948, 10 March 49.

British National Electrics Ltd, Newarthill, Motherwell 24 February 1949

Sadia 7 February 1946 [on back, John Booth & Sons (Bolton) Ltd, Hulton Steelworks, advertising their part in the Mulberry Harbour]

Santon Ltd, Newport 25, Monmouthshire 22 July 1948. Hotric, Broxburn, West Lothian 25 April 1946.

Sadia Electric Water Heaters List 20 (Fourth Edition) Aidas Electric Ltd Sadia Works, Rowdell Rd, Northolt, Middx With letter dated 3 April 1951.

Flexo Plywood Industries Ltd., Flexo Works, S.Chingford E.4. Approximate Current Comparative Price List August 1948
Sample of Flexvemet; sixteen gauge aluminium faced with a decorative veneer.

Cork Manufacturing Co.Ltd. South Chingford London E4
Sample of "Chingford" cork grade 3F thickness 1/4"

Erith & Co.Ltd Drainpipes 1950

Claygate Old English Fireplaces 11th edition November 1951
Claygate Fireplaces Ltd., Claygate, Surrey

Ormak Hardwood "Facia Boarding" Price List 1 June 1960

Atkinson & Kirby Ltd, Wigan Rd Ormskirk Lancs.

Ormak Price List 1 May 1961
[Mahogany has gone up, Clear Western Red Cedar down.]

WITH COOPERS HILL ESTATE CORRESPONDENCE ETC.
Robbialac Colorizer Paints Trade Price List 1st February 1957
J.H.Sankey & Son Ltd., Essex House, Kings Rd, Brentwood,
Essex

Gifco Sink Units The General Iron Foundry Co.Ltd. Gifco
House, Brooks Wharf, Upper Thames St, London EC4

Gifco Porcelain Enamelled Steel Sinks, acid amd alkali resist-
ing, sound deadened.

Ambex the All Purpose Surface Gifco Pricing Chart

Cemp Ornamental Ironwork, Croydon, Surrey Booklet and two
leaflets Supplied by Gifco

Ranalah Ornamental Gates Ltd., 43 Devonshire Place Brighton
Three leaflets, 2 presented by The Norlond Service (Builder's
Merchants) Ltd.

W.C.Youngman Ltd, Wandsworth Works, Wandsworth Rd London SW8
Second-hand plant list February 1959

IN FOLDER MARKED GENERAL
Building Research Station, Garston, Watford, Herts.

Ministry of Works leaflet 31 1959 Heating Stoves etc.

M. of Works leaflet 51 Watertight Basements Parts 1 & 2

HMSO leaflet Facts & Information on Building

HMSO Principles of Modern Building Vol.2 Floors & Roofs

A.Barnes office supplies for building trade, Copying House,1a Regent Rd Leicester

Manifoldia office stationery West Bromwich, Staffs.

Printed stationery Woodford Agency 160 Hermon Hill E18

Kalamazoo Ltd Northfield Birmingham 31 stationery

Edgleys Ltd office furniture 151 Fleet St EC4

N.C.Brown Ltd office furniture June 1965 Eagle Steelworks Heywood, Lancs

Burroughs Adding Machine Ltd, card – 746/8 Eastern Ave Ilford

Office Equipment Co. 113 High Holborn WC1

Numeria calculator BOSCO 10 Coleman St EC2

Reliance (Nameplates) Ltd, Richmond Bridge Works Twickenham

Dampcoursing Ltd 34 St James St Walthamstow E17

Insulight glass blocks Pilkington Bros Ltd St Helens Lancs.

Ruberoid roofing Commonwealth House 1-19 New Oxford St WC1

Marleydek PVC/asbestos bonded roof decking Marley, Sevenoaks, Kent

Marley System Building March 1968

Marley Eagle Beams, Marley Concrete Ltd, Guildford

Marley Storage Walls

Marley Tile (Holding) Co.Ltd Annual Report 1965

Finlock Gutters & foamed slag concrete blocks Tunbridge Wells

Portcrete Stonetex stone; with business card from Gravesend

Monohex Concrete Paving, Horton Rd, West Drayton April 1965

Californian Screen Blocks Ltd 52 Holloways Lane Welham Grn

Waights [concrete] Moulds Limes Avenue, Oakfield Rd SE20

Bribond Signs Ltd, Victoria Rd, Burgess Hill August 1967

Permutit water softeners, Gunnersbury Ave W4 April 1962 – 65

Duro water softeners Edmunds Ltd Station Rd Epping Essex

Pilkington's Tiles Ltd Clifton Junction Manchester 1965

East Anglian Tiling Co.(Brooker) 76 Springfield Rd Chelmsford

Richafix ceramic tile fixatives, Tunstall, Stoke-on-Trent

British Ceramic Tile Council fixatives, Federation House, Stoke-on-Trent

Nic-o-bond tile cement, Nicholls & Clarke, Niclar House E1

Metal Windows Nicholls & Clarke

H.C.Hill Ltd 9 Silverdale SE26 Sanitary fittings 1966

Knowles sanitary fittings for premises affected by 1964 offices, shops and railway act

Knowles Vitriflex joints for pipes, 13-21 Knights Hill SE7

Hepseal clay pipes June 1966 Hepworth Iron Co.Ltd. Hazlehead Stocksbridge Sheffield

Flexpipe, Bowaters Associated Industries Ltd, Ellesmere Port.

Foamflex pipe insulation Dunlop Semtex Ltd.

The Gypsum Mines, Mountfield, Robertsbridge, Sussex, makers of Sirapite lightweight plasters January 1960

Commer Cars Ltd Data Book No.84 19 July 1966 & letter from Ray Powell Ltd Fairlop Rd E.11

Bedford HA van White of Ongar (Garages) Ltd High St 1965

Vymura Wall Covering ICI Templar House 81-87 High Holborn WC1

Artex ceilings Brookside Industrial Estate Rustington Sussex

Jonespan Lattice Beams T.C.Jones & Co.Ltd 93-95 Wood Lane W12

Allen Gates General Iron Foundry Co.Ltd 156 Bermondsey St SE1   Thinsteel drain covers

Metal Letters J.W.& C.J.Phillips Ltd Pomery St New Cross SE14

E.J.Cook & Co.(engineers) Ltd 54 South Side SW4 22 Oct 1965

Letters offering surveying, drawing, house designs, insurance, demolition, Laxton's building price book, 1966 Contract Journal Directory & Year Book, Gold Star Ductless cooker hoods, advertising in Evening News, & mortage service "when the bank says no."

IN FOLDER MARKED BRICKS, STONE
The Ruberoid Co.Ltd, 1 New Oxford St WC1

Fireplaces in Maclit Random Facing October 1960 Claygate Fire places Surrey

Granville English Stone Fireplaces
Haines & Warwick Ltd, Old Church Rd, Romford

Enclosed – business card from B.Finch & Co.Ltd showrooms, Finch Corner, Eastern Avenue, Ilford.

Wandsworth Stonemasonry Works, 78 Wandsworth Rd SW8
Letter soliciting inquiries.

Pilkington's Easifix Tiles March 1968
Pilkington's Tiles Ltd, PO Box 4 Clifton Junction, Manchester

Ensor Flues system
Ensor & Co.Ltd. The Pool Works, Woodville, Burton-on-Trent

Lignacite Hollow Party Wall Blocks
Lignacite Group Sales, 128 Baker St W1

Entrainit mortar plasticiser & air entraining agent
Proctor & Gamble Ltd., Building Specialities Dept.,
Newgate House, Newcastle upon Tyne 1

SeRidge & Red Bank Terminals for domestic gas appliances
Red Bank Manufacturing Co.Ltd., Measham via Burton-on-Trent

Do It Yourself York Stone Fireplace Kits January 1967
Rowe & Pascoe (prop.Geo E.Cloke Ltd) Elmsted Neasden Lane
NW10

Hammill Brick Co.Ltd June 1963 – October 1965
Eastry, Sandwich, Kent

Burwell Brick Co. (Gault facings) October 1964
Harvest House, Princes St, Ipswich, Suffolk (branch of Fisons)

IN FOLDER MARKED PAINTER
Super Leytex wall finish
Leyland Paint & Varnish Co.Ltd, Leyland, Lancs & London

Watertite C water proofer for timber
Duresco Products Ltd., Charlton SE7

Cementone No.7 1966
Cementone Works, Wandsworth, SW18

Caenstone exterior stone texture paint August 1966
Keystone Paint & Varnish Co.Ltd, Hindley, Lancs.

Decorative Paints Price List 1st February 1966
Walpamur Co. Ltd., Darwen, Lancs.

Artex Products (Manufacturing) Ltd notification of change of
address from Brookside Industrial Estate, Rustington to Artex
Avenue, Newhaven, Sussex.

Snowcem 1965
Cement Marketing Co.Ltd., Portland House, Stag Place, SW1
& G.&.T.Earle Ltd, Hull.

Szerelmey Waterproof Encaustic
Szerelmey Ltd, Szerelmey House 273/277 Rotherhithe New Rd
SE16

Fleximent ready-mixed plaster filler
Fleximent Ltd., Mill Hill Grove, Acton W3

Dampel miracle treatment for damp patches
Plycol Ltd Slough, Chester, Glasgow, Bristol, Belfast, Dublin

Pestcure Timber Preservative September 1960
Geo.E.Gray Ltd. Joinant House, Eastern Avenue, Ilford.

Polygalv non-drip thixotropic primer April 1964
Polybond Ltd. Warsash Rd, Warsash, Southampton

Synthaprufe waterproofer & adhesive
National Coal Board Proprietary By Products Branch, Powell
Duffryn House, Docks, Cardiff

Nitromors Paint Removers
Wilcot (Parent) Co.Ltd, Fishponds, Bristol.

Xpelair, Woods of Colchester Ltd, Braiswick Works, Colchester
August 1961

Marley Flex Vinyl Asbestos Floor Tiles samples June 1964
Marley Sevenoaks Kent England

Quantity of warm air central heating leaflets from Edmunds of Epping Ltd c1965

Parkray fires Gifco 156 Bermondsey St SE1 1965

Husqvarna convected warm-air central heating A.H.Bibbey Ltd High Wych Sawbridgeworth

Galgate Surrounds for gas room heaters August 1965
Claygate Fireplaces Ltd. Common Rd, Claygate, Esher & Galleon Fireplaces 216-218 Red Lion Rd, Tolworth, Surbiton, Surrey.

Marley Econoflex Floor Tiles samples September 1965
Marley Floors, Sevenoaks, Kent, England

Henderson sliding doors and gear 1965-7
P.C.Henderson Ltd, Harold Hill, Romford, Essex

Hillaldam sliding door gear 1967
E.Hill Aldam & Co.Ltd., Britannic Works, Red Lion Rd, Tolworth, Surrey.

Solent Whitewood Furniture Ltd
Norway Rd Hilsea Portsmouth Jan 1968

Sound Used Scaffolding Plant and Materials leaflet July 1968
H.W.Bewley Ltd, 124 Balls Pond Road, London N.1

Plant Hire Catalogue Autumn 1968/9
H.W.Bewley Ltd 124 Balls Pond Road, London N.1

Allen Gates catalogue June 1968 The General Iron Foundry Co. Ltd. 156 Bermondsey St London SE1

Stelco Industries, 13/15 Wilson St, London E.C.2
Metal Windows etc Leaflet. No date.

TOGETHER:
Erith & Co.Ltd 455 Old Ford Rd Bow E3
List of materials stocked.

W.J.Simms Sons & Cooke Ltd., Haydn Rd, Sherwood, Notting-ham Quality Doors. (Stamped by Erith)

RIW Liquid Asphaltic Composition
RIW Protective Products Co.Ltd. 325 Whitehorse Rd Croydon Surrey. (Stamped by Erith)

Carlite Pre-mixed lightweight plaster 1966
British Gypsum Ltd Ferguson House 15/17 Marylebone Rd NWl

Vitrified Clay Pipes and Fittings. Feb 1965
Erith & Co.Ltd. Bow Depot.

Arch File containing the National Building Agency + "Build-ing" Commodity File from 27th August 1971 to 20th April 1973

Cases Fencing Taffs Well Ltd 1977 [used to divide 75 and 73 Monkhams Avenue]

Accordial U.K.Ltd Kebbell House Carpenders Pk Watford Herts (new address) Movable Acoustic Walls & Sliding/Folding Partitions.

Hufcor (Partitions) Ltd Castle Donington Derby Acoustic Accordian Partitions May 1978 (Henderson Doors Ltd Harold Hill)

Hufcor Acoustic Operable Walls June 1978 (Henderson)

Crittall Windows Ltd, Braintree, Essex; Luminair stock slider range April 1979

Crosby Windows, Gloucester Trading Estate, Hucclecote, Glos. July 1980 [for Medstead?]

Marley Buildings Ltd, South Ockendon Essex
Rep. F.R.W.Baldwin 40 Roundmead Ave Loughton

APPENDIX E
OTHER BUILDERS' BROCHURES

PERRY'S HOUSE at the Daily Mail Ideal Homes Exhibition Olympia 1931. Includes list of firms whose products were used in the building.
[1926 Perry Bros building contractors 48 Uxbridge Rd Ealing
 1933 Perry's (Ealing) Ltd 16 Uxbridge Rd
 1937 Perry's (Ealing) Ltd 75 Uxbridge Rd
 Then developing widely in the Banstead and Great Burgh area.
 Versions of the exhibition house were erected at Tudor Close
 and 27 Hillside, Banstead Surrey. Both this leaflet and that
 for Dome Hill Estates show houses with authentic pale
 timbering, but all are now stained Victorian-style black.]

THE LOVELL HOUSE 1932 Stand No.180, National Hall, Ideal Home Exhibition, Olympia April 5th-30th. Messrs Y.J.Lovell & Son, 6 Bathurst Street, Lancaster Gate W.2 & Gerrards Cross, Bucks.

JEFFERY HOUSES LTD. 22 & 26 Chapel Rd Worthing 1935

E.HORACE THOMPSON, F.S.I. architect and chartered surveyor, The Estate Offices, High Pine Close, Weybridge October 1936

DOME HILL ESTATES LTD. Hamilton House, 19 Buckingham Gate, SW1
"The Tudor Home"; Dome Hill Est., Surrey Hills, Caterham c1937
Includes £100 voucher towards purchase.
[Built using reclaimed materials from demolished "Tudor" buildings. Off Harestone Valley Rd; later houses added but still exclusive and quiet apart from the roar of the mower and the snarl of the strimmer. Those built with old timbers and bricks obvious including happily OTT bungalows, but some "improvement" including the big Tudor-style seated porch illustrated in brochure walled in and made dull. Last mention of the firm at Buckingham Gate in directory 1942, though the late 17th century house had been damaged by a bomb on Wellington Barracks 17 April 1941. Recent building now on the site.]

T.F.NASH PROPERTIES LTD. Collier Row Rd, Romford Essex 1938

A.W.CURTON LTD. Edgware Golf Club House, Stone Grove, Edgware Rd Edgware Middx 1939

E. & L. BERG LTD. Buckland House, Esher Surrey 1955

E. & L.BERG Ltd 1956

E. & L.BERG LTD. 1958

E. & L.BERG LTD. 1962

G.T.CROUCH LTD Sutherland House, Surbiton Crescent Kingston-upon-Thames 1963

DAVIS ESTATES LTD 350 Kilburn High Rd London NW6
Davis House of the year 1963

COOPER ESTATES LTD Wilmington House, Wilmington, Dartford Kent
1964

FEDERATED HOMES LTD 1965 *

FEDERATED HOMES LTD Crown House, Morden, Surrey
Devon Chalet no date 60s?

TAYLOR WOODROW HOMES LTD 60s Town Houses, Church Rd Upper Norwood.

HOLMDENE COURT SOUTHLANDS GROVE BICKLEY Town houses 60s?
Architects Alan H.Devereux & Partners 3 Gower St WC1
Contractors F. & H.F.Higgs Ltd 2 Herne Hill Rd SE24

NOTES

Chapter 1

1   Now Margery St WC1

2   70 year lease. Draft agreement signed 2 April 1818, seal affixed 9 April. First three years while building peppercorn rent, remainder £525 to be paid on Ladyday 25 March. Information from Royal Commission on Historic Monuments. Most of the Whiskin estate finally fell to the planners in 1965, and the site of Coburg St is now occupied by the centre stretch of Skinner St.

3   Middlesex Deeds Register 10/799 London Metropolitan Archives

4   Later covered by the playground of Bowling Green Lane Board School, opened 1875. As the land has not been built on the burials probably remain beneath.

5   The History and Description of the Parish of Clerkenwell by Thomas Cromwell, Sherwood 1828 pp150-1.

6   Pulled down for Tottenham Road Board School, opened 1874.

7   Guildhall Library Trade Card Collection.

8   St Dionis Backchurch was dilapidated because the parish was not allowed to restore it, due to the Union of City Benefices Act. Demolished after protests in 1878 and St Dionis Parsons Green built with proceeds. Some of the old church's fittings were installed in the new, including the font in which William's youngest son was baptised. The fate of the immense chandelier has not been discovered. It may have been disposed of in the sale of fittings by tender held 16.4.1878 by Fuller Horsey & Co. 11 Billiter Square EC.

9   Statutes 15 & 16 Victoria 1852 Chapter 85. An act to amend the laws concerning the burial of the dead in the Metropolis (1st July 1852) repealing Metropolitan Interments Act 1850. Discontinuance of burials may be ordered in any part of the Metropolis, Quaker and Jewish burial grounds being excepted. Certain rights to relatives of those already buried there, also rights re vaults. Doesn't apply to cemeteries and new burial grounds, or St Paul's or Westminster Abbey, where burial is at the Queen's pleasure. New burial grounds to be approved by the Secretary of State. Between 3 and 9 ratepayers of the parish to form a Burial Board, expenses to be paid out of the Poor Rate. Several parishes may "concur" to produce one burial ground. Finishes with list of parish grounds which are to be closed.

10   Christine Margaret Buggé

11   Public Record Office BT31/1556/5024
12   Guildhall Library Ms 28977 Bundle 3
13   "   "   "   "
14   London Coroners' Inquests 1873 City No.34 Corporation of London Record Office
15   There is a picture of the Bell in City of London Past by Richard Tames pub. Historical Publications. It was rebuilt a few years later in dark red brick, along with the rest of the west side of Addle Hill. The site has recently been redeveloped in a gentle Georgian pastiche whose brickwork blends with the old St Paul's Choir School in Carter Lane.
16   Demolished.

Chapter 2

1   Census 1891 Summary Tables.
2   In the Hackney area John Woodyer Pailthorpe put in Build and Drain applications for 17-27 Harrowgate Rd in 1865; 57-63 Loddiges Rd (dem.) in 1863; 245-269 Wick Rd on the corner with Sidney/Kenworthy Rd in 1881.
3   Westminster Archives 842/1
      Queen's Hall   Robert Elkin   Rider 1944   Wes.Arc.786.26
      P.R.O. CREST 35 2142 – 44, CREST 38 1710
4   The Builder 14 Feb 1891 p128; 21 Feb 1891 p153; 28 Feb 1891 p174; 7 Oct 1893 p269; 2 Dec 1893 p420; 30 Dec 1893 p490; T.E.Knightley's obituary 16 Sept 1905 p303.
5   L.M.A. GLC/AR/BR/07/0269
6   The narrow strip of compulsorily-purchased land drawn in the Leyton Tithe Map eventually grew into the immense Temple Mills Sidings, now vanished and supplanted by new uses.
7   Gentleman's Magazine Vol II p2 c5
8   Corporation of London Record Office Plans 31DG
9   William Rayner was born into a family of Hackney bricklayers 30 November 1806 and married Louisa Jane Prestage of Bethnal Green about l833. Rayner developments took place in South Hackney c1851 – 1875, in Gravesend c1865 – 1903, in Stratford, Leyton, Leytonstone, Wanstead and Snaresbrook c1881 – 1915. Members of the Rayner family are recorded in residence on all sites. William died in 1885 at Gravesend; an executor of his will was F.W.Willmott of Fitzgerald Rd Wanstead, another builder who started out in South Hackney. William's third son Adolphus Charles became mayor of Gravesend and died there in 1903.

His fourth Edwin Isaac died at 19 Spratt Hall Rd in 1923. All left wills based upon property, Edwin's including the Picture Palace cinema, 80 Leyton High Rd which has now been transformed into an Indian Restaurant.

For information on the building lease system see Gentlemen in the Building Line by Isobel Watson, Padfield Publications 1989.

10 Corp.Lond.Rec.Office Large Plan Roll 28

11 Dangan originally Marlborough, Gordon originally Wellington.

12 Frederick Beadle later became part owner of Beadle and Langbein's piano factory in Arlington Road, Camden Town. Its site is now occupied by a cinema turned Bingo hall.

13 App.114 & 162 L.B.Redbridge Local History Lib.

14 Square 75 Grave 298

15 L.B.Waltham Forest 4311 & 4380

16 This name eventually became an asset when Ras opened a factory, Buggé's Insecticides Ltd, in London Rd Sittingbourne c1930 (dem. 1994), in fact some assumed that the name was purely commercial.

At about the same time, Ras, Florence and their three surviving children moved to a large house, Eversley, at 87 London Rd and another factory was later opened at Gads Hill Gillingham.

17 Also known as Finchley Junction or Church End and now the Northern Line Finchley Central.

18 The head of a family of licenced victuallers recorded at The Orange Tree 234 Euston Rd, the Bird in Hand 88 Masborough Rd Hammersmith and the Westminster Arms 10 Praed St W

19 James Ellwood arch. & surv. Priory Rd Hornsey N
J.Pappin Rosebery Rd Muswell Hill N

20 The Kiwi Polish Co. Ltd. Newton & Wright Ltd, manufacturers of X-ray and electrical medical apparatus, moved there from 471-475 Hornsey Rd in 1937. A passage into Ballards Lane with iron overthrow marked Newton Wright Ltd remains.

21 Built by Ideal Homes Southern Ltd, Goldsworth House, Goldsworth Park Centre, Woking GU21 3LF. Houses first recorded as inhabited for Electoral Register 10 October 1995.

Chapter 3

1 George Trollope & Sons, 7 Hobart Place Eaton Square, West Halkin St Belgrave Square, 5 Victoria St & 14 Mount St SW
See Epping Forest Then & Now by Winston G.Ramsey & Reginald L.Fowkes pub After the Battle p223

Plot sale particulars Redbridge L.H.Lib. Clements Rd Ilford
2   85 – 97 & 145 Monkhams Lane Building App. 1027 & 919
      113 – 121 Monkhams Avenue App. 1420 & 1455
3   161 – 163 Monkhams Lane App. 1691
4   London's Lea Valley Jim Lewis Phillimore p116
5   App. 2074
6   App. 2051 Now 36 and 36a The Broadway
7   App. 2093 2146
8   App. 2187
9   App. 2207
10   Diconwyn, 2 The Green App.2209. Sheppard Bros. Snakes Lane
      and Horn Lane Woodford Green.
11   T.H.Osborn & Sons High Rd Woodford, Claud R.Osborn St Osyth
      Buckingham Rd S.Woodford, H.H.Starke 45 Ingatestone Rd,
      J.C. Lee, Ravenswood Wanstead Place.
      Flaxman & Wright took offices at 4 The Broadway which re-
      tained the old counter and shelves until the fifties; it is now a
      Sue Ryder Charity Shop. R.F. & W.Peachey of Boundary Rd &
      Blenheim Rd Walthamstow had a Belgrave Works, just like the
      great Trollope & Colls.
12   101 – 111 App.2591, 113 – 119 App.2657, 121 – 123 App.2697
13   App.2868
14   App.2276
      Isaac Edmondson was born c1830 in Penruddock Cumberland.
      He married Hannah Nicholson at Temple Sowerby
      Westmoreland on 28.6.1856 and their son James was born in
      Clerkenwell 1857. He described himself as a carpenter in the
      1861 Census, but by the birth of his daughter Annie at 64 Great
      Percy St in 1868 he was a builder. In 1872 he was at 105 Mildmay
      Rd N. In 1881 his business address was Rosebank 7 Park Villas
      Albion Rd Stoke Newington, but he was living at 40 Petherton
      Rd Highbury. By 1885 the firm was I.Edmondson & Son and
      James married the same year, being recorded in residence at
      Rosebank in 1888. In 1891 Isaac was at 140 Green Lanes and
      James at 12 Aberdeen Terrace, Aberdeen Park Rd. Edmondson's
      developed at Highbury, Wood Green, Muswell Hill, Westcliff,
      Harringay, Woodford Green, Winchmore Hill, Sydenham,
      Golders Green, Bourne Hill Southgate and probably other ar-
      eas. Isaac died at Belgrave Villa, The Cliffs, Southend (part of
      the Cliff Town Estate of Peto, Brassey and Betts) on 21.1.1905.
      James's children were Albert James 1886, Percival Harry 1888,
      Elsie Maud 1890 and Cyril Arthur 1892, and two sons died in the

1914-18 war. Directories record James at Fairclough Hall, Weston, Herts in 1926 and at Woodberry, West Overcliff Drive, Bournemouth in 1923 & 1931. He died 7.6.1931 leaving nearly a quarter of a million pounds, of which at least £10,000 went to charity. His surviving son was Major Sir Albert James Edmondson, M.P. for the Banbury Division of Oxfordshire.

15 App.2238

16 Coincidentally, up to 1889 his father had been in business as a manufacturer and dealer in sacks, tarpaulins etc. at 19 Cullum St.

17 Early house names on the Monkhams Estate.
The Green. 1 Kingsthorp, 2 Diconwyn, 3 St Helens, 4 Glenluce, 5 Rest Harrow, 6 Aviemore.
Monkhams Avenue. 7 Keneric, 11 Idmiston, 13 Holmwood, 21 Boscobel, 23 Aderf (the lady of the house was called Freda), 25 Croysdill, 27 Ranfurly later Burleigh, 29 Lyncroft, 31 Wendover, 33 The Glen, 35 Broxstowe (dem.), 39 Hazeldene, 41 Allandale, 43 Darfield, 45 Hawfield, 47 Woodstock, 49 Torridan, 51 Firsinga, 55 Hillside, 57 Northwood, 59 Orpey, 63 Inglenook, 65 Denehurst 75 Bonniecot, 77 The Firs, 79 Braeside, 81 L'Ancresse, 83 Campana later Merchiston, 91 Mascot, 93 Oakwood, 95 Ridgwood, 97 Maycroft, 99 Trevone, 101 Aldington, 103 Eastnor, 105 Glenmore, 107 Arden, 109 Beechcroft, 111 Glenholme, 123 Meyrick, 125 Rowans, 127 Keston 2 Lindisfarne, 4 Wickersley, 6 The White Cottage, 10 Kilmorey?, 12 Maxwell, 14 Bossinney, 16 Marshfield, 18 Bidston, 20 Myliss, 22 Corbyn, 36 Adderley, 40 Kelvedon, 42 Braemar, 44 The Pyghtle, 70 Melrose, 72 Oxenford, 74 Newstead, 76 Shepreth, 82 The Shack (dem.).
Monkhams Drive 3 Newlyn, 5 Waratah, 7 Claremont later Symra, 9 Selbrook, 11 Orotava, 13 Trollheim, 15 Aysgarth, 19 Thrapston, 21 Ruthven, 23 Brynawelon, 25 Dunollie House, 27 Clare Lodge, 29 Helenslea, 31 Dartymoor, 33 Glengarriff, 35 The Craig, 37 The Bryn.
2 Glencarse, 4 Hillside, 6 Lyncott, 8 Dunkeld, 10 Melbourn Bury, 12 Lynton, 14 Rosemount, 16 Louisville, 18 Fernbank, 20 Fritton Lodge, 22 San Fermo, 24 Prestwich, 26 Dunottar, 28 The Gables (dem.), 30 Aviemore.
King's Avenue 13 Craigalvah, 21 St.Ives, 23 The Knoll, 25 Belmont, 53 Walberswick, 55 Oakdene.

20 Hillhead, 22 Mount View, 50 Oakhurst, 52 Fordhurst, 54 Avonhurst, 56 Lyndhurst.

18   Examples of Edmondson's thundering red and white shopping parades can also be seen at Highbury, Muswell Hill, Winchmore Hill, Golders Green and Sydenham. There must be many more awaiting discovery.

19   App. 2363 2522 2535 2656 (later 2 & 4 Monkhams Ave) 2708 2767

20   App.2691

21   Hansard 1909 Vol 5 p 1224

22   Hansard 1909 Vol 6 p 37-41

23   The Finchley Press, Muswell Hill Mercury and Highgate Post.

24   App.2737

25   App.2922

26   The Yorkshire Herald July 23, 24 & 25 1928

27   Hackney Archives Dept. has microfilm of the borough's early planning applications, accessibly indexed.

28   Barclay Bros. timber merchants, 3rd floor, 16 & 17 Devonshire Square EC. A third brother, John Matthewson Barclay, was also involved in the firm.

Chapter 4

1   Plan 2331 for 3 – 11 King's Avenue Woodford is marked "Printed by Velography 24 Oct 1905 Norton & Gregory Ltd., Castle Lane, Buckingham Gate S.W.1"

2   Richard owned a combined penknife and ruler which must date from this time, marked "Joseph Westby Engineers Machine Tool Makers Sheffield. Shells, Armour Piercing Projectiles, Patent Obturators for Naval Garrison & Field Guns – Stock Crucible Electric & Open Hearth Process".

3   Information; The Royal Arsenal O.F.G.Hogg pub.Oxford 1963

4   Now lower school of the Girls' Central Foundation.

5   Jack Travers Cornwell V.C. aged 16, mortally wounded on H.M.S.Chester, died 2.6.1916. Buried Manor Park Cemetery See The East End Then and Now pp 79-83 pub. After the Battle, Church St E15

6   Housing issued by The Ministry of Health Housing Dept. Vol l July 1919-June 1920 Vol 2 July 1920 – June 1921 Harry Simpson Memorial Library, University of Westminster.

7   George Rowe Woodruff, 1 Braydon Rd, Stoke Newington. Thomas Osment, 54 Mount Pleasant Lane, Upper Clapton.

Oliver Richard Chillingworth, 45 Oldhill St, Stoke Newington.

8   Metropolitan Borough of Hackney Housing Committee Minutes, Hackney Archives. Information drawn from H/H/1 to H/H/5.

9   H/H/5 p32 23 Nov 1926

Chapter 5

1   The main sources for this chapter have been the minutes of the Poplar Special Committee on the Housing of the Working Classes (Tower Hamlets Local History Library POP/1352-1354) and the Royal Commission on Historic Monuments Survey of London volume on Poplar (copies at Tower Hamlets L.H.Lib. and L.M.A.). The Poplar Borough Surveyor's Dept. letter books have also been interesting and they are indexed. (Tower Hamlets POP/ 1538 – 1540).

2   A derelict cul-de-sac of tiny mid-Victorian houses. From about 1846 18 Grundy St was the home of a carpenter and builder called George Reader, the son of a pork butcher of 274 Poplar High St. He died 7.12.1875 at 65 Market St, where his son George continued the business. There was no relationship to the Reader brothers. The A.Reader who carted away clinker from the borough destructor (Borough Surveyor's Letter Book POP/1540 April 1922) was probably born in Gravesend.

3   7th George 1V Chapter XC

An Act for making a turnpike road from St John's Chapel in the Parish of Saint Marylebone to the north-east end of Ballard's Lane, abutting upon the North Rd in the Parish of Finchley, with a branch therefrom, in the County of Middlesex. Passing through St Marylebone, St John Hampstead, Hendon & Finchley, terminating at NE of Ballards Lane, abutting upon North Rd in the Parish of Finchley ... branch to commence from North point of a certain road now making and known by the name of Avenue Rd leading from Primrose Hill Rd in a straight line through the lands or grounds of his grace the Duke of Portland, in said parish of St Marylebone, and joining said Main Rd at or near West End of Belsize Lane (St John's Hampstead).

Commencing at NE end in Ballard's Lane... no land to be dug or disturbed until it shall become necessary....Tolls 3d – 8d, payable only once a day. To commence on third Monday after passing. ..in force for 21 years, then to the end of the next session of parliament....trustees to meet at Eyre Arms Tavern. 5th May 1826.

4   Possibly Augustus Hoffman auctioneer and appraiser of 21 Upper St Martin's Lane.
5   The Story of Golders Green F.Howkins 1923 Barnet Local History Library L 942.187 Maps Barnet L.H.L., Tithe map & app.PRO IR29/21/29 & 30
6   Photograph of the farm avenue in Hendon by Stewart Gillies & Pamela Taylor pub.Phillimore
7   Again sourced from Housing Committee Minutes & Royal Commission report.
8   In an article in the Sunday Times 17 Oct 1920 Dr Addison also blames this situation on the pre-war building slump (courtesy of Lloyd George), and the absence of new apprenticeships during the war when building virtually stopped. He quotes the fall in the number of bricklayers as from 116,000 in 1910 to 53,00 in 1920.
9   William Simms builder, plumber, boiler setter & furnace builder 139 Brook St E1 (now east end of Cable St.)
10   Perry & Co,(Bow) Ltd 56 Victoria St SW1, 35 Finsbury Square EC2, Tredegar Works Ordell Rd Bow E3
11   Named from the mediaeval convent it passed, its site roughly between Priory St and Bromley High St. The remaining church chancel was destroyed by bombing and the lychgate in the last fragment of churchyard was not part of the Priory.
12   After Harper Twelvetrees of the Imperial Chemical Works Three Mill Lane who founded the Bromley Literary Association.
13   The General Strike May 1926; Its Origins & History R.Page Arnot repub.1975 by E.P.Publishing Ltd, East Ardsley, Wakefield W.Yorks.

Chapter 6
1   Poplar Board of Guardians minutes 1926 – 1929 indexed. Tower Hamlets L.H.Lib. A short history of St Andrews Hospital Bromley by Bow E3 1871-1971 E.Hacker. Bishopsgate Library.
2   The Laindon Farm Colony was founded in 1903 for Poplar Guardians by American industrialist and philanthropist Joseph Fels. Leaflet, Poplar Labour Colony at Dunton 1904, THLHL LP223. During the imprisonment of Poplar Council in 1921, the Colony brass band serenaded Lansbury outside Brixton Prison. LMA Po BG 152/6. When Poplar Board of Guardians disbanded 1928, taken over by LCC. Now Dunton Park caravan site.
3   George and Elizabeth Stevens, cowkeepers, married at St John

at Hackney 18 June 1814, and in 1843 she was renting a large part of South Mill Field and Hackney Marsh from the Tyssens. In 1861 their son Henry's widow Eliza was at the dairy 152 Homerton High St. Eliza's son Henry Slingsby took over while her son William Edward became a building contractor and carman, working from 24 Bridge St (Ponsford St). He built Stevens Avenue, two appealing little terraces numbered 1 – 22 and 23 – 36, bearing plaques inscribed W.E.S. 1895 and 1896. If all builders did this research would be much easier. The family owned a certain amount of property around Homerton.

4   Build and Drain index Plan 3020 Hackney Archives 117/202
5   Tower Hamlets L.H.Lib. POP/1354
6   "   "
7   "   "   12.4.1929
8   "   "   Cuttings 100.
9   East London Advertiser 4.10.1929
10   By Nina Thornicroft, attending as Jack Reader's fiancée.
11   By Edgar Reader
12   After former owner St Bartholomew's Priory Smithfield.
     Sources for Canons Drive development; Hendon R.D.C. and U.D.C. planning applications at L.B.Harrow Building Control; Greater London by Edward Walford, Cassell; Semi-detached London Alan A.Jackson Wild Swan Publications Ltd 1991; Suffolk Punch George Cross Faber & Faber 1934; The Development of Edgware between the Wars Suzanne Stone Dissertation 1992 Barnet Local History Lib.
13   Edgware Local Directories 1936/8, Barnet Local History.
     Albert John Butcher F.R.I.B.A. 2 Express Mansions, Station Rd
     Sandon Bros bldrs 4 Canons Close
     H.A.J.Capps bldr Little Babbitts, Cavendish Avenue
     Sword Daniels bldrs 105 Station Rd
     F.W.Bristow & Son Ltd bldrs Chestnut Avenue
14   David Salter A.N.A.E.A, Leslie Leigh & Co. 129 High St Edgware.

Chapter 7
     Sources; Seventy Glorious Years: a history of local government in Chingford Rex Pardoe 1965
     Chingford at War S.Warburton pub Chingford B.C. 1946
1   The Chingford Tithe Map can be seen at Waltham Forest Local History Library, Vestry House, Walthamstow.

2   Edward, Wallace, Lewis and Henry Good from Coggeshall Essex were the sons of Walter Good, master tailor from Devon. In 1869 Edward married Charlotte Johnson at St Mary's Walthamstow and by 1874 he and at least one of his carpenter brothers were in business at 5 Grosvenor Terrace, Pembroke Rd, Walthamstow from whence they carried out local building development. In 1878 the yard was at Gladstone Villa, Pembroke Rd. At the 1881 Census Edward was employing "15 men and 1 lad" and brothers Lewis and Henry were living in Alexandra Rd, later moving to Clarendon Rd. In 1894 Good Bros were builders' merchants at 316 Hoe St, with a wharf by the railway in Boundary Rd. In 1896 Wallace was living at 3 Fraser Rd, which is marked "1891 Edward Good". In 1908 Councillor Edward Good J.P. was living at a large Restoration house called Clevelands, 285 Hoe St (now converted into flats), and the business premises at Pembroke Rd, Boundary Rd, Queen's Rd and 316-324 Hoe St accommodated building, wholesale ironmongery, builders' supplies including lead, glass & paint, hosiery and bootmaking. The firm was also involved in buying land and in continuing development including picture houses; the Empire at Bell Corner, the Empress at 468-474 Hoe St which is just about still standing, and the Queen's behind their own Hoe St premises.

Edward died in April 1922 at Carisbrook 487 Lea Bridge Rd (dem.). In many ways his career echoes the Protestant work ethic of Twentyman and Edmondson; strong, practising Nonconformity; frugality, hard work and increasing prosperity; involvement in local government and good works. He and Charlotte died within days of each other and were buried at Queen's Rd Cemetery, where other family members have since joined them beneath the white marble monument outside the chapel. His parents Walter and Rhoda Kezia Good are buried in plot 1563A. Reports in the Walthamstow Guardian on 21 & 28 April 1922 recorded Edward's energy, virtues and achievements, though the "council's homage" included several tributes of the "you might not agree with Mr Good but ..." variety. Charlotte Good left £167 3s 11d and Edward Good £14,676 13s 9d, and had Charlotte survived him he would have left her thirty shillings a week and the life use of enough furniture for two small rooms. The remainder of his estate was left to his trustees on behalf of his family with first entitlement to his grandson William Richard, a posthumous child. His sons Edward Johnson Good and Thomas Walter Good carried on the businesses and in 1930 the builder's merchants' was inherited by Thomas's sons, Leslie Thomas and Harold Lewis. They gave land for a rose garden at the end of Priory Avenue Chingford in memory of their father.

3 Contractor George James Anderson 1856-1935 pavior, wharfinger, mason, road, cartage and general contractor. Warehouse built for him at 76 Poplar High St 1909, and a "graceless" house with "suburban aspirations" (Survey of London) at 68a East India Dock Rd 1910 by Poplar architect William Clarkson. Moved to Dungiven, Cambridge Pk Wanstead, then Moreton House, Woodford Rd Snaresbrook, a Victorian pile which his family referred to as The Morgue. Grandson George Eric married Eileen Buckley who lived at Shortlands next door; after polytechnic, apprenticed to Reader's, became family friend, received distinction of having teddy bear named after him. Firm closed in fifties, when George James's sons retired.

4 Arthur Peachey & Co.Ltd 26a Hoe St E17
Albert George Tufton, Belle Vue, Hale End Rd E17. Belle Vue was built at the beginning of the 19th century and surrounded by extensive gardens, including a lake. By the 1920s the grounds had been developed. The house was demolished in 1935 and twelve maisonettes numbered 36-56 Hillcrest Rd were built on its site.

5 Now Waltham Way.

6 Reader's also advertised in the Chingford Express, and yet another method is revealed in a draft letter at the back of Richard's 1931 diary; "I have received a Route Guide showing where the buses go to, which does not interest me, having booked with your Mr Abrahams 1 space in each of 20 new Di Lux [sic] Buses, forming a new service between Victoria & Chingford Mount (which I notice are not yet on the road.)" These were the new LT 165 buses for the London General Omnibus Company's 38 route. The service had been running from Victoria to Chingford since 1912 and was extended to the Royal Forest Hotel in 1922. However, due to the steepness of Chingford Mount the northbound route ran via New Rd, Larks Hall Rd, Kings Rd and Station Rd, while the southbound buses went down the Ridgeway and the Mount. The LT 165 buses went into service in May and June 1931 and tackled the Mount, up which they could be heard

labouring from bottom to top. The eyes provided by Picture Post gave waiting passengers an eerie frisson as they peered over the brow outside the Old Church; the adverts for Everybody's Weekly made them look half asleep.

Information from David Ruddom via the London Transport Museum.

7   Chingford Planning Dept Application 1155 for 23-169 New Rd 1 May 1926 from The Artistic & Expert Building Co.Ltd. 4 St Andrew Rd Walthamstow E17, signed William George Lee. On 12 September 1928 Ernest Thornicroft wrote to the council re planning permission for a glass lean-to outside his french windows. The writing on the plan looks as if it might have been done by Richard Reader.

8   Records of suppliers of materials for Chingford have not survived.

9   Edwin Robert Boswall builder, 60 High St Walthamstow, the son and grandson of Bethnal Green cabinet makers. They were an offshoot of the East London Boswalls who dealt in tripe from the late eighteenth century until 1938.

10   Notebook, probably Richard's; "October 12th 1931 to March 1st 1932. Must sell 9 houses. Stan says we won't 10/-" (ten shillings). Stan may be G.J. Anderson's son. Same book contains estimation of money earned over the last ten years, which could have something to do with an entry in Jack's diary for 1931; "Thursday 8 January Dad 4 o'clock Income Tax."

11   Now the United Reformed, monument nearest door. "In ever loving and affectionate remembrance of my dear wife Eleanor Vera Lucy Reader who passed away 20th December 1934 aged 30 years. Dearly loved and sadly missed by all who knew her."

12   Chislehurst & Sidcup Council minutes Oct 1935 – Mar 1936 p548 L.B.Bromley Local History Library.

13   W.P.Render, Barclays Bank Chambers, Highbury Corner N.5.
     T.J.Mortimer & Sons, 12 Palmerston Rd, Walthamstow E17.

14   Many name changes are made for good postal reasons, but it is not obvious why Dove House Close should become Dove House Gardens, and the former Dove House Gardens, Gomm's Rd after the farm and then Lansdowne Rd.

15   Mr Cyril J.Newman.

16   Petty Cash for Chingford 1938/39 included windowcleaning, coke (for office and messroom), petrol, rent agreement forms, typing paper and a pail from grocers and ironmongers Trant &

Grundy, on the corner of New Rd and Chingford Mount Rd. They delivered weekly orders to all three Reader homes.

Chapter 8

1   Arthur Ingram's Estate Office was in Wades Hill on the corner of Hill Crest. The Cresswells were a distinguished local family; Henrietta Cresswell wrote a book on Winchmore Hill "Memories of a Lost Village" in 1912.
2   Oliver Richard Davis, Ideal Housing Co. 6 The Green N21 and 70 Wynchgate N14
3   Erected 1868 by Esther Doe in memory of her ironfounder husband and silk manufacturer father. For 12 spinsters.
4   Arthur Bates was handling the firm's legal affairs by 1934, and probably before that. He was born in 1874, the son of a provision merchant, and was admitted to the Law List in 1896. By 1899 he was at 10 Basinghall St EC, by 1917 at 3 Pancras Lane. He lived in the Croydon and Purley area, and his brothers were a builder, an architect and a farmer.
5   Knowles's Killalkali (KKK) made by John Knowles & Co. (London) Ltd builders' merchants. Used in plastering.
6   Evelyn De Bock Porter FRICS. The District Valuer's Office, Seven Sisters Rd was part of Inland Revenue and responsible for revenue and compensation valuations. Southgate Urban District and Municipal Borough minutes can be seen at Enfield Local History Library, Southgate Town Hall, Green Lanes N13
7   Victoria County History of Essex
8   A.Peachey & Co.Ltd 615 Forest Rd E17
    Ben Horn Ltd 36 Waverley Ave E4
9   Alfred Savill & Sons, surveyors, land, estate & house agents & auctioneers 51a Lincoln's Inn Fields WC2 & 13 Old Bond St EC2
10 C.H.Tysoe, 231 Westward Rd E4
11 Complimentary diaries, notebooks, calendars and gifts were widely handed out at the end of the year by firms expressing appreciation for custom received. Jack possessed an orange pottery cigarette box marked The Norlond Service underneath, also a cream-coloured ashtray made of the same material as Norlond's fireplaces. Christmas fare such as turkeys and bottles of scotch also came Reader's way, but the war put an end to the practice.
12 A siren suit was a warm all-in-one garment which could be zipped up quickly over night clothes before going to the air raid shelter.

13 Code Name Mulberry Guy Hartcup David & Charles 1977. The Artificial Invasion Harbours Called Mulberry Printed The Viking Group June 1980 pub Sir Bruce White. Mulberry Harbour 1944 – 1994, supplement to New Civil Engineer 1994 pub Thomas Telford Ltd.
These sources and many more available in the Imperial War Museum Reference Library.

14 There was no 64 in Wellington Avenue. The site of 62 was originally intended for a pair of semis.

Chapter 9

1 Licence for painting 7 and 15 Castle Rd N12 dated 9.7.1947

2 William Clarkson & Partners auctioneers 2 & 3 Philpot Lane, Fenchurch St EC3 & 87 East India Dock Rd, Poplar E14

3 By 13 June 1947 this firm had become Bailey & Walker of 7 Victoria St.

4 George Hennings-Hamer (Windows) Ltd 6 Duke St, St James's SW1

5 Hooper Cushen & Co. surveyors valuers estate agents and insurance brokers 173 West Ferry Rd Millwall E14 & 27 Clements Lane EC4

6 Butters Bros & Co Ltd crane makers, electric, steam & hand derricks & all other types of cranes & winches. Mc Lellan St Kinning Pk Glasgow & Trafalgar House Waterloo Place London SW1.

7 1946 F.H.Marshall & Co Ltd cabinet makers & furniture makers, offices 126 & 128 Lansdowne Drive E8, Mackintosh Lane E9 & Cassland Works Bramshaw Rd E9; 1949 Mackintosh Lane E9; 1950 no entry.

8 The old East India Dock Rd built from 1802 onwards has almost entirely vanished due to road widening, bombing and redevelopment, but Palm Cottage built 1834 still survives next to Sturry St. It may owe its reprieve to having been Doctor Byrne's surgery until 1973. In 2000 other survivors are north side, the former Sailor's Home between Jeremiah St & Duff St, the George Green Schools 1884, 197-267 (local photographer William Whiffin was at 237 in 1924); south side, 4 – 52, the Phoenix Inn, the Missions to Seamen Institute at 154, Poplar Baths, All Saint's Church and the Manor Arms.

9 This beautiful office block was built between 1935 and 1937, architects Albert W.Moore and Nicholas & Dixon-Spain. It was then the second largest building in the City, covering more than

41,000 square feet. In 2000 its site is part of a huge excavation between Fenchurch St, Mincing Lane and Rood Lane, with St Margaret Pattens looking uncomfortably as if it might fall into it. British Land's Plantation Place is to rise there, with the astounding Minster Court next door to live up to. To enjoy departed glories see the prospectus leaflet for Plantation House in Guildhall Library Ref.Store 1460.2

10   This was an exaggeration.

11   Building applications 2495, 3175, 3800. Redbridge L.H.L.

12   Named after R.Bernard Elliott, choirmaster at St John of Jerusalem South Hackney.

13   By John Madge, pub.,Bureau of Current Affairs, Carnegie House 117 Piccadilly W1 Number 50 March 20 1948. Harry Simpson Library University of Westminster.

14   Erith & Co.Ltd builders' merchants 530 High Rd E11

15   At that time local accounts seem to have been opened for each site; bankbooks extant are for branches in Bow 1920-1922, Golders Green 1923-1925, Poplar 1923-1929.

16   A charitable housing society initated by the Rev. Basil Jellicoe who laid the foundation stone 29 May 1935. Completed 1936, consisted of 68 dwellings and a shop. Address c/o Messrs Laurence Collins & Fearnley-Whittingstall of Sardinia House, 52 Lincoln's Inn Fields.

17   Kearley & Tonge Ltd wholesale grocers & provision merchants Mitre Square EC3.

18   Blenheim Rd E15 built between 1884 and 1888, applications lost in Waltham Forest Planning Dept fire 1982. 1890 Essex Directory – Joseph Tyler dairyman, Blenheim House. The tiles on the front look more Deco than Victorian.

Chapter 10

1   Brassey was also responsible for the same line as far back as Woodford, the East London Railway between New Cross and Bishopsgate, and the London, Tilbury and Southend Railway.

2   They were probably lost during the Planning Department's move to the new council offices in Epping.

3   In the process, it was discovered that maps in the deeds and therefore probably the OS map itself, were inaccurate, and the site was smaller than on the plans put in. At least 10 or 12 plots had to be adjusted in both roads.

4   LCC Minutes July-Dec 1890 p831; Report of Standing Committee.

5   Guidebook to the bunker written by Judy Cowan December 1994.
6   Plans for quite a few houses in the area are missing from the Council Planning Department.
7   Mr Harold Fitchett.
8   Numbers 253 and 255 Waltham Way were still being rented out in September 1969.

Chapter 11

1   ECRO Chelmsford D/F33/11/22
2   ”   A882
3   This document was full of good intentions but has arguably not achieved a great deal in the way of preservation. Today, its sole apparent tooth limits the height of front walls, though not their style or materials.
4   A.R.Sheppard Ltd. Maybank Wks Maybank Rd S.Woodford E18 1ET
5   Obituary of R.F.Reader; West Essex Gazette Ongar Edition 24 March 1978.
6   The lathe had an interesting life after 1973. It was taken down to Dick's house at Nine Ashes, then picked up in Nick's Morris 1000 ex-GPO van and driven to his house in Farnborough Hants, where he set it up in a shed but never got it working. He then lent it to a musical instrument repairer in Clerkenwell until he would need it again. Some years later he requested its return and found it had been given to someone else. With the help of an orchestral van driver it was retrieved and moved to the garage of 75 Monkhams Avenue, later to another garage down in Dyfed, and finally to a musical instrument repairer in rural Suffolk, where it remains.

With the Compliments of

Reader Brothers (Builders) Limited

36 Coopers Hill,
Marden Ash,
Ongar, Essex.   *Tel. : Ongar 2423*

INDEX

Barnfield Mews Chelmsford 199, 200, 209, 210
Bate, Katherine 97
Bates, Arthur sol 142, 144, 146, 149, 169, 172-3, 184, 189
Batten, Ernest 173, 176, 208
Beach, Richard & Elizabeth 1
Beadle, Annie 23, 33 26, 91, 114, 125, 180
Beaumont Cemetery E1 6
     Fyfield 190
Beech St EC2 122
Bell Tavern Addle Hill EC4 13
Bertie, Hon Francis Leveson 21
Bessborough, Lord 166
Bevin, Ernest 82
Biggs undertaker 7
Billson St E14 77
Birches, The, Nine Ashes 189, 202
Bird, S.J. & partners 184
Bishops Rd (Bishops Way) E2 7
Blake, T.S. arch 127
Blenheim House, Blenheim Rd E15 176, 178, 201, 204-5
Bohemia Theatre Ballards Lane 31
Bombing 1914-1918 61, 64
     1939-1945 149, 160, 173, 175
Bostwick, T.H. labourer 204
Boswall, E.R. blder 120, 127
Boutillier, Arthur le, 128
Bower, Eleanor Ann 1
Boyle, Douglas Bruce 197
    Josephine 124, 135, 147, 150, 159, 183, 200, 200
    Malcolm Charles 184, 207
    Michael Robert, 183, 200
Brassey, Thomas rlway blder 182, 242
Bretzfelder, Alfred blder 75
Bristow, Andrew Alfred Collyer sol 22
     F.W. & Son bldrs 102
British Steel Frame Co 175
British St E14 (Harbinger Rd) 98
Broadfields Avenue N21 139, 140, 142, 143, 153
     Estate Winchmore Hill 139-143, 152-157
Broad Oak, Woodford Green 43
Bromley, F.K. of Russell & Bromley 166
Broomfield Rd Chelmsford 198, 199
Brown, W.H. of Harts House 44, 45
Britannia Rubber Works, Devons Rd E3 97
Brunner, Mond & Co. explosion 62

BUILDERS OF REPUTE: THE STORY OF READER BROS.

Builders of Repute: the Story of Reader Bros.